Urban Waste and Sanitation Services for Sustainable Development

Urban sanitation and solid waste sectors are under significant pressure in East Africa because of the lack of competent institutional capacity and the growth of the region's urban population. This book presents and applies an original analytical approach to assess the existing socio-technical mixtures of waste and sanitation systems and to ensure wider access, increase flexibility and improve ecological sustainability. It shows that the problem is *not* the current diversity in waste and sanitation infrastructures and services and variety of types and scales of technology, of formal and informal sector involvement, or of management and ownership modes. The book focuses instead on the lack of an integrative approach to managing and upgrading the various waste and sanitation configurations and services so as to ensure wider access, flexibility and sustainability for the low-income populations who happen to be the main stakeholders.

This book provides students, researchers and professionals in environmental technology, sociology, management and urban planning with an integrated analytical perspective on centralised and decentralised waste and sanitation configurations and tools for improvement in the technology, policy and management of sanitation and solid waste sectors.

Bas van Vliet is assistant professor at the Environmental Policy Group of Wageningen University, The Netherlands.

Joost van Buuren is emeritus academic staff of the Sub-department of Environmental Technology of Wageningen University, the Netherlands.

Shaaban Mgana works at Ardhi University (ARU) Department of Environmental Engineering, Dar es Salaam, Tanzania.

Urban Waste and Sanitation Services for Sustainable Development

Harnessing social and technical diversity in East Africa

Bas van Vliet, Joost van Buuren and Shaaban Mgana

Routledge
Taylor & Francis Group
LONDON AND NEW YORK

First published 2014
by Routledge
2 Park Square, Milton Park, Abingdon, Oxfordshire OX14 4RN

and by Routledge
711 Third Avenue, New York, NY 10017

First issued in paperback 2016

Routledge is an imprint of the Taylor & Francis Group, an informa business

British Library Cataloguing-in-Publication Data
A catalogue record for this book is available from the British Library

Library of Congress Cataloging-in-Publication Data
A catalog record has been requested for this book

ISBN 13: 978-1-138-68717-2 (pbk)
ISBN 13: 978-0-415-83377-6 (hbk)

Typeset in Times
by Apex CoVantage, LLC

Contents

Tables

Figures

Acknowledgements

The heart of this book is a collection of studies executed by East African researchers in collaboration with researchers at Wageningen University. The editors would like to thank all members of the PROVIDE team for their support and commitment without which this volume would not exist. On behalf of this team the editors would like to express their gratitude to the Interdisciplinary Research and Education Fund of Wageningen University (INREF) for its funding of PhD studies and exchanges between African and Dutch researchers. The collaboration in this project with Ardhi University in Dar es Salaam, Kenyatta University in Nairobi, and Makerere University in Kampala was highly appreciated. WASTE Advisors on Urban Environment and Development in Gouda, in particular Arnold van de Klundert, generously shared with us their extensive network of scientists and practitioners in East Africa at the start of the project. Gabor Szanto in his function of project manager has given an invaluable input to the progress and the outcomes of the PROVIDE project. Lastly, the editors thank Corry Rothuizen at the Environmental Policy Group at Wageningen University and Khanam Virjee and Charlotte Russell at Routledge for their help in the final editing and processing of the manuscript.

Wageningen, May 2013

Bas van Vliet, Joost van Buuren, Shaaban Mgana

1 Introduction

Harnessing social and technical diversity for sustainable development

Joost van Buuren, Shaaban Mgana and Bas van Vliet

1.1 Introduction

Sub-Saharan Africa is the world's region with the most urgent problems with respect to sanitation and solid waste management. This book focuses on East Africa, which, in terms of economic conditions, can be seen as representative for the largest part of the Sub-Saharan region. The East African Community (EAC) comprises Tanzania, Kenya, Uganda, Rwanda and Burundi. These countries are characterised by rapid growth of the population, from a total of 115 million in 2005 to 139 million in 2010, with an expected 237 million by 2030. Across the countries, the percentage of the population living in cities in 2010 ranged from 11% (Burundi) to 26% (Tanzania). Urbanisation is expected to grow further to 20% in Burundi (lowest) and 39% in Tanzania (highest) by 2030. This rapid urbanisation puts an immense pressure on provision of urban infrastructure services, such as water supply, sanitation and solid waste management. The situation is compounded by the bifurcated nature of infrastructure development, with relatively good services in the central and business areas of cities and poor services to those who live in the widely spread informal settlements. Though during the last decade the percentage of people in the EAC countries below the poverty line has slightly decreased, the absolute number is estimated to have increased to 53 million people (38% of the population) in 2010. It is, in particular, the poor dwellers of informal settlements who suffer from the lack of adequate water supply, sanitation and solid waste provision (Society for International Development (SID) 2012: 30).

A 2008 report about the achievement of the Millennium Development Goals (MDG) in water supply and sanitation in Africa pointed out that the number of persons served must double from 350 million in 2006 to 760 million in 2015, which still leaves 400 million persons unserved. This implies for Africa an overall sanitation coverage target for 2015 of 66%. Despite the widely spread awareness of the public health benefits, the expectations of reaching the MDGs – in particular, in the domain of sanitation – are bleak (AMCOW, AfDB, The World Bank, & WSP 2008). More specifically, in the EAC countries, the sanitation provision is still far from satisfactory, with coverage percentages ranging from only 32% (Kenya) to 55% (Rwanda) in 2010. Between 1995 and 2010, the percentage of the population that gained access to sanitation amounted to 14%, which shows that progress is slow. For Tanzania and Uganda, this figure was not made available (UNICEF & World Health Organization 2012).

Most East African countries signed, in 2008, the eThekwini Declaration (Second African Conference on Sanitation and Hygiene 2008). With this policy document, governments commit themselves to important measures to achieve progress towards reaching the MDG sanitation targets. Among them is the allocation of 0.5% of their GDPs to sanitation. Some progress has been made since then, but the pledged budget turned out to be especially hard to allocate in the countries of the EAC. Accordingly, it seems unlikely that the expected acceleration towards the MDG targets will be achieved in time.

In the domain of solid waste management, international target setting and monitoring of national performance is much less pronounced than in water and sanitation. Here, the situation is full of challenges, as well, as this book will show. Urban waste management in East Africa is characterised by insufficient collection methods, failing equipment and waste dumping, along with low levels of recycling and reuse and the littering of waste within and beyond the city boundaries. There is only one up-to-date sanitary landfill in the entire East African region. All other waste disposal sites are not much more than uncontrolled dumpsites. In addition, the present infrastructure contributes very little to the recovery of valuable materials, such as reusable water, fuels and fertilizers from wastes.

The challenges of a drastic increase of access, of improved performance in terms of public health and environment and of increased recovery of resources from waste and sanitation streams can only be met if environmental governance at multiple levels is fundamentally improved. That improvement is the main topic of this book.

Throughout the past half century, local and international actors have made large efforts to improve sanitation and solid waste management in Africa. These efforts have been based on a variety of assumptions and beliefs about how a good and rapid development had to be approached. In the early years of post-independence, the young governments were expected to put an end to grave inequities with respect to access to infrastructure. As progress soon turned out disappointing, various new views on infrastructure development emerged. The use of expensive large-scale technologies borrowed from, and often promoted by, the North was seen as an impediment rather than an opportunity to meet the needs of all, and especially the poor segments of society. Instead, appropriate small- and intermediate-scale technologies adapted to the local possibilities and legitimised by community participation had to be applied. As the national means for infrastructure development turned out to be very limited, governments had to deliver at least the *basic needs* of the poor. *Privatisation* was recommended as a means to rapidly provide scarce investment capital and know-how. New directions for *good governance* were imposed, pleading for more transparency, accountability and capacity building. In addition, new methodologies for infrastructure analysis and planning emerged, such as the concept of Integrated Sustainable Waste Management, to further a more systematic approach to development in sanitation and solid waste management.

The failure of meeting the Millennium Development Goals for sanitation and solid waste management shows that in many Sub-Saharan African countries, the recommended approaches have as yet not produced the expected breakthroughs. The challenge of this volume is to contribute to a more profound understanding of the causes of this failure and to more effective and more sustainable approaches towards waste and sanitation infrastructure operation and development. The key notion here is institutional diversity and multiple spatial and technical scales. The approaches mentioned above address governments, the formal private sector or communities, but seem to have less of a vision of the complexity of stakeholder roles and relationships in the implementation and operation of various infrastructures in practice. How are these roles performed? What are the trends in the relationships between these multiple actors? Can this diversity of players together realise what government and/or private sector alone cannot? And can they do it in a sustainable way? The underlying assumption of this book is that they can. It is based on the potential of network governance for infrastructure development and operation that is adapted to local circumstances under the complex political and economic conditions in Sub-Saharan Africa.

1.2 PROVIDE

The present volume is the result of a multi-disciplinary research project, Partnership for Research on Viable Environmental Infrastructure Development in East Africa (PROVIDE). PROVIDE was initiated in Kenya, Tanzania, Uganda and The Netherlands in 2004 to contribute to the understanding and improvement of environmental infrastructures, notably in sanitation and solid waste management, and to further develop the Modernised Mixtures approach (MMa) based on empirical studies. While the MMa was developed for and during studies on environmental infrastructure innovation in Europe (Van Vliet 2006; Hegger 2007), the PROVIDE project was initiated to find out if and how it could become applicable in the context of developing countries (Spaargaren 2006). The geographical scope for all studies was East Africa and, in particular, the urban centres bordering, or with an urban run-off into, Lake Victoria. The project took off with a research framework that combined an integrated flows approach to environmental infrastructure, with a four-level view on involved actors, as well as the contribution of multiple scientific disciplines.

The integrated flows approach views environmental infrastructure as socio-technical institutions functioning through an interplay among flows, technologies, actors and institutions. The flows associated with environmental infrastructure development are, in the first place, the material flows of solid wastes and wastewater, but also the flows of money and information that come along with the material ones.

The flows of wastes and wastewater are conceptualised as being constituted by various components, such as food wastes and plastics. The material flows all follow a chain of processes, such as collection, sorting, transporting, treatment and reuse. Each process in such a chain, such as the treatment of sewage in a septic tank, is associated with a technology (the septic tank), one or more actors (households, builders, emptiers, governmental policy makers), spatial requirements, rationalities and rules (e.g., about the required size). In order to operate a chain of processes, actors enter into relationships with each other and make agreements. In the field of solid waste management, such agreements (in some form) exist between households, primary collectors, itinerant buyers of recyclables, waste transporters and operators of the disposal sites. Similar relationships exist in the domain of sanitation. The shaping and operation of the abovementioned processes are formal and informal economic activities that engender flows of money and information through society.

The handling of waste and wastewater flows implies practices at multiple levels of society. This is true for the material flows, for the associated flows of money and information, and also for governance and institutions: legislation, policy making and chain management. The levels at which PROVIDE aimed its research were: 1) households and communities, 2) cities, 3) the national state and 4) the international community.

The PROVIDE research ran from 2006 to 2011 and was a collaboration between Wageningen University in The Netherlands and three universities in East Africa: ARDHI University in Dar es Salaam, Tanzania; Kenyatta University in Nairobi, Kenya; and Makarere University in Kampala, Uganda. The project brought together scientists in the fields of environmental policy, environmental technology, development economics and environmental system analysis. Throughout the project, the involved researchers made efforts to learn from their partners in other disciplines so that the interdisciplinary results of the project as a whole would exceed the results of the individual studies.

As the initiators of the PROVIDE project considered that the development and operational performance of urban infrastructure would primarily depend on improvement of governance, the emphasis in the project had to be put on the roles and relationships of the actors that shape and operate the infrastructure chains; the researchers could then take the results as raw material for recommending new policies and practices. Accordingly, the practices of various actors at multiple levels in urban sanitation and solid waste management were the key study objects. These actors were households, formal and informal private service providers, NGOs and CBOs, local government and international development agencies. As the PROVIDE project was meant to be relevant to East Africa as a whole, the study areas had to be spread over the various countries of East Africa. For practical reasons, the field work for the project and this book has been carried out in the cities of Mwanza (Tanzania), Kisumu (Kenya) and Kampala and Jinja (Uganda), bordering Lake Victoria. In addition, case studies were done in the capital cities Dar es Salaam (Tanzania) and Nairobi (Kenya).

Five African researchers obtained their PhD degrees in the framework of PROVIDE. Their work lies at the basis of Chapters 4 through 8 of this volume. The book as a whole is a product of the collaboration between these African academics and several other scholars associated with PROVIDE and environmental research in developing countries.

1.3 Outline of the book

The book begins with two chapters that present the core theoretical concepts and the technological chains associated with waste and sanitation provision in the urban centres of East Africa.

In Chapter 2, Van Vliet, Van Buuren, Oosterveer and Spaargaren introduce the Modernised Mixtures approach to the provision of environmental services, the core theoretical concept of this volume. They do so by first reviewing strategies that have been developed over time to combat the deficiencies of urban infrastructures. The chapter discusses the role of the state in providing waste and sanitation services in East Africa, drawing on models of the developmental and network state and the theory and practice of decentralisation of service provision. These models of governance are then linked with approaches of technology development and implementation designed to enhance the provision of waste and sanitation services in developing contexts: appropriate technology and integrated sustainable waste management and, on a more applied level, participatory planning tools. The chapter infers that the discussed approaches are predominantly technology- and infrastructure-centred, while the wider debate on governance in East Africa rarely focuses on governance of waste and sanitation systems. The final part of the chapter situates MMa as a reflexive modernisation approach that is related to Ecological Modernisation Theory. Under an MMa there is no blueprint for the provision of environmental services, neither in technical nor in governance terms. The objective is to create a 'fit' between different infrastructure options and the prevailing socio-economic, ecological, technological and political conditions. When applied to the assessment of infrastructure, the approach abandons dogmatic lines of thinking about technology and management as either centralised or decentralised. In the design of policies, MMa begins with an analysis of stakeholder roles, their relationships and prevailing rationalities and builds on institutional and technological diversity to find new – and strengthen existing – network governance arrangements in waste management and sanitation. The chapter ends with questions about whether and how the modernised mixtures that will be analysed in this volume can be conceived as necessary stepping stones of a wider transition towards sustainability.

Chapter 3, a contribution of Van Buuren, Mgana, Salukele, Okot-Okumu, Zurbrügg and Zeeman, looks at sanitation and solid waste management in East Africa from a technological and systems perspective. The first part reviews the present systems of sanitation and solid waste management in Tanzania, Kenya and Uganda; the second part sketches possible resource-oriented approaches to the management of urban flows. The existing infrastructure usually lacks a systems perspective and the environmental performance is low: Latrines and septic tanks, for instance, lack a proper system of sludge management; if they are emptied, the sludge is dumped and heavily pollutes the environment. The chapter discusses material chains in waste (water) management as elements in a Modernised Mixtures approach. The elaborated chains are faecal sludge management in unplanned settlements, wastewater reuse and the reuse of biowastes from municipal solid waste. In addition, new developments in sanitation and solid waste management techniques relevant to Sub-Saharan Africa are briefly described. The chapter ends with recommendations for African research and the use of participatory methods in technology selection.

After the abovementioned conceptual chapters on, respectively, governance and technology, the book continues with five chapters that present the field research of the PROVIDE project.

Oberlin Solomon and Spaargaren highlight in Chapter 4 the roles and perceptions of households in waste management in informal settlements. For a long time, this role was ignored; households were considered simply as receivers of centrally provided services. Based on research in informal settlements in Dar es Salaam, this chapter shows the way new practices, actors and relationships establish themselves where centralised formal waste management fails. Community-based organisations have taken up primary collection in some wards, and they service households that are willing to pay. Illegal waste pickers collect recyclables and give households some cash in return. However, waste burning, burying and local dumping have also turned into daily routines. Survey results show the perceptions of households offering their ideas on service improvements they are hoping for and how these could be achieved. These results underpin the recommendation that waste management authorities should definitely take households on board as actors for change.

Chapter 5 focuses on the changes of solid waste services in Kampala city after the partial privatisation around the year 2000. Burger and Katusiimeh document the effects of privatisation on the system performance and the changing demands for the services of old and new providers, making a distinction between demand of high-, middle- and low-income households. Formal privatisation led to an overall increase of door-to-door services and reduction of the utilisation of the neighbourhood skips and local waste dumping. Both before and after privatisation there was a demand for informal sector services in primary collection. The nature of these services, however, changed. In the present situation, informal collectors mainly service the shopkeepers, with their relatively high quantities of wastes. The authors suggest applying the Modernised Mixtures approach in strengthening emerging public-private-informal partnerships in Kampala and propose several technical and governance measures for further service improvement.

In Chapter 6, Tukahirwa, Mol and Oosterveer argue that although the role of CBOs and NGOs in providing sanitation and solid waste management services to marginalised or hardly accessible areas in East Africa is widely celebrated, little is known about their performance. This chapter explores and compares their provision of urban sanitation and solid waste services for the poor in capital cities Nairobi, Kampala and Dar es Salaam. Using ideas of modernised mixtures and institutional pluralism, the authors clarify the role of civil society institutions, among other urban environmental service arrangements. Differences are found in CBO or NGO involvement in sanitation and solid waste provisioning, in the socio-economic characteristics of service recipients and non-recipients and in levels of appreciation of these services.

Majale, Oosterveer and Mireri address in Chapter 7 the role of local governments in sanitation and waste services. Local governments in East Africa witness declining capacities in environmental service delivery. To ensure adequate levels of sanitation and solid waste management, they turn increasingly towards private and civil actors. However, this requires municipal authorities to develop a broader set of strategies when tackling sanitation and waste management challenges. This chapter assesses two of these. The first one is the supervisory, monitoring and evaluation role that local authorities have to take up when new actors enter into service delivery, and the second is the creation of alliances with other municipalities on a regional scale. The conclusion confirms that promising perspectives exist in both innovative strategies.

Chapter 8, by Letema and Van Vliet, combines the discussion on scales of management and participation with that of scales of technology and infrastructures. A study of sanitation planning in Kisumu (Kenya) and Kampala (Uganda) shows how various scales and kinds of sanitation infrastructures (on-site, community on-site, satellite sewer and conventional sewer) are owned, managed and maintained by various actor configurations. After assessing and evaluating such socio-technical configurations with the Modernised Mixtures approach, the chapter ends with presenting routes for improved sanitation planning. These routes are based on criteria of environmental and public health, accessibility and flexibility that surpass the conventional criteria used in sanitation planning.

In Chapter 9, the editors conclude on the findings of the collection of empirical studies in waste and sanitation in East African urban centres. It is argued that the Modernised Mixtures approach that has been developed and applied in the underlying research for this volume proves to be helpful in conceptualising, assessing, mapping and prescribing waste and sanitary systems in cities where social, institutional and technical mixtures are the norm rather than the exception. It is also helpful as a conceptual model for organizing a research agenda along the dimensions of technical and spatial scale, planning and decision-making, operation and maintenance and closing of material cycles, as well as in searching for appropriate innovation pathways along one or more of these dimensions. The mixtures that are the object of study in this volume can be conceived as stepping stones of a sustainability transition in waste and sanitation service provision, but to employ them as such, a change in conventional urban governance and international support programs is required. For the Modernised Mixtures approach to flourish, it needs a networked mode of governance, which would allow for acknowledgment and support of multi-stakeholder participation in managing environmental system chains. In sum, apart from harnessing social and technical diversity in waste and sanitation service provision, the chapter posits that this volume presents the building stones for the sustainable development of such infrastructures in East Africa and for the Sub-Saharan Africa region as a whole.

References

African Ministers' Council on Water (AMCOW), African Development Bank (AfDB), The World Bank, & Water & Sanitation Program (WSP). (2008). *Can Africa afford to miss the sanitation MDG target? A review of the sanitation and hygiene status in 32 countries.* Retrieved from https://www.wsp.org/sites/wsp.org/files/publications/Can_Africa_Afford_to_Miss_the_Sanitation_MDG_target.pdf

Hegger, D. (2007). *Greening sanitary systems: An end-user perspective.* PhD thesis. Wageningen: Wageningen University.

Second African Conference on Sanitation and Hygiene. (2008). *The eThekwini Declaration and AfricaSan Action Plan – WSP.* Retrieved from http://www.wsp.org/sites/wsp.org/files/publications/eThekwiniAfricaSan.pdf

Society for International Development (SID). (2012). *The state of East Africa 2012*. Nairobi, Kenya.

Spaargaren, G. (2006). *PROVIDE: Partnership for research on viable environmental infrastructure development in East Africa* (Full Project Proposal INREF 2). Wageningen: Wageningen University.

UNICEF & World Health Organization. (2012). *Progress on drinking water and sanitation: 2012 update*. Retrieved from http://www.unicef.org/media/files/JMPreport2012.pdf

Van Vliet, B. (2006). *The sustainable transformation of sanitation*. In J. P. Voss, D. Bauknecht & R. Kemp (Eds.), *Reflexive governance for sustainable development* (pp. 337–354). Cheltenham: Edward Elgar.

2 Network governance and waste and sanitation service provision

An introduction to the modernised mixtures approach

Bas van Vliet, Joost van Buuren, Peter Oosterveer and Gert Spaargaren

2.1 Introduction

There is a growing consensus among scholars and decision makers that contemporary waste and sanitation service provision in urban East Africa fails to meet the requirements of public health and environmental quality. With population growth rates in Kenya, Tanzania and Uganda of around 3% for the period 2005–2015 (Oosterveer 2009) and even higher growth rates in the urban centres of these countries, it is clear that even if existing infrastructures were able to serve the current urban population, they would be not sufficient in the near future. It seems impossible to pinpoint one particular reason for this failing service provision. Explanations have been collected from historical analysis (i.e., Abbott 2012; Nilsson 2006), technology assessments (Letema 2012), and studies of governance from colonial to contemporary times (Oosterveer 2009).

Historical analysis has found some explanation in the fact that the urban infrastructures, such as the piped water, sewerage and waste disposal systems, were initially built to serve only the affluent groups in colonial society, rather than the African population at large. These central systems have all the characteristics generally associated with large technical systems – namely, the sunk costs and inertia in institutions and ideas (Nilsson 2006). In Kampala and Kisumu and many other cities in East Africa today, the layout and coverage of sewer systems still resemble the colonial urban patterns designed in the 1930s (Letema 2012), but these cities have grown substantially since then and have been unable to extend these systems to provide access for all.

Assessments of existing technical systems for waste and sanitation services (Tilley, Lüthi et al. 2008; Letema 2012) have clarified that many of the large-scale systems are ill-designed for the conditions of urban Africa and that they are badly maintained. Abundant is the empirical evidence of non-functioning sewer pumps and overloaded treatment installations, stolen covers of manholes, skips overloaded with waste, or waste littering the open spaces and streets due to the lack of timely collection and storage facilities. The smaller-scale, 'appropriate' or low-tech facilities that have been put in place by international donor organisations, NGOs, CBOs and users themselves do not always function well either. Simple pit latrines may work in rural areas where housing density is low; this provides the necessary space for digging new pits whenever the ones in use are full, and the soil absorption capacity for pit latrine leachate will not be exceeded. In an urban context, such latrines are often overused and not maintained. They pollute groundwater as soil absorption capacity is exceeded and, therefore, have become a threat to public health and the urban environment.

In a search for explanation of current problems in waste and sanitation, urban governance studies have focused on the role of the state in provisioning basic services to the urban population in Africa. They revealed that, after independence in Africa, the hopes of development led by a capable state turned soon into disappointment, especially among the poor. The developmental states in Africa after independence turned out to be working predominantly for the interests of specific elites instead of putting the public good first. Africans came to live under so-called *neo-patrimonial regimes*: states that displayed a formal distinction between public and private sectors, although in practice political actors misused formal procedures and public resources so as "to allow their use for private ends" (Oosterveer 2009: 1063). One answer to this situation, instigated by the Washington consensus (IMF and the World Bank), was to radically cut down on the state apparatus and to privatise the state-owned companies, many of which were responsible for the management of urban infrastructures of domestic waste, water supply and sanitation. This approach has led to the introduction of much-needed foreign capital investments in dilapidated infrastructures of major cities, but not to increased access of the urban poor to basic services at large. In most cases, the economic elites in urban centres may have benefited more financially from the handing over of public goods to private entities than the recipients of services did in terms of improved service delivery or enhanced access to services.

This brief overview of explanations for the failures of urban services provision in East Africa may give us an in-route to the presentation of possible strategies that have been developed over time to combat malfunctioning of urban infrastructures or the inequity in access to existing services. The aim of this chapter is not to add arguments to the growing literature stressing the failures of urban service provision by the state or the market (Abbott 2012; Bakker, Kooy et al. 2008; Kessides 2005). Rather, it tries to build on a number of existing socio-technical approaches for the sustainable provision of waste and sanitation services and situate them in the changing governance contexts in urban East Africa. It results in an approach for the assessment and planning of urban waste and sanitation infrastructures and services (Modernised Mixtures) that takes into account the interplay of the spatial, social and technical dimensions that are identified in the existing approaches towards urban service provisions.

The chapter is built up as follows: We start with discussing the role of the state in provisioning waste and sanitation services to the urban poor, drawing on models of the developmental and network state and the theory and practice of decentralizing service provision in East Africa. We link these models of governance with approaches of technology development and implementation that have been introduced over the past decades to enhance waste and sanitation services provision in developing countries' contexts: appropriate technology, Integrated Sustainable Waste Management and, on a more applied level, several methods that support the selection process of more appropriate models of waste and sanitation service provision. Drawing on these experiences and connections between governance and technology development, we present the Modernised Mixtures approach and discuss its potential to more adequately address the challenges mentioned.

2.2 Network governance in waste and sanitation service provision

The modern history of waste and sanitation services provision in urban East Africa cannot be discussed without zooming out to review urban governance and the changing roles of the state over the last 50 years. Since their independence in the 1960s, the new states of East Africa have been coping with the inheritance of not only the infrastructures that were built in colonial times, but also the state institutions and the modes of governance that were built around them (Abbott 2012; Nilsson 2006). In most cities during colonial times, the availability and access to modern infrastructures like water and sewer systems were restricted to the European elites. In Kisumu and Kampala, for instance, a spatial duality was created by 'sanitary zoning': Central sewer systems were built in the centre area reserved for immigrants (townships), leaving the peri-urban, unplanned areas for native African communities – the 'unsanitary' sections of the city. In Kisumu, a sanitary 'buffer zone' between the colonial townships and the unplanned native zones was created to avoid contamination of the sanitary zone by unsanitary practices. Townships were administered by councils, with a mandate to provide municipal water and sanitation services. The councils charged property taxes and service charges, and the colonial government invested in the building of sewer systems. Native councils were responsible for the African areas, where people lived a semi-rural life. No property or service taxes were charged, nor did sufficient capacity exist, to provide formal services in these areas (Letema 2012).

Such spatial divisions and socioeconomic exclusion of native African communities from modern infrastructures were among the first issues to be abolished after independence. The colonial state apparatus, including the materialised division between groups in society, was to be replaced with a new model of the state: the developmental state. This developmental state is based on the stated ideal model of a written constitution, a rationally established legal system and an administration based upon clear rules and competent civil servants. It also taxes citizens in order to supply welfare services and provides a sense of identity and "nation-hood" to secure social order, while arbitrating or repressing dispute (Bracking 2005 in Oosterveer 2009). Like the emerging welfare states in the former European colonizing states, the African developmental states were seen as rationally dividing decision-making processes from bureaucratic implementation of decisions, with the aim of the economy to grow and to extract surplus that can be reinvested in building and maintaining the state apparatus and the major infrastructures supporting economic growth and public welfare.

The ideas about the roles of the developmental state also affected urban planning. After independence, the formerly African areas that had been excluded from 'modern' infrastructure planning were to be included in large scale planning schemes, such as the Kampala Transport Master Plan (1968), Development Plan (1972) and the Structure Plan (1994). The plans aimed to redevelop the former African peri-urban areas, and to extend and connect them to modern and large scale transport, waste, water, energy and sanitation infrastructures. The subsequent plans covered seven times the size of the 1951 colonial planning area for Kampala, and their geographical scope expanded from 7 to 25 hills. In Kisumu, the boundaries of city planning were extended in 1972, and similar large-scale plans were made in 1969 and 1983 (Letema 2012: 56).

For many reasons, these plans remained what they were: plans. First, the new states lacked the capacity and the financial resources to invest in the development of the settlements. Quite soon after independence, it became apparent that the developmental states in Africa did not deliver on their promise of economic growth and nation-building. During the 1970s and 1980s, the African states became increasingly burdened by inefficient state-owned enterprises, a large and ineffective civil service and high external debts (Fritz and Rocha Menocal 2006 in Oosterveer 2009). Funding of major urban slum upgrading and infrastructural projects was initially secured by loans from international donors and the World Bank, but over time, the expansion and maintenance of the big works fell short. Quite prominent was the lack of capacity at municipal level to operate and maintain the systems and the increasing political interference with the allocation of investment funds. Moreover, much of the peri-urban areas targeted in the large scale plans were not public but private lands (Letema 2012: 57), which impeded the planning and implementation of public infrastructure works. Lastly, cost recovery schemes for running the infrastructures after their construction have, in general, been lacking. Similar to the provision of services by the colonial state, the developmental states considered waste and sanitation services as public goods, and therefore to be subsidised from public funds. From the 1960s on, the municipal authorities, however, were unable to continue funding a system whose services "were not tailored to the needs, preferences and income level of the African population" (Nilsson 2006: 382). The financial and human resources in East African countries were insufficient to match the increasing demand for environmental services that was resulting from the growing urban population (Oosterveer 2009).

The 1990s brought in new ideas on the role of the state and that of private parties in building infrastructures and delivering services to the urban population. The so-called Structural Adjustment Programs, instigated by IMF and the World Bank, entailed that governments would size down their state apparatus through privatisation of para-statal companies and introduction of competition in the delivery of formerly public services. Introducing market principles in services provision was considered to be more efficient and eventually more effective to serve the growing populations in the urban centres of Africa. The state should be of minimum size and use the market as the main allocation principle to deliver the services to the urban population. In reality, this approach did not fulfil expectations. Political interferences with the private service companies were not interrupted at all, and the ideal of a minimal state could not be achieved because the regulation of markets needs a considerable state apparatus. The regulatory task for controlling privatised utilities appeared to be more complex and demanding for the state organisation than it was when state monopolies were responsible for the utility-based provision (Kessides 2004). Besides, the Structural Adjustment Programs failed as a strategy to serve the poor in African societies. If private companies invested in infrastructures, they ensured that their investments were recovered through tariffs that the poor could not afford to pay.

Around the turn of the century, and especially after the issuing of the Millennium Declaration by the General Assembly of the United Nations (in 2000), the debate on development and aid partly moved away from Structural Adjustment Programs, allowing for new approaches towards the role of the state in African developing countries to be considered. There are two main political directions that can be distinguished in the present debate. One is the "neo-developmental state" which reinvigorates state institutions, giving them a stronger role (again) in the provision of services. The other is a "networked state", entailing the establishment of some form of network governance, assigning to the state only a limited, but well-defined, role as centre of a network of service providers, with each of them having their own tasks (Oosterveer 2009).

In terms of urban environmental services, the neo-developmental state is based on strong governmental institutions, supported by a legal framework that is strictly upheld against political interference. Privatisation is not excluded, but should not be limited to allowing contracts to large (foreign) companies either, and should include a role for smaller local companies and NGOs/CBOs. The state is there to protect and secure the poor's access to environmental infrastructures. Strong municipal governments are also considered best able to bridge the gap between the formal laws and regulations and their limited implementation in practice (Oosterveer 2009).

In contrast to the neo-developmental state, the networked state means that the state is not a priori at centre stage in economic development or the delivery of urban infrastructures. Depending on sector and local conditions, state institutions may partner with public, private or civil society parties to provide the infrastructures and services needed in certain local circumstances. The role of the state is primarily in facilitating rather than in steering urban development. This approach allows for participation of various stakeholders in the provisioning of services, including end-users, community-based organisations and the informal sector. Especially in sectors of waste and sanitation, the latter groups prove to be essential in providing services to the very poor in unplanned settlements. Smaller communal infrastructures, such as those described by Mara and Alabaster (2008) and Mara et al. (2007), need network approaches to urban environmental governance because they facilitate the co-production of solutions that fit local conditions (Oosterveer 2009: 1066).

This development at the level of African urban governance from colonial, (neo)developmental and networked states can be mirrored in the development of sectoral strategies to improve public service provisions – in particular, sanitation and solid waste services. In the following section we discuss appropriate technology, Integrated Sustainable Waste Management (ISWM) and several recently developed infrastructure planning and design methods.

2.3 Appropriate technology

Since their independence, East African states have made efforts to break with the colonial paradigms of urban infrastructure provision within a developmental mode of governance. However, as has been outlined above, it appeared extremely difficult to uphold the large-scale modern infrastructures that were built to serve the colonial elite in the urban centres, let alone to extend them to allow for wider access, especially in the sub-urban areas. From the beginning of the 1970s, a new 'appropriate technology' paradigm in development aid related to infrastructure provision emerged, which was highly inspired by the "small is beautiful" work of Schumacher (1973) and Dickson's "alternative technology" (1974). Appropriate technology stands for a radical break with large-scale western infrastructures and is developed to meet basic human needs with technology that is locally based, understandable, labour intensive, easily maintainable and has very low requirements in terms of capital or (foreign) expertise. As opposed to applying high-tech Western solutions to solve complex problems on a centralised level (as was done, for example, in Kampala, where a succession of the latest Western technologies has been installed at the central waste water treatment plant), the appropriate technology movement stands for low-tech solutions for local problems, mainly in the suburban and rural areas where there is a continuing lack of proper sanitation, water provision or waste management. Generations of engineers and development workers have been trained within this new paradigm, and they have supported numerous local communities, schools, CBOs and NGOs in the design and maintenance of local technological solutions for waste and sanitation. It resulted not in large-scale infrastructures but in man-powered (bicycle) water pumps, home composting schemes and ventilated pit latrines: all typical, small-scale technologies that are affordable to the rural and urban poor.

The appropriate technology paradigm has certainly booked interesting results; to many, however, it remained too much a simple, second-best technology paradigm, useful in situations where the finances, technological capabilities and organisational capacities are severely limited. Partly, the paradigm suffers from an image problem: low-tech solutions are conceived by many as a poor man's solution, at best. Once income levels rise and high-tech large-scale solutions come within reach, the 'modern' technologies are preferred over appropriate technologies. In the case of sanitation, this is illustrated by the water-flush toilet, which is seen as the ultimate and globally desired toilet system, despite its inappropriateness, in many conditions, due to its space, water, sewer and treatment requirements (Black and Fawcett 2008). More substantively, however, the paradigm does not provide an answer to questions of governance and environmental service provision beyond the local level that are typically raised in urban settings. The paradigm lacks a vision for serving densely populated areas where large-scale infrastructures are already in place or unavoidable because of the lack of space to generate or process environmental flows locally. In practice, we see small-scale technologies now being implemented in rural and suburban areas, next to developments on an intermediate scale and next to large-scale waste and sanitation schemes being rolled out on an urban and even national scale. In developing countries in general, and in East African urban centres in particular, alternative systems for sanitation and solid waste management are not jeopardised by the dominance of already existing, large-scale, 'conventional' socio-technical systems. Instead of large systems replacing the small-scale options (as we have seen in past trajectories of modernisation in urban centres of Europe), we observe in urban centres of East Africa the consolidation of a mix of scales, technologies and modes of governance in urban infrastructures delivery. This is partly the result of different development strategies that have run parallel to each other, without mutual coordination; parallel to community support for local sanitation solutions by NGOs in informal settlements, there have been multilateral support programs for upgrading sewer systems in the same city. It can even be argued that this is a continuation of segregated provision of urban infrastructures for the centre and for African settlements, as we know it from the colonial past. In the current practice of East African cities, it means that strategies to develop urban infrastructures for waste and sanitation need to incorporate the existing variety in scales, technologies and management structures, rather than focussing on one infrastructure or assuming single-user needs.

2.4 Integrated sustainable waste management

In some respects, the Integrated Sustainable Waste Management (ISWM) approach that was developed in the 1990s (IJgosse, Anschuetz et al. 2004; Scheinberg 2011; Van de Klundert and Anschütz 2001) builds upon the ideas of the appropriate technology movement. ISWM is rooted in the practice of development workers collaborating at a grassroots level with city dwellers, informal waste pickers and processers in low and middle income countries. It shares the emphasis of the appropriate technology movement on labour-intensive, small-scale, low-tech solutions for waste management. As Wilson and Scheinberg (2010: 1055) put it:

> *(. . .) we need to shift the norm – moving our collective mind-set from technology-focused solid waste management (SWM) to the broader and more inclusive ISWM. To say that technology must be appropriate is a step forward, but that is not enough; rather it is about the appropriate place and role for technology in a discipline and area of practice where governance assumes ever greater significance.*

Rather than a strategy focussed on technical solutions, ISWM addresses the various 'stakeholders' in waste management, the 'elements' of the waste chain from generation to disposal, and a wide spectrum of broadly defined 'aspects': technical, environmental, institutional, financial, sociopolitical and sociocultural

(Scheinberg 2011). The term 'integrated' means that all stakeholders, elements and aspects need to be addressed when developing waste management strategies towards sustainability. As such, the ISWM approach is indeed a much more socially and institutionally embedded strategy compared to the traditional engineering solutions. Local conditions and actors matter for the design and choice of elements of the entire solid waste chain. However, the governance part is not well articulated. The recurrent model of ISWM, as in Figure 2.1, lists the important stakeholders, aspects and elements, but does not reveal what is needed to work towards sustainability, except for process time.

Despite the claim that the ISWM approach is extending appropriate technology towards governance, what this governance actually entails only comes forward in the projects that have been executed under the banner of ISWM. Typically these projects include a participatory process involving all stakeholders mentioned in the scheme. Together with these stakeholders, a baseline assessment is made of the elements and aspects of the waste management system in place. Then, a plan of action, including a system of cost recovery, is constructed, discussed with stakeholders and negotiated with city authorities, after which implementation and monitoring follows (Van de Klundert and Anschütz 2001: 31).

Similar to what we have seen in the previous section on appropriate technology, local actors and users, rather than large formal infrastructure and service providers, are brought on stage in the development of sustainable waste and sanitation services. Although ISWM definitely has its focus on grassroots activities and (informal) local actors, it does include the stakeholders and elements of the larger waste management chain, at least in its analysis and its action plans. So where the appropriate technology approach is restricted to the local level and to small-scale technologies, in ISWM, the technological solutions for solid waste collection and processing have more often been considered as part of a larger chain of activities.

Lastly, ISWM stands for a management strategy that takes into account stakeholders, elements and aspects in some integrated form, but fails to articulate how such integration should be governed. In this respect, the approach is mainly beneficial for the assessment of actors, technologies and factors needed for a change towards sustainability, rather than pointing out what roles various actors would have, or what policies are needed to make that change.

2.5 Infrastructure planning for sustainability

The ISWM approach stipulates an active role of stakeholders in the planning and decision making for environmental infrastructure, combined with a search for enhanced sustainability. Independent from ISWM, several tools for this purpose have been elaborated during the last decades. Their characteristics are various and can be described as generic versus site-specific, as well as focused on different objectives, on different parts of the material waste chain and on different societal levels: national, city, community and household. Generic tools assess, for example, the sustainability of systems independent from specific situations of implementation, while site-specific tools are made for planning and decision

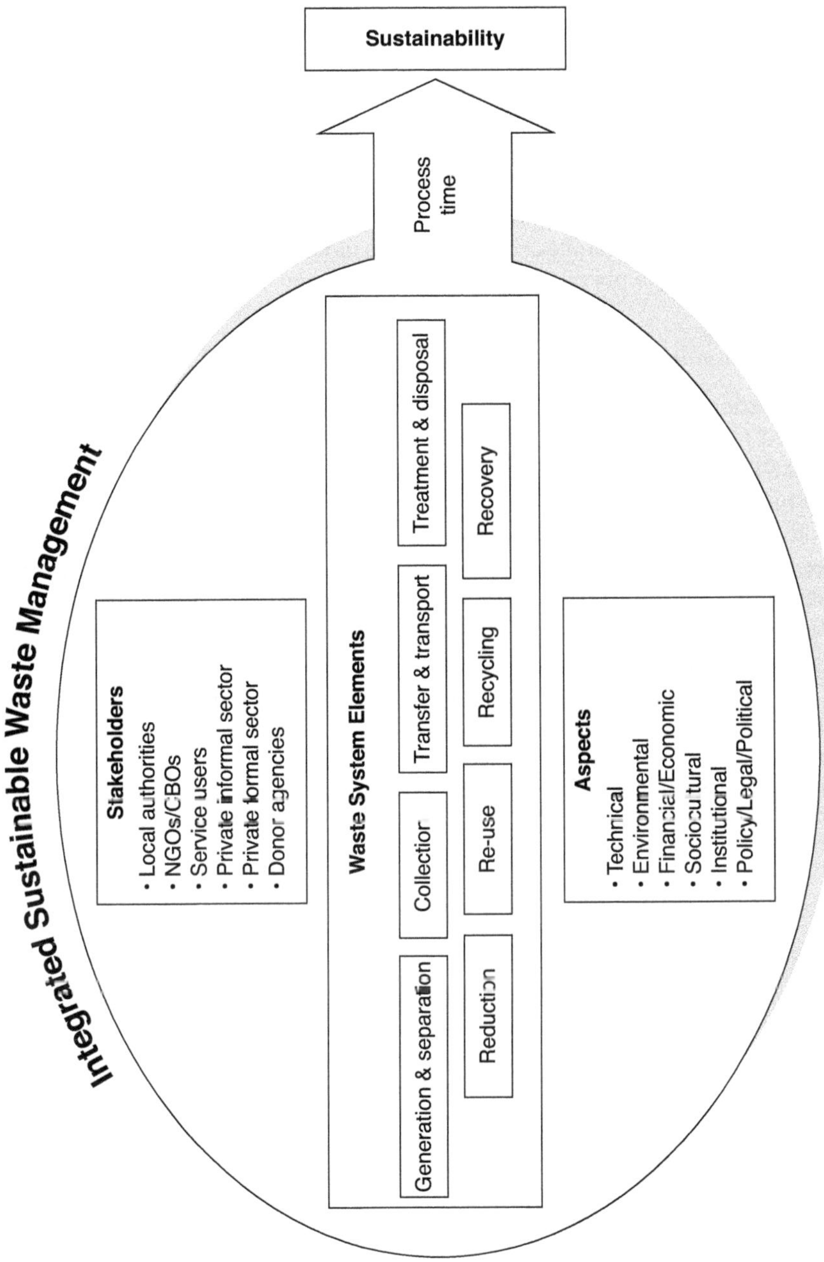

Figure 2.1 Integrated Sustainable Waste Management.

Source: Van de Klundert and Anschütz, 2001

making in a specific country, city or community. We limit our discussion to the site-specific tools.

Critical issues of conventional sanitation and solid waste management planning procedures include the failure to integrate the various parts of waste(water) management systems, the lack of environmental sustainability, the lack of acceptance of implemented systems, the biased selection of technology and the lack of management capacity building. Innovative planning and decision-making methodologies should therefore apply an integrated systems approach, optimise the environmental sustainability of systems, rely on stakeholder participation and empowerment, and use multi-criteria selection of technical systems. The next subsections elaborate on planning tools for sanitation and solid waste management.

2.5.1 Sanitation planning

A few participatory planning tools in the field of sanitation are discussed here (Table 2.1).

PHAST (Participatory Hygiene and Sanitation Transformation) (Sawyer and Simpson-Hébert 1998) explains how to guide communities in a step-by-step participatory planning process towards more adequate hygiene behaviour and improved water and sanitation facilities. Experts have to bring in technological information on sanitation, but the stakeholders rank systems and make a choice. The focus on behavioural change and sanitation facilities puts the emphasis strongly on end users and their toilets in rural areas and informal urban settlements.

SANEX (Sanitation Expert) (Loetscher 1999) is a computerised decision aid in the field of low-cost sanitation that consists of a technological database and a selection algorithm. SANEX selects feasible sanitation systems for a situation under study after having been fed with 52 characteristics of that situation. For the feasible technologies, a cost and functionality comparison can subsequently be

Table 2.1 Tools for participatory sanitation system selection.

Tool name	*Nature*	*Focus*	*Target audience*
PHAST	Planning guide for stakeholders and facilitators	Behaviour change and empowerment related to hygiene, water supply and sanitation in rural and informal settlements	Facilitators in community water, sanitation and hygiene
SANEX	Computerized database and algorithm	Choice of appropriate sanitation and wastewater treatment technologies	Engineers, planners
HCES	Database and planning and procedure	Participatory selection of sanitation systems	Engineers, planners and communities
SANCHIS	Database and planning and procedure	Participatory selection of sanitation systems, primarily in cities	Engineers, planners and communities

made so that the most preferable system is identified. The strength of SANEX lies in making the link between implementation conditions and feasible technologies. Although the tool could be used in the context of a participatory multi-stakeholder planning and decision-making process, it seems most useful for consultants in the preparation of projects and in academic training.

The Household Centred Environmental Sanitation approach (HCES) (Lüthi, Morel et al. 2009; Tilley, Lüthi et al. 2008; Zurbrügg and Tilley 2007) comprises a 10-step plan for the participatory design and implementation of new sanitation systems in urban communities. After local governments, NGOs and beneficiaries assess the current sanitation status and user priorities in consultative workshops, the heart of the approach is the identification of sanitation configurations based on the Compendium of Sanitation Systems and Technologies (Tilley, Lüthi et al. 2008). This compendium is a toolbox with a comprehensive set of possible sanitation user-interfaces (toilets) and collection, transport and treatment technologies. Many configurations may be constructed from this list, depending on local environmental, geographical and socio-economic conditions. Once selected, the proposed configurations are checked for feasibility, followed by planning and implementation.

SANCHIS (Sanitation Choice Involving Stakeholders) (Hendriksen, Tukahirwa et al. 2011; Van Buuren 2010) combines stakeholder dialogues with multi-criteria decision making about sanitation systems. SANCHIS focuses on urban rather than rural sanitation and consequently puts much emphasis on technological choices in wastewater transport, treatment and reuse technologies. Stakeholders obtain an instrument to judge sanitation systems with respect to a full range of criteria: functionality, health, environmental sustainability, social manageability and economic desirability. SANCHIS is meant to bridge the gap between expert knowledge about technical systems at city scale and the local knowledge of the communities in which these systems have to be implemented and maintained.

2.5.2 *Solid waste management planning*

Participatory methods, such as stakeholder dialogues, are widely used in planning and improvement of solid waste management infrastructure; in particular, to improve the cooperation between stakeholders (e.g., between local government, households and informal collectors and waste pickers, or between compost producers and farmers) (UNEP International Environmental Technology Centre 2009). To inform decisions, especially at the level of cities and countries, a rich variety of scientific guidebooks and expert planning instruments has been developed, such as the UNEP International Sourcebook (UNEP International Environmental Technology Centre 1996) and EASEWASTE (www.easewaste.dk). A computerised tool like EASEWASTE focuses on calculation and comparison of the environmental sustainability of waste management systems. The well-known waste hierarchies (such as 'prevent, reuse and recycle, treat and dispose') are a typical result of the work with these tools. However, solid waste management planning tools usually take waste generation for granted and pay little attention to possibilities of waste prevention in the domain of production of consumer goods.

The mentioned planning tools are diverse with respect to the groups they are targeting. Some aim at experts, others guide a grassroots decision-making process and again others intend to bridge the gap between expert and local stakeholder knowledge and apply multi-criteria methods to arrive at optimal technology choices. Most can be conceived as a combination of an expert-driven and bottom-up approach. The selection of "key stakeholders" to involve in the participatory multi-stakeholder process may result in a bias towards the problem assessment and technology choice. The outcome of the 10 HCES steps, for example, is more likely a household or neighbourhood on-site sanitation system, rather than larger-scale infrastructures in which bigger stakeholders play a role.

Stakeholder involvement is supposed to result in accepted and functional outcomes of the planning process; capacity building and community empowerment could be important secondary effects. The participatory approach could incite changes to the economic and governance arrangements that constitute the infrastructure. However, the existing methods basically consider the governance surroundings, in institutional and ideological senses, as a given fact and are not equipped to problematise them, nor improve them. The Modernised Mixtures approach that will be elaborated in the next section attempts to incorporate both issues of participatory decision making on technological design and the institutional environment in which such decisions are taking place.

2.6 Network governance and the Modernised Mixtures approach (MMa) in East African urban centres

In this chapter, we first presented views on the governance of urban infrastructures in Africa, followed by a number of approaches and methods for the provision of waste and sanitation infrastructures and services for the urban poor. Notwithstanding their attempts to include strategies, stakeholders and procedures for participation, the latter approaches do originate from, and are mainly centred around, the development and implementation of hardware: technologies and infrastructures for waste and sanitation services. The debate on the neo-developmental state and network governance in post-colonial Africa concerns the role of the state and public and private actors in fostering socio-economic development, but has not yet specifically addressed the governance of waste and sanitation systems. In this section we aim to synthesise network governance thinking and participative approaches towards infrastructure service provision. We present a Modernised Mixtures approach (MMa) that combines the social, managerial, spatial and technical dimensions that come to the fore in all of the studies of waste and sanitation provision being presented in this volume.

The Modernised Mixtures approach (Hegger 2007; Letema, Van Vliet et al. 2012; Scheinberg and Mol 2010; Van Vliet 2006; Van Vliet, Spaargaren et al. 2010) is built upon the notion that there is no blueprint for the provision of environmental services, neither in technical nor in governance or management terms. It builds on ideas that allow for various combinations of actors and technologies, depending on local contexts, rather than on the more dogmatic frames like "small is beautiful" or the neo-developmental mode of governance. The approach is referred to as 'mixture' because it is modular and addresses the several features of socio-technological strategies for waste and sanitation provision, the multiple scales of provisioning technologies and infrastructure and hybrid governance solutions.

The term 'Modernised' seems provocative because it has connotations of the typical large-scale infrastructure roll-outs in the 1960s and 1970s that have been legitimised as being part of a process of bringing (Western) 'modernity' to the still 'underdeveloped' regions of the world (Abbott 2012). Rather than referring to such patterns of *simple* modernisation, the MMa is built on notions of reflexive modernisation (Beck, Giddens et al. 1994), a process of reform that is based on a re-evaluation rather than an expansion of our modern institutions. In fact, the origins of the MMa stem from Ecological Modernisation Theory (Mol, Sonnenfeld et al. 2009; Spaargaren and Mol 1992), in which 'simple modernity' is reflexively modernised by using ecological principles and perspectives. According to the ecological modernisation theorists, one should not abolish, but reconstruct the instruments of modernity – the modern institutions of science and technology, as well as state, market and civil society actors – to foster an environmental reform process. Modernised Mixtures, then, refer to "those socio-technical configurations of (. . .) infrastructures in which various features of *simple* modern systems have been deliberately and reflexively reconstructed to deal with contemporary social, economic and environmental challenges" (Hegger 2007: 48, emphasis added).

This new, hybrid paradigm can be characterised by its multidimensional character in technological (scale, process and combination of water and waste flows) and governance respects (involvement of end-users, civil society actors, financial arrangements and organisational set-up), as is visualised in Figure 8.2 in this volume (based on Spaargaren, Oosterveer et al. 2005; Hegger 2007; Van Vliet, Spaargaren et al. 2010). In addition, MMa opts for an integrated approach, including all steps in the urban solid waste and the sanitation chains; combining multiple scales in organisation, management and governance; and requiring the inclusion of technical as well as social scientific knowledge. The objective of introducing MMa is to create a 'fit' between different infrastructural options and the prevailing socioeconomic, ecological, technological and political conditions. To realise this objective, one has to develop a profound understanding of the specific (urban or semi-urban) settings in which these infrastructures are to be realised. This understanding will allow the involved stakeholders to decide which technological options (and combinations) are realistically possible in the context of their particular cities or neighbourhoods. This means that each city, or even each neighbourhood, will require a specific mixture of technologies and governance arrangements. Hence, promoting MMa means promoting a modular approach to urban environmental facilities and not a one-size-fits-all solution.

The MMa approach can be utilised as an assessment or as a prescription tool. As we will see in this volume, the approach is used as an assessment tool in the first place. The social and technical dimensions of a waste management or sanitation system can be assessed from an integrated perspective, allowing for combinations of large- and small-scale social and technical features that would otherwise be missed. Different from what the appropriate technology approach would suggest, small-scale technologies could be provided and maintained by big actors; the reverse could also be observed – for instance, in the case of waste infrastructure managed by its users in community co-operatives. Such assessments are valuable because they open up the more dogmatic lines of thinking about the management of urban infrastructures, where it is either the state responsible for the big infrastructure works or the community organisations and NGOs providing the appropriate technologies for the poor. Chapters 4 through 8 in this volume will each present much more diversity in management and technology combinations than the opposing centralised or decentralised approaches assume, by enrolling informal collectors in city-wide waste management (Chapter 5) or by including NGOs and CBOs in sanitation and solid waste management (Chapter 6). Local governments may enrol private or civil actors to ensure waste and sanitation provision, but may at the same time need to collaborate on a higher level of inter-municipal collaboration to govern these new alliances (Chapter 7). And in Chapter 8 it is shown how new intermediate scales of technology and institutional arrangements may be incorporated in central sanitation planning.

Next to identifying socio-technical configurations, MMa has been used as a guideline for the improvement of urban environmental infrastructures. In these instances, such as in the case of waste management in Dar es Salaam (Chapter 4) or sanitation infrastructure in Kampala (Chapter 8), proposals for improvement were made based on three main criteria: proposed mixtures should be (a) ecologically and institutionally sustainable, (b) accessible (particularly for the poor), and (c) institutionally and technically flexible, resilient and robust.

Accessibility refers to the extent to which specific groups within the urban population, such as women, poor or elderly, are included or excluded from receiving sanitary infrastructures and services due to financial, physical or cultural reasons. Flexibility points at the way a sanitation system might fit into more encompassing systems to be developed in the future, while also describing how the systems behave in times of climatic, political or economic instability. The sustainability requirement can be conceived as institutional and environmental sustainability. Institutional sustainability concerns the extent to which a new system becomes embedded in existing sociopolitical and cultural systems at the local and national level, while improving their performance. Environmental sustainability refers to the achievements in waste prevention (reducing the need for final disposal of the waste) and in reduction of demand for inputs – in particular, water and energy.

The criteria were further developed through stakeholder workshops and applied in expert multi-criteria decision making procedures to elaborate their particular connotation in specific contexts and their relative importance. This enabled a comparison between different options (similar to the procedures proposed in ISWM, HCES and SANCHIS presented above). These results also provide inputs for a matrix, where social, institutional, spatial and technical criteria are set and indicators for measurement can be applied.

Recent research applying the MMa has illustrated the importance of better understanding the specific characteristics of everyday lives of the stakeholders, in particular of the households involved (Solomon 2011). Social practices of households, such as their (in)formal economic activities, cultural practices and internal division of tasks and responsibilities, all have direct consequences for how they relate to these facilities and services. Many failures of recent innovation attempts can be explained by their proponents having ignored the social practices of end-users, and MMa should explicitly pay attention to these practices if this approach aims to avoid similar mistakes.

In terms of governance of urban environmental infrastructures, we posit that forms of network governance would make a better match with the ideas behind the MMa approach than the neo-developmental state would do. A networked form of governance allows for the needed diversity in the management of environmental flows, in terms of the actors involved and the responsibilities they have. For instance, social actors and institutions involved in the generation and primary collection of sanitation and solid waste differ in some essential ways from those involved in secondary collection, treatment and disposal. While the primary steps are dominated by domestic rationalities and household practices, the secondary steps are primarily characterised by system rationalities of technological and economic nature. The presence of these different rationalities requires a mode of governance that does not prescribe the state or any other actor to dominate in the decision making on provision or management of urban infrastructures. In some cases, the city council would indeed be the most appropriate actor to provide the services of sludge disposal and treatment, while in other locations, private actors or communities would be the best option for taking up these responsibilities. Also, the locations where upstream and downstream rationalities may meet are of particular importance for infrastructure governance. An example of such a meeting point is the skip (waste container) located in neighbourhoods, studied in Chapters 4 and 5. At this location, the different practices and their associated rationalities have to become mutually adjusted and accommodated in order to enable a more effective, integrated operation and management of infrastructural systems and their environmental flows (Oosterveer and Spaargaren 2010). As these locations might differ over the systems of waste and sanitation services in urban East Africa, also the modes of governance may differ, which again pleads for the more flexible network governance that allows for institutional diversity, rather than fixed state-based governance settings.

2.7 Modernised Mixtures approach as a strategy for system innovation in waste and sanitation infrastructure provision

While this chapter posits the MMa as a useful approach to assess current varieties of socio-technical configurations in waste management and sanitation, the question is whether Modernised Mixtures should also be conceived as a (necessary) stage in the sustainable development of waste and sanitation systems. This is a question that requires a view on long-term environmental reforms in infrastructures or on system innovation and the different patterns and stages of socio-technical change. Such a view has been developed by a vast number of scholars who have contributed to the theory of socio-technical transitions (amongst others: Geels 2002; Smith, Stirling et al. 2005; Spaargaren, Oosterveer et al. 2011). In brief, transition theory is a multiple-level and multi-actor approach to long-term socio-technical system change. It distinguishes three different levels: the landscape, the regime and the niche. The *regime* level takes central stage in the theory of transitions: it is the configuration of technologies, meanings, practices and policies in place that stabilises a particular socio-technical system and, therefore, comprises the target of system innovation. On a higher level, the *landscape* entails context variables, such as macro-economy, political culture, demography and natural environmental conditions, which channel transition processes and change only very slowly. As a strategy towards regime change, transition theory proposes the development of socio-technical *niches,* which are situated below the regime level. Niches are breeding grounds, protected by tax or law exemptions, subsidies or other means, for the development and experimentation of new socio-technical configurations. In niches, new sets of actors may collaborate, develop social practices around new technology and infrastructures and learn from these experiences. Socio-technical systems may also change through the breaking up of particular regimes under pressure from wider social and environmental developments (landscape-pressure) or through failures in their function as system stabilisers. This would allow for radical system change from the top along with changes from the bottom, as in the case of niches.

Connecting this transition theory with the MMa offers the perspective for a longer-term view on developing more sustainable and more accessible urban environmental infrastructure in East African contexts. This chapter has presented the Modernised Mixtures approach as a reflexive modernisation answer to urban environmental system innovation. In terms of transition theory, we posit that modernised mixtures can be conceived as niches that serve as a stepping stone towards regime change and system innovation, as well as alternatives for present regimes. As a consequence, the authors in this volume all have chosen to study cases where there are hybrid scales of technology involved, mixed management schemes, multiple governance levels or new forms of stakeholder participation in waste and sanitation services. Not only to show that that there is much more than either large-scale centralised or small-scale decentralised technologies and management systems, but – more importantly – to find out how future socio-technical regimes could be configured, given the current niche innovations in waste and sanitation systems. By studying the current mixtures, we hope to learn more about the feasible future socio-technical regimes that are emerging or could possibly emerge. In Chapter 9, the findings of the empirical studies of waste and sanitation services in East African urban centres will be utilised to build up further insights on such long-term sustainable development of waste and sanitation infrastructures.

References

Abbott, J. (2012). *Green infrastructure for sustainable urban development in Africa.* London: Earthscan.

Bakker, K., Kooy, M., Shofiani, N.E., & Martijn, E-J. (2008). Governance failure: Rethinking the institutional dimensions of urban water supply to poor households. *World Development,* 36 (10): 1891–1915.

Beck, U., Giddens, A., & Lash, S. (1994). *Reflexive modernization: Politics, tradition and aesthetics in the modern social order.* Cambridge: Polity Press.

Black, M. & Fawcett, B. (2008). *The last taboo: Opening the door on the global sanitation crisis.* London: Earthscan.

Dickson, D. (1974). *Alternative technology and the politics of technical change.* Glasgow: Fontana/Collins.

Geels, F. W. (2002). Technological transitions as evolutionary reconfiguration processes: A multi-level perspective and a case-study. *Research Policy,* 31 (8–9): 1257–1274.

Hegger, D. (2007). *Greening sanitary systems: An end-user perspective.* PhD thesis. Wageningen: Wageningen University.

Hendriksen, A., Tukahirwa, J. T., Oosterveer, P.J.M., & Mol, A.P.J. (2011). Participatory decision making for sanitation improvements in unplanned urban settlements in East Africa. *Journal of Environment & Development,* 21 (1): 98–119.

IJgosse, J., Anschuetz, J. et al. (2004). Putting integrated sustainable waste management into practice: Using the ISWM assessment methodology as applied in the UWEP plus programme (2001–2003). WASTE, Gouda, The Netherlands.

Kessides, I. N. (2004). *Reforming infrastructure: Privatization, regulation and competition.* Washington DC: World Bank.

Kessides, I.N. (2005). Infrastructure privatization and regulation: Promises and perils. *The World Bank Research Observer,* 20 (1): 81.

Letema, S., van Vliet, B. & van Lier, J. (2012). Satellite sanitary systems in Kampala, Uganda. *Environmental Engineering Science,* 29 (5): 291–296.

Letema, S. C. (2012). *Assessing sanitary mixtures in East African cities.* PhD thesis. Wageningen: Wageningen Academic Publisher.

Loetscher, T. (1999). *Appropriate sanitation in developing countries.* PhD thesis, University of Queensland, Brisbane, Australia.

Lüthi, C., Morel, A., Kohler, P. & Tilley, E. (2009). *People's choice first, a 4-country comparative validation of the HCES planning approach for environmental sanitation.* Bern, NCCR: North-South Dialogue 22.

Mara, D., Drangert, J.-O., Anh, N., Tonderski, A., Gulyas, H., & Tonderski, K. (2007). Selection of sustainable sanitation arrangements. *Water Policy*, 9: 305–318.

Mara, D. & Alabaster, G. (2008). A new paradigm for low-cost urban water supplies and sanitation in developing countries. *Water Policy,* 10: 119–129.

Mol, A.P.J., Sonnenfeld, D. A., & Spaargaren, G. (eds.) (2009). *The ecological modernisation reader.* Oxford: Routledge.

Nilsson, D. (2006). A heritage of unsustainability? Reviewing the origin of the large-scale water and sanitation system in Kampala, Uganda. *Environment and Urbanization,* 18 (2): 369–385.

Oosterveer, P. (2009). Urban environmental services and the state in East Africa; between neo-developmental and network governance approaches. *Geoforum,* 40 (6): 1061–1068.

Oosterveer, P. & Spaargaren, G. (2010). Meeting social challenges in developing sustainable environmental infrastructures in East African cities. In B. van Vliet, G. Spaargaren & P. Oosterveer (Eds.), *Social Perspectives on the Sanitation Challenge* (pp. 11–30). Dordrecht: Springer.

Sawyer, R. & Simpson-Hébert, M. (1998). PHAST step-by-step guide: A participatory approach for the control of diarrhoeal disease, WHO, Geneva, Switzerland.

Scheinberg, A. (2011). *Value added: Modes of sustainable recycling in the modernisation of waste management systems.* PhD thesis. Wageningen: Wageningen University.

Scheinberg, A. & Mol, A.P.J. (2010). Multiple modernities: Transitional Bulgaria and the ecological modernisation of solid waste management. *Environment and Planning C: Government and Policy,* 28 (1): 18–36.

Schumacher, E. F. (1973). *Small is beautiful: A study of economics as if people mattered.* London: Blond Briggs.

Smith, A., Stirling, A., & Berkhout, F. (2005). The governance of sustainable socio-technical transitions. *Research Policy,* 34 (10): 1491–1510.

Solomon, A.O. (2011). *The role of households in solid waste management in East Africa capital cities.* PhD thesis. Wageningen: Wageningen Academic Publisher.

Spaargaren, G. & Mol, A.P.J. (1992). Sociology, environment, and modernity: Ecological modernization as a theory of social change. *Society & Natural Resources,* 5 (4): 323–344.

Spaargaren, G., Oosterveer, P., & Loeber, A. (Eds.). (2011). *Food practices in transition: Changing food consumption, retail and production in the age of reflexive modernity.* London: Routledge.

Spaargaren, G., Oosterveer, P., Van Buuren, J., & Mol, A.P.J. (2005). *Mixed modernities: Towards viable environmental infrastructure development in East Africa.* Wageningen: Wageningen University, Environmental Policy Group.

Tilley, E., Lüthi, C., Morel, A., Zurbrügg, C., & Schertenleib, R. (2008). *Compendium of sanitation systems and technologies.* Dübendorf, EAWAG.

UNEP International Environmental Technology Centre (1996). *International sourcebook on environmentally sound technologies for municipal waste treatment.* Osaka/Shiga, UNEP.

UNEP International Environmental Technology Centre (2009). *Developing integrated solid waste management plan* (Training Manual Vol. 4 ISWM Plan). Osaka/Shiga, UNEP.

Van Buuren, J.C.L. (2010). Sanitation choice involving stakeholders. PhD Thesis, Wageningen University, Wageningen, The Netherlands.

Van de Klundert, A. & Anschütz, J. (2001). *Integrated sustainable waste management – The concept. Tools for decision-makers.* Gouda: Waste.

Van Vliet, B. (2006). The sustainable transformation of sanitation. In J. P. Voss, D. Bauknecht & R. Kemp (Eds.), *Reflexive governance for sustainable development* (pp. 337–354). Cheltenham: Edward Elgar.

Van Vliet, B., Spaargaren, G. & Oosterveer, P. (Eds.). (2010). *Social perspectives on the sanitation challenge.* Dordrecht: Springer.

Wilson, D.C., & Scheinberg, A. (2010). What is Good Practice in Solid waste Management? *Waste Management & Research,* 28 (12): 1055–1056.

IJgosse, J., J. Anschuetz, et al. (2004). Putting integrated sustainable waste management into practice: Using the ISWM assessment methodology as applied in the UWEP plus programme (2001–2003). WASTE, Gouda, The Netherlands.

Zurbrügg, C. & Tilley, E. (2007). *Evaluation of existing low-cost conventional as well as innovative sanitation systems and technologies* (Workpackage 3 – Assessment of Sanitation Systems and Technologies). NETSSAF, Deliverable 22 & 23. Project No. 037099, EAWAG.

3 Sanitation and solid waste management options for sustainable service provision in East Africa

Joost van Buuren, Shaaban Mgana, Fredrick Salukele, James Okot-Okumu, Christian Zurbrügg and Grietje Zeeman

3.1 Introduction

The importance of good urban sanitation and solid waste management infrastructure has been widely documented (Cairncross and Feachem 1983: 3; Tchobanoglous, Theisen et al. 1993: 3; IETC 1996). Hutton and Haller (2004: 35) show that every dollar spent in Sub-Saharan Africa on improved water and sanitation yields from 5 to 15 dollars in terms of time savings associated with better access to water and sanitation facilities, gain in productive time, costs saved due to less treatment of diseases and deaths prevented. Accordingly, local and international stakeholders spend much effort improving access to adequate household sanitation infrastructure. Most widely known are the programs undertaken to reach the water and sanitation targets of the UN Millennium Development Goals of water and sanitation. This chapter first reviews the state of the sanitation and solid waste management service provision in East Africa and then looks at innovative and effective new approaches from a technological perspective. In particular, the chapter emphasizes the recovery of resources from urban wastes so that waste handling may become a driver for new economic developments and enhance environmental sustainability. In the framework of the Modernised Mixtures approach, adaptive and diverse policies on service provision are proposed based on multi stakeholder participation.

3.2 Sanitation in East African cities

Throughout this volume, sanitation and solid waste management system options are seen as *service chains:* systems that facilitate the flows of materials through the private and public spatial domain of the city. This means that a system option is envisioned as a chain of infrastructure components (hardware) and human actions (software and management) that handles waste flows from the generation source to the final point of disposal or reuse. Depending on the system type, a sanitation chain may include a series of technologies, beginning with a 'toilet' and followed by a device for on-site pre-treatment and storage of faecal material, a transport system, an off-site treatment system and a way of disposal or utilisation of the end products of the treatment. Such a service chain is established and operated by social actors or, otherwise stated, it is part of a socio-technical arrangement. Using a slightly adapted typology proposed by Tilley and co-workers (2008), sanitation service chains can be classified into four groups, namely: (1) waterless on-site options, (2) on-site options with pour-flush toilets, (3) full-flush or pour-flush toilet systems with (partial) on-site treatment and (4) full-flush or pour-flush toilet systems with full off-site treatment. The systems of group 1 are usually found in areas without piped water supply. The domestic water here is hand-carried. The systems of groups 2 through 4, in most cases, serve users with piped water supply and multiple taps in the household. Under each group there is a large variety of systems. System inventories can be found in literature (Franceys, Pickford et al. 1992; Mara 1996a; Tilley, Lüthi et al. 2008). The most important sanitation systems reported from studies in East Africa are shown in Table 3.1. The terms used in this table are explained in the following text.

The table shows the conditions of application and an assessment of the quality level according to the service ladder proposed by the IRC International Water and Sanitation Centre (WHO and UNICEF 2008; Potter, Klutse et al. 2011). Using criteria for infrastructure performance, the ladder attributes a quality ranking from *unacceptable*, applied to the limited and basic, to *improved* facilities. Only the improved facilities and those higher on the ladder have been qualified as contributing to Millennium Development Goals (MDG). The estimates of the served population are borrowed from Szanto, Letema et al. (2012). In the countries studied, the population with adequate (improved) sanitation was estimated in the range of 30 and 35% (2011, Uganda: 34%; Kenya: 32%) (UNICEF 2013). The inadequately serviced group is living in rural areas and urban informal settlements. The systems in use are briefly discussed below.

3.2.1 Latrines

The simple pit latrine (group 1) in East Africa is mostly self-constructed, following many different designs: plain, elevated, with or without concrete slab, etc. Simple latrines equipped with a safe concrete slab at the top of the pit are considered as an improved sanitation system. However, many simple pit latrines do not comply with the MDG criteria for improved sanitation and are therefore assessed as a basic or even limited sanitation technology. The Ventilated Improved Pit (VIP) latrine is an upgraded version of the simple pit latrine, with concrete slab, sturdy superstructure and ventilation pipe against smells and insect nuisance. VIP latrines have been rather widely implemented in a bid to improve the user acceptance and hygienic conditions. They are more expensive than simple pit latrines. According to SEI, South African Knowledge Node on Sustainable Sanitation et al. (2011), South Africa has presently three million VIP latrines. Their big environmental issues are soil and ground water pollution due to leaching and the erroneous handling of their sludge, the latter exacerbated by the use of latrines for garbage dumping. An environmental improvement of simple and VIP

Table 3.1 Sanitation systems in East African cities

Group	*System*	*Typical conditions of application*	*Level*	*Estimated served population*
1	Simple pit latrine (elevated or on ground level)	Urban and peri-urban areas where in-house water supply is lacking. The latrine is often shared by several households	Limited, basic, improved	High percentage in rural zones and urban slums
	VIP latrine (single and double pit)	Urban and peri-urban low-income areas	Improved	3-5% in urban slums
	Fossa alterna (composting toilet)	Rural and peri-urban areas. Effective demand for compost	Improved	Very small %
	Urine-diverting latrine (Ecosan, Skyloo, etc.)	Rural and peri-urban areas, effective demand for compost and urine	Improved	Very small %
2	Pour-flush (PF) single pit	In Uganda, it is mainly urban and often used by higher-income owners, not in the slums	Improved	Very small % (Uganda)
3	PF toilets + bio-latrine + infiltration	Public/shared sanitation and institutions, biogas production, faecal sludge utilised	Improved	Very small %
	Flush (PF/CF) toilet + septic tank + soak pit	High/middle-income households, faecal sludge transported to central sewage treatment plant or dumped	Improved	2.5-20% (Dar es Salaam) 3.2-17.5% (Kampala) 56% (Nairobi)
4	CF/PF + satellite separated sewerage	High-income residential areas and Institutions (prisons), sewage treated in small local sewage treatment plants	Improved	1% (Kampala)
	CF/PF + centralised separated sewerage	Central Business Districts (CBD), some industrial areas, selected residential areas with high-income households and public institutions, sewage treated in small local sewage treatment plants	Improved	6.5-13% (Dar es Salaam) 6% Kampala 36% Nairobi 29% Kisumu

Sources: (Szanto, Letema et al. 2012, Letema, 2012, 17 and 81)

(PF = pour-flush; CF = cistern-flush)

latrines are the single pit and twin-pit composting toilets (e.g., *Arborloo and fossa alterna*) (Morgan 2007). The composting toilets receive both urine and faeces. To bring about (aerobic) composting, leaves, straw, sawdust, ash, soil or compost should be added after defecation to reduce smells and maintain aerobic conditions. The leachate from the pits seeps into the subsoil. The produced compost can be utilized. To allow for easier drying and hygienisation of the pit contents, urine diversion has been introduced. In this case, urine is stored separated from the faeces. Urine-diverting (UD) toilets have been used in East Africa for quite some time. They come under names like Ecosan toilet or Skyloo (Malawi). They are not popular in cities, probably due to the lack of facilities to utilize urine and composted faeces (Ministry of Water and Environment Uganda 2012) and religious beliefs about the necessary use of water for anal cleansing. On the other hand, they have significant environmental and practical strengths, so that, for instance, the municipality of eThekwini in South Africa proposes urine-diverting systems as the only future dry toilet system (SEI, South African Knowledge Node on Sustainable Sanitation et al. 2011). Where dry latrines are used, grey water from bathing and the kitchen is usually drained into the soil near the house. The reuse of grey water is discussed below.

3.2.2 Wastewater and sludge treatment

Off-site or hybrid on-site sanitation systems include transport, treatment and disposal/reuse of faecal sludge (groups 1, 2 and 3) or wastewater (group 4). Faecal sludge from on-site sanitation in East Africa may be handled in one of the following ways, depending mostly on households' or local authority's preferences and affordability:

- permanently abandoning it in disused pits and constructing new pit latrines;
- burying it in newly dug pits adjacent to emptied pits;
- dumping in sewers and in surface water;
- dumping on land without pre-treatment;
- co-disposal with municipal solid waste on landfills;
- treatment in adequately equipped plants.

As the first four methods are likely to cause soil and (ground)water contamination, they are less acceptable, but very common. The impacts of dumping untreated sludge on land (fourth method) much depend on circumstances. The sludge may benefit the fertility of the soil, but, in particular, helminth eggs may remain infectious for a long period and could form a health risk. The fifth method is environmentally acceptable only if the disposal sites are provided with lining material to prevent seepage into the underground and if landfill gas is captured. Such sanitary landfills are rare in East Africa. The sixth method can be effective, but is still rare as well. It is discussed later in this chapter.

Treatment of domestic and institutional sewage (combined black and grey water) occurs in East African cities at various scales. Large cities often have

Table 3.2 Centralized sewage treatment plants in East African cities

Country/city	*Type of sewage treatment plant*
Kenya	
Nairobi	Stabilisation ponds
Kisumu	Trickling filters and stabilisation ponds
Uganda	
Kampala	Trickling filters and stabilisation ponds
Jinja	Stabilisation ponds
Tanzania	
Dar-es-Salaam	Stabilisation ponds and sea outfall
Mwanza	Stabilisation ponds
Arusha	Stabilisation ponds
Tanga	Preliminary treatment followed by sea outfall

centralized sewage treatment plants particularly serving the central (business) districts. Others have several plants that serve particular zones. Most urban sewage treatment plants apply stabilisation pond technology. The centralized treatment plants of Kampala and Kisumu are provided with trickling filters (Table 3.2). In sewered areas, the percentage of the population actually connected is rather low. For Tanzanian cities, this is only 13–27% (Ewura 2010). For Kampala, Uganda, Letema (2012: 18) reported a connection rate of only 5% in 10 sewered areas.

3.3 Solid waste management in East African cities

The main sources of municipal solid waste in Africa are households, markets, street sweeping, shops and institutions (Okot Okumu and Nyenje 2011). In capital cities, industries also contribute significantly. The per capita household waste generation amounts on average is 0.65 kg/d in Nairobi (Kasozi and Von Blottnitz 2010), 0.55 kg/d in nine cities in Uganda and 0.32 kg/d and 0.4 kg/d in Mwanza and Dar es Salaam,[1] respectively. Nairobi (2010), Kampala (2006) and Dar es Salaam (2007) generated approximately 3,120 tonnes, 1,300 tonnes and 3,460 tonnes MSW/d, respectively, in the indicated years. These amounts have risen because of population increases and higher consumption rates.

Compositions of municipal solid wastes in East African cities are shown in Table 3.3. The compositions in nine cities in Uganda and Mwanza city (TZ) are rather similar, showing that food wastes are the main waste category, followed by yard wastes. In Nairobi, the waste contained considerably more paper and plastics than in the other East African cities. According to JICA (2010) quoted in Oyake-Ombis (2012: 183), Kenyan urban waste contains about 10% plastics, which is considerably less than the 16.1% given in Table 3.3 for Nairobi.

Table 3.3 Composition of MSW in cities in East Africa (% by weight)

Component	*Nairobi (Kenya)*	*Nine cities in Uganda*	*Mwanza (TZ)*
	(Kasozi and Von Blottnitz 2010, table 3)	*(Okot Okumu and Nyenje 2011)*	*(Salukele, Mgana et al. 2011)*
Food wastes	50.9	37.8	46.2
Yard wastes	n.a.	33.6	37.6
Paper	17.5	6.7	7.3
Plastics	16.1	7.8	2.8
Textiles	n.a.	1.3	1.5
Metals (cans, etc.)	2.0	0.8	0.9
Glass	2.0	0.7	1
Ashes/sand/debris	n.a.	8.6	2.6
Others	11.4	2.7	0.1

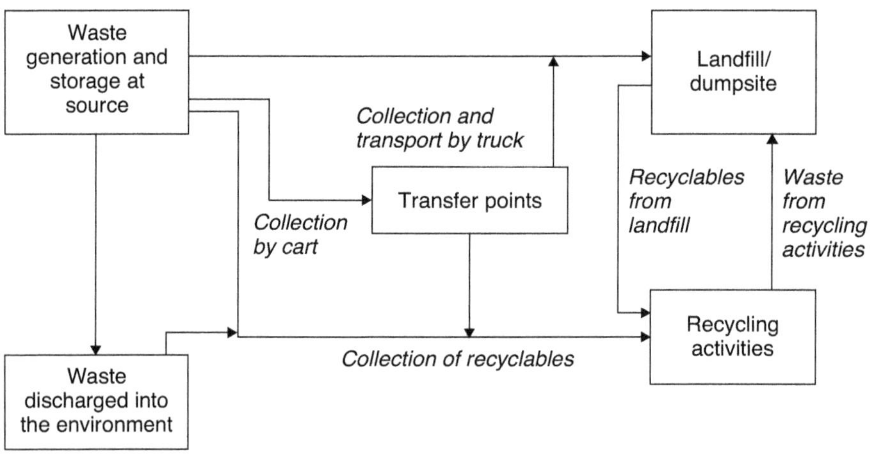

Figure 3.1 Simplified flow diagram of solid wastes in East African cities

The actual service chain of municipal solid waste (MSW) management in the three countries under study is briefly reviewed below, with a focus on the material flows and technologies. This chain is conceived as consisting of the elements storage at source, collection, transfer, transport, treatment, disposal and recycling. Figure 3.1 gives a schematic overview of the actual system. It is a relatively simple system in which the generated waste is either collected or haphazardly dumped into the environment. The collected waste is separated in a stream to a disposal site and a much smaller stream of recyclables to be processed.

3.3.1 Solid waste storage at source

Households in East African cities use several means for storage of wastes, e.g., plastic bags, old plastic buckets, baskets and boxes. The Public Health Act (2009) in Tanzania advocates solid waste separation of different kinds of waste at source; it provides standards to guide the type, size, shape, colour and other specifications of the waste containers used. However, municipalities currently do not adhere to the requirements of this act.

3.3.2 Collection, transfer and transport

The fate of the municipal waste is threefold: a (small) part with a market value is separated and collected for recycling, another (large) part without perceived value is either collected as commingled waste or dumped in the environment where collection services are lacking. Recyclables from garbage separated at source are collected by individual informal recyclers at the household (Figure 3.1). Collected commingled wastes are transported by manual or mechanically driven vehicles to intermediate transfer stations and then to disposal sites or else directly to disposal sites. The mode of collection and transport of wastes depends on the characteristics of neighbourhoods. A mixture of types of waste collection can be observed, such as door-to-door collection, kerb collection and backyard collection. In areas with accessible roads, the collection vehicles are usually trucks, which, when full, make the trip to the disposal site. In less accessible areas, collectors bring the waste from where it is collected to transfer points using push carts and wheelbarrows and transport it onwards by truck to the disposal site. At the transfer points, the waste is stored in different ways. Dar es Salaam City has trailers at some points. Other storage devices are skips, bunkers and chambers. However, often the transfer points are not more than open dumping sites without any measure to protect the surroundings. Waste may stay at such sites for a long period without being collected. The use of skips and trailers avoids the need to transfer the waste onto the trucks and could prevent littering to some degree. A detailed picture of collection modes in Kampala is sketched in Chapter 5 of this volume. Waste trucks in East African cities are often in a dilapidated state. Often they are simple open trucks or skip loaders. Rather sophisticated compactor trucks are also in use, but their application is deemed less appropriate to the dense and wet waste of East African cities. It appears a lasting challenge is to keep waste trucks in running order. Well-provided repair shops often are lacking and bad road conditions lead to frequent tire punctures and breakdowns. Accordingly, the number of trucks available for waste collection in a certain city may vary significantly over time, which has a strong impact on the collected fraction of waste (Henry, Yongsheng et al. 2006). A report covering the period 2002–2007 states that in Kampala 35 five-ton waste trucks were in operation out of a required average of 86 (Office of the Auditor General 2010). The frequency of collection at households is usually once or twice per week. At companies and institutions, collection may be more frequent, depending on individual agreements.

Table 3.4 Collection coverage in a few East African cities

Country/City	*Collection coverage %*	*References*
Kenya		
Nairobi	33	(JICA 2010)
Eldoret	36–54	(Henry, Yongsheng et al. 2006)*
Uganda		
Kampala	40	(Office of the Auditor General 2010)
Nine cities	43.7 (15–60%)	(Okot Okumu and Nyenje 2011)
Tanzania		
Dar es Salaam	40	(Oberlin Solomon 2011)
Mwanza	65	(Salukele, Mgana et al. 2011)

* The collection coverage data quoted by Henry, Yongsheng et al. (2006) are from 1999.

Table 3.4 gives recent data of the overall collection coverage in some East African cities. In Dar es Salaam, the collected fraction has increased gradually from 12% in 1994 to about 40% in 2007. The introduction of privatization of collection and transport has contributed to higher efficiency and adequacy of the collection (Kaseva and Mbuligwe 2005; Oberlin Solomon 2011, Chapter 2). This shows that organisational set-up and management are critical elements of service performance.

3.3.3 Recycling and reuse of materials

Households, waste collectors, waste pickers and itinerant waste buyers handle recyclables all along the waste chain: at the generation sources, during collection and transfer, at the official landfills and at illegal dumping sites. In general, waste recycling is carried out by both the formal and informal sector – that is, informal collectors who are not recognized as part of the official solid waste management system. In some places and for some types of recyclables, formal and informal actors work in competition; in others, in forms of commercial cooperation (e.g., where formal processors buy recyclables from junk shops to which informal collectors sell their recyclables). In East African cities, the recycling and reuse is to a high degree undertaken for the direct financial gains to the involved actor. For many waste components, the societal benefits of recycling outweigh the costs. This positive balance is primarily the result of the avoided costs of waste disposal and reduced use of virgin materials in production. The benefits of recycling grow with decreasing costs of recycling itself (e.g., through more efficient and cheaper technologies). Reliable comparisons of the costs of formal and informal recycling activities are hardly available, probably due to the complex relationships of the two sectors (Scheinberg, Spies et al. 2011). Chapter 5 of this volume shows how in the case of Kampala the informal private sector free-rides on public services, which may reduce its costs.

In East African cities, metals, paper, cardboard and plastics are recycled to produce new materials. In Kenyan cities, metals are picked from waste and used in the many small-scale 'Jua Kali' handicraft workshops (Kasozi and Von Blottnitz 2010).

In Nairobi and Dar es Salaam, composting of biowastes from MSW is practiced at a (very) small scale only (Henry, Yongsheng et al. 2006; Kasozi and Von Blottnitz 2010), although biowastes are by far the biggest fraction in municipal waste. In Dar es Salaam, the municipality discourages home composting to prevent bad smells and insect nuisance. A few somewhat contrasting figures have been published about plastic recycling in Nairobi. Assuming 3 million inhabitants, 0.65 kg MSW/cap/d (Table 3.2) and a 16% fraction of plastics in MSW (Table 3.3), the waste plastics flow of Nairobi would be about 300 tons/d. Mwai (2008) and Practical Action (2005), both quoted in (Oyake Ombis 2012), reported a recycled plastic flow of 20–30 tons/d and 100 tons/d, respectively. This would mean that from 7% to one third of the waste plastic was being recycled. We have no explanation for the differences between the reported values.

As mentioned above, recovery of materials from municipal waste is usually beneficial to society as a whole. On the basis of waste characteristics (Table 3.3), one could conclude that about 80 to 90% of the generated MSW could in theory be recycled, including paper, textiles, metals, plastics, glass and food wastes. A JICA study in Dar es Salaam in 1997, cited by Oberlin Solomon (2011: 43), has shown that about 8% of the generated household waste was recovered for recycling. Kasozi and Von Blottnitz (2010) estimate that in Nairobi 5% (100–150 tons/d) of the generated waste is recovered for reuse and recycling. In Lusaka (Zambia), for comparison, the overall diversion of recyclables was 9% (around 2007), of which a third was recovered by informal collectors (Scheinberg, Spies et al. 2011). Though the overall benefits of recycling activities outweigh the costs and recycling has become common practice in developed countries, East African countries lack most of the industrial activities that could add value to recyclables and policies and regulations that would help to stimulate recycling. Both are a prerequisite to increased material recovery from wastes.

3.3.4 *Solid waste treatment and disposal*

Engineered landfills are the only, rare, practiced waste treatment and disposal technology in the three studied East African countries. They receive wastes directly from generators, from transfer points/stations and rejects from industry (Figure 3.1). Uncontrolled dumpsites are being utilised much more frequently. They lack measures to protect the subsoil and groundwater and prevent atmospheric pollution. Around 2009, Nairobi had 60 illegal dumpsites apart from the official site at Dandora (Ngau and Kahiu 2009 quoted in Kasozi and Von Blottnitz 2010). General problems associated with the landfills and dumpsites are considerable environmental and health damages, the frequent outbursts of public resistance against them and the difficulty of finding alternative or new sites. These problems are increasing, given the rapid rate of filling up due to fast growth of the waste stream and improving collection services. As a consequence, disposal sites have to be closed and new ones to be found in places at longer distances from the city centres, with concomitant hikes of transport fees.

Table 3.5 gives an overview of present disposal sites in some of the major East African cities. Kasozi and Von Blottnitz (2010) estimate that the disposal costs at the

Table 3.5 Disposal sites for MSW in East African cities

Country/city	*Disposal sites in use (SL = sanitary landfill)*
Kenya	
Nairobi	Dandora, Ruai SL (future)
Uganda	
Kampala	Kiteezi SL
Other cities	Open dumpsites
Tanzania	
Dar es Salaam	Pugu Kinyamwezi (64 ha)
Mwanza	Buhongwa (94 ha)

future sanitary landfill of Ruai (Nairobi) (3,400–5,000 Ksh/ton; 45–67 USD/ton[2]) will be four to five times higher than the actual costs at Dandora. The discharge fees at Pugu Kinyamwezi (Dar es Salaam) at the moment vary between 1,000 and 4,000 TZSh/ton (0.67–2.67 USD/ton) (Oberlin Solomon 2011: 42). Kampala is the only city in the East African region equipped with a sanitary landfill – meaning that the site is protected, leachate is treated and landfill gas captured. This site at Kiteezi handles 400 to 600 tons of waste daily, at a tipping fee of 10,000 UGX/ton (3.73 USD/ton).

3.3.5 Waste prevention

In several African countries, plastic bags have been banned because they pose an environmental threat. Since 2007, in Kenya the use of bio-plastic bags has been introduced in a bid to reduce the stream of waste packaging material. This project is now deemed a failure due to insufficient support from key stakeholders (Oyake Ombis 2012: 159–182). Little is recorded about other measures for waste prevention through deliberately changed consumption.

The performance of municipal solid waste management in East African cities shows many shortcomings; the key one being that rarely more than 50% of the generated urban MSW is being collected and disposed (Table 3.4). The other 50% is being dumped directly, often in the middle of residential zones. The same malpractice holds for industrial and hazardous wastes. This leads to grave public dissatisfaction. At that, it should be noted that this poor performance cost not less than 10% of the municipal budget in Nairobi in 2010 (Oyake Ombis 2012: 15). The situation used to be much better (before about 1980), but has deteriorated severely since, because of rapid growth of the urban population, changing lifestyles, lack of financial resources, lack of capacity to apply technology-intensive waste handling methods and poor governance (Okot Okumu and Nyenje 2011; Oyake Ombis 2012: 13). For some time, governments have put emphasis on decentralization and privatization to counteract this situation, and here and there improvements are discernible (Zurbrügg 2013, Chapter 5) .

3.4 Modernised Mixtures: Towards multidimensional transformations

The preceding sections show that sanitation and solid waste management systems in East African cities can be seen as dualistic. Local government provides only a small part of the households with a sewerage and drainage system. Most other households are responsible for their own sanitation, which implies that they install the simple pit latrines that are affordable to them. Joyce and co-workers (2010: 10) show that households in low-income countries of Sub-Saharan Africa shoulder about 30% of all capital expenditure in water supply and sanitation. This is a total expenditure of 450 million USD annually (period 2001–2006). In solid waste management, the dualism is somewhat different from sanitation. Here, in the range of 50 to 60% of the waste is not collected, affecting the poor neighbourhoods in particular. Where a collection system is operated, door-to-door collection and collection from skips coincide to a certain extent with respectively richer and poorer areas (Table 5.2 in this volume).

Abbott (2012) analyses the bifurcated urban infrastructure in Sub-Saharan African cities as a colonial legacy and proposes a new vision on infrastructure as a prerequisite to overcome the present miserable situation in informal and low-income settlements. Instead of considering environmental infrastructure as a minimal service to prevent outbreaks of epidemics, it should be seen as a driver to development. Its economic feasibility should be considered at city level and not at household level, and it should strive for environmental sustainability by closing material cycles. Especially in the domain of recycling, many opportunities for economic improvement are missed (Abbott 2012: 274; Oyake Ombis 2012: 246). The latter is rapidly gaining recognition, at least in academia and among environmental NGOs. Activities in this direction are discussed below.

The present infrastructure, apparently, is not uniform, but mixed in various dimensions of technical scale, management, user participation and resource recovery. It is very unlikely that a multi-dimensional transformation will lead, eventually, to a uniform urban sanitation and solid waste management infrastructure. Rather a pluralistic, multi-provider, multi-scale, multi-technology and participatory system of provision will emerge (Scheinberg, Spies et al. 2011): a modernised mixture. But different from the present infrastructure, a transformed infrastructure does not have to distinguish its technologies according to social class and income levels. The actual discussion about environmental infrastructure in Africa strongly emphasizes the need for effective governance to enable the necessary transformations towards more equitable access and to the utilisation of urban material flows as resources. Strategically, proposals are made of strengthening local government and clarifying the roles and relationships of the various players, better regulations and their enforcement, enhanced participation of users and businesses, integration of the informal and formal sectors, behavioural change to end open defecation and illegal dumping of wastes and, last but not least, a stable mobilization of financial resources to sustainably operate services, especially in low-income areas (Kasozi and Von Blottnitz 2010; SEI, South African Knowledge Node on Sustainable Sanitation et al. 2011; Toubkiss 2010). Governance and the needed institutional changes are, amongst others, the subject of Chapter 2, and the following empirical chapters of this volume. The next sections of this chapter will focus on chains of processes, or loops, in sanitation and solid waste management that convert wastes to valuable end products.

3.5 Closing loops in sanitation

The key issue of a long-term change towards environmental sustainability is treating all urban solid and sanitation wastes as resources. Urine, faecal sludge, black water, grey water and storm water have potential value to local water and food chains and energy supply. Solid wastes include valuable materials that could be fed to industrial and agricultural chains. It has been shown above that in East African cities these potential resources are scarcely valorised at the moment. Closing loops of resource streams often requires separated transport of wastes, effective treatment and quality control and onwards transport to the place of reutilisation (i.e., steps that linear waste management does not have). Consequently, extra costs are incurred that have to be earned back via the monetary and non-monetary benefits of the resource reutilisation. The economic feasibility of resource utilisation is often scale dependent. The following categories of scale are applied: household, neighbourhood/district, wide-area urban/agricultural and industrial reutilisation (Adewumi, Ilemobade et al. 2010). Here, emphasis is laid on valorisation of faecal sludge and reuse of different forms of urban wastewater.

3.5.1 Valorisation of faecal sludge

East Africa has a great need for improved handling methods for faecal sludge from latrines and septic tanks. The problem is, however, that rarely a chain of collection, treatment and utilisation or disposal of sludge is in place.

The challenge of collection lies in reaching the latrines in often very densely built areas, emptying the pits and doing this at acceptable costs. Emptying methods range from manual emptying via simple mechanized techniques, like the Vacutug, to vacuum trucks. Recent developments in this domain can be found in a report by SEI (2011). A new pit emptying device is the Gulper pump, which has been successfully tested recently in Tanzania (Mgana 2012) and is likely to replace the now abandoned manual MAPET technique.

Reutilisation of sludge as compost requires dewatering and hygienisation. Faecal sludge can be treated in several ways, such as entrenching along with agroforestry (SEI, South African Knowledge Node on Sustainable Sanitation et al. 2011), anaerobic digestion, windrow composting, dewatering on planted and unplanted sludge drying beds, solar drying and other, more mechanized, drying and hygienisation techniques. The method to be selected depends on the characteristics of the sludge to be treated, such as the water, salts and plastics content and the methane generation potential. A new development reported from South Africa is a machine for drying and pelletisation of latrine sludge (SEI, South African Knowledge Node on Sustainable Sanitation et al. 2011).[3]

A promising treatment method for relatively wet sludge is planted drying beds onto which sludge from latrines and septic tanks can be dewatered and simultaneously hygienised. The bed separates dry matter, which stays on top of the planted bed, and leachate, which percolates through the bed and is further treated in, for example, stabilisation ponds (Strauss, Larmie et al. 1997; Koottatep, Surinkul et al. 2004). By virtue of long sludge retention times, high pathogen removal can be achieved so that the produced biosolids are suitable as soil conditioner (Koottatep, Polprasert et al. 2005; Kengne, Dodane et al. 2009). An important advantage of this type of drying beds over conventional sand beds is that they need less land. An effective demand for the compost product is needed as an important driver for the faecal sludge chain. This issue is discussed below.

3.5.2 Source control, treatment and reuse of urban waste water

Planned middle- and high-income urban zones in East Africa usually are equipped with piped water supply. In these zones, (pour-) flush toilets generate black water, and kitchens, bathrooms and washing machines generate grey water. The quantities and qualities of these streams depend on household wealth and number of taps, toilet types and washing and bathing equipment. Industries may contribute wastewater flows as well. These streams may, either apart or in combination, be considered for utilisation of water, nutrients, energy and sludge. Reuse of effluents and sludge from wastewater treatment plants requires source control. This means that the producers of the wastewater should prevent, as much as possible, pollution of the wastewater with substances that are difficult and costly to treat, or endanger its reuse. In the next section, the treatment and reuse of black water, grey water and sewage are briefly discussed. Some attention is given to the scale of operations.

Black water

Black water consists of toilet flushing water loaded with urine, faeces and anal cleansing material. Its reuse requires thorough treatment. For its on-site treatment, mostly horizontal-flow septic tanks are used. The treatment efficiency of these septic tanks could be improved by the use of an additional in-built upflow filter (Polprasert and Rajput 1982; Raman and Chakladar 1972). Possible clogging of the filter has been mentioned as a disadvantage. An alternative to the septic tank with a higher treatment efficiency is the baffled anaerobic reactor, as applied in Vietnam (Viet, Morel et al. 2008). A third development is the UASB septic tank: an anaerobic treatment system with which biogas can be captured for utilisation (Lettinga, De Man et al. 1993; Van Buuren 2010: 115). The quality of septic tank effluent is insufficient for direct reuse. If drain fields are used for post treatment, the effluent could contribute to the growth of trees and garden plants. Vertical-flow constructed wetlands (e.g., reed bed filters) could be a suitable method to improve the quality of septic tank effluent. Nyakang'o and Van Bruggen (1999) have reported an example of this system in Kenya.

A new development is the emergence of the biocentres (Binale undated). A biocentre includes a communal (pour-flush) toilet and bathroom facility combined with commercial services and an on-site anaerobic digester. In Tanzania, biocentres are currently applied to public institutions, like secondary schools and prisons, for production of biogas in addition to waste treatment and agricultural reuse of effluent. Since, however, the biogas production from solely diluted faecal matter tends to be too low for communal cooking, other feedstocks, like animal manure and sludge from pit latrines and septic tanks, are added. For the organic fraction of municipal solid waste and animal manure, biogas yields of 80–200 m^3 per wet tonne are reported. The biogas replaces wood and charcoal, typical sources of energy in the East African region. As a consequence, avoidance of CO_2 emissions, in addition to lower emissions of methane from animal manure, are indirect environmental benefits of biocentres.

Grey water

The reuse of treated grey water could save limited sources of freshwater (Morel and Diener 2006; Nhapi 2004). Notably, the grey water flow is about two thirds of the total domestic flow, and it is less polluted compared to black water, since faeces and urine are absent. Accordingly, the concentrations of pathogenic organisms, nitrogen and pharmaceutical residues are much lower. Kitchen wastewater may be so polluted that it could better be kept separated from the other grey water to simplify its treatment. The required treatment depends on the discharge/reuse purpose and the local conditions. Primary treatment methods for grey water for low- and middle income countries are coarse filtration, grease and grit traps and sedimentation tanks (septic tanks). Feasible methods for secondary treatment are anaerobic upflow filtration, horizontal and vertical flow unplanted and planted filters and pond systems. The effluent of primary cum secondary treatment facilities could be used for irrigation and aquifer recharge (Morel and Diener 2006: 40). An example of grey water reuse in Sub-Saharan Africa can be found in Djenné (Mali) where 600 households were connected to a grey water system to avoid pollution of the streets. After grease/grit removal, the effluent is infiltrated. Another system in Mali services 11 large households and consists of bathing water treatment by means of a grease and grit trap, followed by a vertical flow multimedia filter. The effluent is reused in a grey water garden (Morel and Diener 2006: 54, 57).

Reuse at neighbourhood scale in households (e.g., for toilet flushing) presupposes a dual household water reticulation. This will probably be prohibitively expensive and risky in low-income countries.

Sewage

Sewage (black plus grey water) can be treated *on-site* by the various types of septic tanks plus soak pits (mentioned above for black water), and post-treated (e.g., with constructed wetlands). Off-site treatment and reuse requires collection by means of sewers, which account for about 75% of the costs of this type of wastewater management (Van Buuren 2010: 239). Some developments to reduce the costs of sewerage are briefly indicated below.

As shown in Table 3.2, stabilisation ponds are the dominating off-site sewage treatment technology in East Africa. In some places, other technologies are used such as trickling filters, suspended growth activated sludge process plants and constructed wetlands. UASB technology is increasingly applied, mainly for industrial wastewater in South Africa (Wolmarans and De Villiers 2002). Important strengths of this technology are the generation of biogas as a fuel, a low excess sludge production, small spatial footprint and low costs (Van Haandel and Lettinga 1994). The technology could be attractive for sewage treatment where the large areas for low-rate treatment technologies like stabilisation ponds and constructed wetlands are unavailable. Providers working with UASB systems should be aware of the requirement of regular maintenance of this technique. Constructed wetlands deserve consideration as a sewage treatment method, especially at capacities smaller than 500 m^3/d (Balkema, Njau et al. 2010). In particular, the vertical-flow subsurface systems are widely applied now in developing countries for secondary treatment after pre-sedimentation of sludge. They can also be applied for the treatment of raw sewage (Molle, Lienard et al. 2005) and grey water (Morel and Diener 2006).

As long as land is not a limiting factor, stabilisation ponds and constructed wetlands seem the most appropriate technologies for wastewater treatment plants under East African conditions. Subsurface-flow constructed wetlands can be economically competitive with ponds (Okurut 2000 cited in Balkema, Njau et al. 2010: 137). The costs of these planted filters increase, however, with the costs of the graded sand and gravel with which the wetland has to be filled at the building site.

Treated sewage can be reused (e.g., for crop irrigation, for aquifer recharge and in households and industries as a secondary source of supply water). Different forms of planned reuse pose different requirements to the quality of the reused water and consequently come with their specific costs of treatment and distribution. The main driver of wastewater reuse is water stress, with its concomitant high costs of fresh water. Though the stress in East African countries is still less than in South Africa, wastewater reuse could become important in the near future to relieve local and seasonal fresh water scarcity, as is being shown in South Africa (Adewumi, Ilemobade et al. 2010).

In East Africa, the scale of urban sewage collection and treatment systems is now becoming a design variable. In Kampala, the National Water and Sewerage Corporation has initiated a move to decentralize sewage treatment to catchment levels as noted by Letema (2012). Probably, a mix of centralized and decentralized systems based on the various prevailing local conditions has a greater chance of success than purely centralized or decentralized systems. This search for an optimum combination of system scales can be seen as an example of what the Modernised Mixtures approach supports.

3.5.3 New sanitation technologies

So far, the cycles for valorisation of sludge and wastewater have been briefly discussed. In addition, some important technological developments in sanitation are indicated.

Household waterless latrines

The various types of waterless pit latrines in use in East Africa are discussed above. They have a common problem of contamination of soil and groundwater as the leachate seeps into the underground. A major improvement would be lining of the pits: soil and groundwater contamination would be prevented and the faecal matter could be collected for treatment and reutilisation. A disadvantage to the user would be a more frequent need of emptying as liquids can no longer leave the pit. Diversion of bathing water would mitigate the rapid filling of the pit. A relatively inexpensive kind of lining would be a durable plastic material that would be applied to the pit after excavation. Studies about new pit designs are reported in SEI (2011).

Waterless composting and urine-diverting (UD) toilets

As mentioned above, composting and UD toilets are not common in East African cities. Indispensable prerequisites for both toilet systems is the availability of materials to cover the excreta after toilet usage and an effective demand of the end products. The popularity of urine-diverting toilets might be improved if a service could be created to collect the separately stored urine, after which it could be properly treated and utilised. Such a service could be integrated with the collection of solid wastes. The rate of filling of the excreta container of a UD toilet is considerably less than the conventional pit latrine, since urine and anal cleansing water are excluded from it. As a consequence, the costs of pit emptying are avoided.

Cost reduction in sewerage and drainage

The discharge of unwanted water in East African cities takes place through separated systems for wastewater (sewerage) and stormwater (drainage). As shown above, sewerage has limited application in East African cities because of its high costs and inappropriateness in zones with a scarce water supply. As sewers built according to European standards are expensive, several approaches have been proposed to reduce the costs without reducing functionality. Those approaches are simplified sewerage and settled or small-bore sewerage. The costs reduction can be achieved through technical measures, such as the use of pipes with smaller diameters for effluent of septic tanks, laying out sewers below yards and sidewalks at less than the conventional depth, and construction of fewer and smaller manholes, pumping stations and siphons (Mara 1996b; Melo 2005; Van Buuren 2010: 211). Other measures to save on sewerage costs are involvement of communities in the planning, construction and operation of local sewers (Hasan 2002). Letema (2012) has elaborated on the role of satellite (decentralized) sewer systems in Kampala. In particular, in these decentralized systems, wider application of the cost reduction concepts described in the aforementioned references could lead to a better affordability of sewerage.

In East African cities, stormwater is drained via gullies and channels as a way to protect roads and residential areas against the destructive power of flooding. Depending on local and seasonal water scarcities, it can be important to consider the possibilities of rainwater harvesting. The harvested water could be utilized for fresh water supply in households, gardens, horticulture, for recharge of aquifers, and so on. Harvesting of rainwater for utilisation diminishes the amounts to be drained, thereby reducing the costs of drainage systems.

3.6 Closing loops in municipal solid waste management

In solid waste management, usually the waste hierarchy is used as a guideline for improvements (Kiely 1996; Van Buuren and Potting 2011: 57). This hierarchy is based on environmental impact considerations and prioritizes the 3 Rs (Reduction, Recycling and Reuse) over treatment and disposal and serves as the basis of modern waste management policies.

3.6.1 Biowaste reuse

As shown above, waste recycling and reuse are widely practiced in East African cities, much less as a result of deliberate government policy than as a way for the poor to earn a livelihood. The recycled materials are mostly paper, cans and plastics. Recycling of wastes requires the existence of a working service chain from households via waste buyers and processers to the clients of these processing companies. Enforcement of policies, effective institutions and appropriate technologies that strengthen these chains could certainly lead to an increase of the rate of recycling and reuse, to a reduction of the waste flows to be treated and an improvement of the income situation of waste recyclers. It has been shown that the manufacturing of high quality products from wastes is greatly helped by waste separation at source – that is, at the households and other waste generators (Okot Okumu 2012). As presently biowastes (kitchen, market, park maintenance wastes) constitute in the range of 50 to 80% of the municipal solid wastes in East African cities, enhanced recycling could significantly reduce the amounts of these wastes to be landfilled and deliver compost attractive to horticulture and agriculture (Hoornweg, Thomas et al. 1999). Up to the present, most composting in East Africa is carried out at a small scale, applying the windrow composting technique. In Uganda there are at least 11 urban solid waste composting pilot plants that are operating under the Clean Development Mechanism, and there is a plan for expansion to more towns (Okot Okumu 2012). The key issue for an increasing reuse of biowastes is the effective demand of the compost product close to the production site. Compost is a soil conditioner, rather than a fertilizer, as it contains relatively small amounts of nitrogen and phosphorus. It augments the organic matter content of soils, which is important for a healthy soil life, for maintenance of a suitable soil moisture content and protection of plants against diseases. It is used in Africa in household gardening, plant nurseries, parks and landscaping (Ekelund and Nystrom 2007). The demand of large quantities produced from municipal wastes can be influenced by effective marketing, but will certainly depend on the quality of the compost and the economic characteristics of local agriculture. Large plantations may have the purchasing power to apply significant quantities of bulk compost, which small tenant farmers may lack. To the authors' knowledge, no recent studies about compost demand around East African cities and towns are available. Accordingly, nothing definitive can as yet be concluded about the quantitative potential of biowaste reuse in East Africa. Though aerobic composting is most often used for biowaste treatment to compost, anaerobic digestion may be particularly promising as its biogas is very welcome as a source of energy (Voegeli, Lohri et al. 2009). A combination of anaerobic digestion and composting may become a new option for biowaste processing in East Africa.

3.6.2 Solid waste treatment and disposal

Uncontrolled dumping sites are the sole treatment and disposal facility in nearly all East African cities and towns. Accordingly, a first improvement would be to retrofit these dumping sites to controlled dumping sites, with avoidance of ground water pollution and sanitary landfills with capture and utilisation of landfill gas. This would certainly require a considerable investment. Application of bioreactor landfilling could be a further improvement, as it potentially leads to a smaller spatial footprint and higher benefits of landfill gas utilisation than conventional sanitary landfilling (Reinhart, McCreanor et al. 2002; Jiang, Yang et al. 2007). Other promising technologies would be anaerobic digestion and composting of biowastes. The role of incineration of wastes is probably limited to special wastes like hazardous industrial and clinical wastes because of the high costs and required skills associated with this technology.

3.7 Technological research needs and tools for technology selection

The preceding sections evidenced several research needs. Firstly, the transition to the above mentioned sludge, wastewater and solid waste recycling chains needs a strong effort with respect to a combination of technological and social issues. In general, suitable technologies are on the market, but their application in East Africa has to be adapted to local conditions, and this requires solutions for extant bottle-necks. An example is the UASB treatment of sewage. The technology is widely applied (e.g., in tropical Latin America), but in Africa the relatively modest but regular maintenance needs seem to be a major impediment to its application. A solution may be found in securing better funding for maintenance, but the selection of a design that is less sensitive to irregular maintenance could increase the success rate. Secondly, more effective and cost-saving methods should be applied to the practice of collection of latrine and septic tank sludge, sewer construction and operation and solid wastes collection and recycling. As indicated above, many possibilities are described to reduce the costs of sewer construction, but these need to be tried out, monitored and analysed in specific situations. Thirdly, African experience should be built up in relatively new treatment technologies, such as constructed wetlands for wastewater; controlled irrigation with effluents from treatment plants; and anaerobic treatment of black water, sewage, municipal biowastes and other bioorganic wastes. Building experience includes the crucial element of reporting about new treatments, also when they are not successful; practitioners can learn a lot from that. Centres for such technological

Table 3.6 Tools for participatory technology selection in developing cities

Tool name	*Nature*	*Domain of application*	*Reference*
PHAST	Planning guide for stakeholders and facilitators	Hygiene education and sanitation	(Sawyer, Simpson-Hébert et al. 1998)
SANEX	Computerized database and algorithm	Sanitation and wastewater treatment	(Loetscher 1999)
HCES and EAWAG Compendium	Database and planning procedure	Sanitation and grey water treatment	(Tilley, Lüthi, et al. 2008; Zurbrügg and Tilley 2007)
SANCHIS	Database algorithm and procedure	Sanitation, wastewater treatment and drainage	(Van Buuren 2010; Hendriksen, Tukahirwa et al. 2011)

(Acronyms: PHAST = Participatory Hygiene and Sanitation Transformation; SANEX = Sanitation Expert; HCES = Household-Centred Environmental Sanitation; SANCHIS = Sanitation Choice Involving Stakeholders).

research in East Africa are, among others, Kenyatta University in Nairobi, Makarere University in Kampala and, in Dar es Salaam, Ardhi University and the University of Dar es Salaam. Strong interdisciplinary and international research groups need to be formed and funded to further develop these topics. Evidently, there are promising opportunities for South-South academic cooperation.

Biased technology selection by a small group of experts and decision makers has been blamed for the failure of sanitation and solid waste handling technologies. In order to make technologies fit the physical, social and economic conditions of their application, the selection procedure needs to be better informed and involve all relevant stakeholders. For this purpose, several tools have been developed and applied (Table 3.6). Such tools may comprise one or more of the following elements: a database with description of technologies, a selection method and a procedure of participatory decision making. The latter includes actor analysis as a basis for knowing who the relevant stakeholders are. The selection method has to help experts making a screening between feasible and non-feasible technologies for the situation under study prior to organizing stakeholder participation. Their role as part of the overall planning of environmental infrastructure and their application are discussed in Chapter 2.

3.8 Conclusions and outlook to the future

In East African cities and towns, a substantial part of the population is still not provided with adequate sanitation and solid waste management infrastructure. The Modernised Mixtures approach would entail increasing the access to and environmental performance of these services, counting on the strengths of diversity of technological and social systems of provision. In the unplanned settlements, sanitation and solid waste management are presently to a high degree a matter for the households themselves and their community organisations. Enhancing the access of those unserviced to a perhaps basic but yet adequate service must be the first priority. Such basic services should not be seen as an endpoint, but as a first step in an incremental development process. The infrastructure in these areas lack integration into larger chains at neighbourhood or city level, as is, in particular, evident for pit latrines and septic tanks. Rarely is the sludge accumulated in these devices handled in an environmentally safe way. The required treatment and valorisation of wastes require enhanced involvement of the local government, not with the aim to provide services but to organize the closing of material cycles. Modernising the existing technological and management mixtures should imply creating a wider and qualitatively better choice of sanitation and solid waste management infrastructure to the end users. Extending piped water supply to all households in a city would open the possibility of using pour-flush toilets instead of pit latrines, but at the same time it would lead to an enormous grey water generation. This system change would have to be accompanied by provision of low-cost sewerage schemes, adequate treatment and possibly reuse of effluent. In informal settlements, such a change would have to be preceded by agreement on the locations of houses, roads and other infrastructure. Besides neighbourhood upgrading, some relocation and compensation to the relocated would be necessary. The marketing of attractive, high quality, urine-diverting toilets and accessory services could open opportunities for expanding the use of this toilet type and the valorisation of urine and dried faecal matter. In solid waste management, government support to and cooperation between the stakeholders could strengthen the economic output of the recycling sector. Waste separation at source and composting at various scales could deliver high quality compost and a strong reduction of the waste flow to landfills, thereby alleviating the pressure of finding new landfill sites.

Notes

1. In the Netherlands in 2008, the per capita generation of MSW amounted to 563 kg/cap/yr (1.54 kg/cap/d) (Abbema, Brouns et al. 2010).
2. KSh to USD rate of 76 KSh/USD (mid-market rate at 31–12–2009) (www.xe.com/currencytables/?from=KES&date=2009–12–31).
3. See also: http://www.parsep.co.za/Malyasia-Poster1.pdf

References

Abbema, A., Brouns, L. et al. (2010). *Jaarboek 2010 Afval!,* Uitgeverij Noordhoek bv The Netherlands.

Abbott, J. (2012). *Green infrastructure for sustainable urban development in Africa.* London: Earthscan.

Adewumi, J. R., Ilemobade, A. A. et al. (2010). Treated wastewater reuse in South Africa: Overview, potential and challenges. *Resources, Conservation and Recyling*, 55: 221–231.

Balkema, A., Njau, K. N. et al. (2010). Socio-economic analysis of constructed wetland systems for hygienic sanitation in Tanzania. *Water Practice and Technology*, 5 (1).

Binale, A. (undated). Umande trust bio-centre approach in slum upgrading. Retrieved from http://hal.archives-ouvertes.fr/docs/00/75/59/05/PDF/Aidah_Binale_-_UMANDE_TRUST_BIO-CENTRES.pdf

Cairncross, S. & Feachem, R. G. (1983). *Environmental health engineering in the tropics.* London: J. Wiley & Sons.

Ekelund, L. & Nystrom, K. (2007). *Composting of municipal waste in South Africa – Sustainability Aspects.* Uppsala, Sweden: Uppsala Universitet.

Energy and Water Utilities Regulatory Authority (EWURA-Tanzania) (2010). Water Utilities Performance Report for 2008/2009. Part A: Regional Water Utilities and DAWASCO – April, 2010.

Franceys, R., Pickford, J. et al. (1992). *A guide to development of on-site sanitation.* London: World Health Organisation.

Hasan, A. (2002). A model for government-community partnership in building sewage systems for urban areas. The experiences of the Orangi pilot project – Research and training institute (OPP-RTI), Karachi. *Water Science and Technology,* 45 (8): 199–216.

Hendriksen, A., Tukahirwa, J. T. et al. (2011). Participatory decision making for sanitation improvements in unplanned urban settlements in East Africa. *Journal of Environment & Development,* 21 (1): 98–119.

Henry, R. K., Yongsheng, Z. et al. (2006). Municipal solid waste management challenges in developing cities – Kenyan case study. *Waste Management,* 26 (1): 92–100.

Hoornweg, D., Thomas, L. et al. (1999). *Composting and its applicability in developing countries, urban waste management* (Working Paper Series #8). Washington, DC: The World Bank.

Hutton, G. & Haller, L. (2004). *Evaluation of the costs and benefits of water and sanitation improvements at the global level.* Geneva: WHO.

IETC (1996). *International source book on environmentally sound technologies for municipal solid waste management.* UNEP/IETC: Osaka/Shiga.

Jiang, J., Yang, G. et al. (2007). Pilot-scale experiment on anaerobic bioreactor landfills in china. *Waste Management,* 27: 893–901.

JICA (2010). *Preparatory survey for integrated solid waste management in Nairobi City-Kenya* (Volume 2). CTI Engineering and NJS Consultants Company Ltd.

Joyce, J., Granit, J. et al. (2010). *The Impact of the Global Financial Crisis on Financial Flows to the Water Sector in Sub-Saharan Africa* (Report 28). Stockholm: SIWI.

Kaseva, M. E. & Mbuligwe, S. E. (2005). Appraisal of solid waste collection following private sector involvement in Dar-es-Salaam. *Habitat International,* 29 (2): 353–366.

Kasozi, A. & Von Blottnitz, H. (2010). *Solid waste management in Nairobi: A situation analysis* (Draft 17 February 2010). City Council of Nairobi.

Kengne, I. M., Dodane, P.-H. et al. (2009). Vertical-flow constructed wetlands as sustainable sanitation approach for faecal sludge dewatering in developing countries. *Desalination,* 248 (1–3): 291–297.

Kiely, G. (1996). *Environmental engineering.* Boston: McGraw Hill.

Koottatep, T., Polprasert, C. et al. (2005). *Nutrient recycling and treatment of fecal sludge through constructed wetlands and sunflower plant irrigation.* Conf. Environmental Management of Urban Infrastructure and Industry in Asia, Ho Chi Minh City, CENTEMA. November 11 and 12, 2005.

Koottatep, T., Surinkul, N. et al. (2004). Treatment of septage in constructed wetlands in tropical climate – Lessons learnt after seven years of operation. *Water Science & Technology,* 51 (9): 119–126.

Letema, S. C. (2012). *Assessing sanitary mixtures in East African Cities.* PhD thesis. Wageningen: Wageningen Academic Publishers.

Lettinga, G., De Man, A. et al. (1993). Anaerobic treatment of domestic sewage and wastewater. *Water Science & Technology,* 27 (9): 67–73.

Loetscher, T. (1999). *Appropriate sanitation in developing countries.* PhD thesis. Brisbane: University of Brisbane.

Mara, D. D. (1996a). *Low-cost urban sanitation.* Chichester, UK: John Wiley & Sons.

Mara, D. D. (Ed.). (1996b). *Low-cost sewerage.* Chichester, UK: John Wiley & Sons.

Melo, J. C. (2005). *The experience of condominial water and sewerage systems in Brazil: Case studies from Brasilia, Salvador and Parauapebas.* The World Bank, BNWP and WSP.

Mgana, S. (2012). *Gulper pump faecal-pit emptying technology operation and management: Low cost sanitation option.* Dar-es-Salaam, Tanzania: Water Aid.

Ministry of Water and Environment Uganda. (2012). *Water and environment sector performance report.*

Molle, P., Lienard, A. et al. (2005). How to treat raw sewage with constructed wetlands: An overview of French Systems. *Water Science & Technology,* 51(9): 11–21.

Morel, A. & Diener, S. (2006). *Greywater management in low and middle-income countries, review of different treatment systems for households and neighbourhoods.* Duebendorf, Switzerland: Swiss Federal Institute of Aquatic Science and Technology (EAWAG).

Morgan, P. (2007). *Toilets that make compost. Low-cost, sanitary toilets that produce valuable compost for crops in an African context.* Stockholm: Environmental Institute Ecosanres Programme.

Nhapi, I. (2004). *Options for wastewater management in Harare.* London: Taylor and Francis Group.

Nyakang'o, J. B. & Van Bruggen, J.J.A. (1999). Combination of a well functioning constructed wetland with pleasing landscape design in Nairobi, Kenya. *Water Science & Technology,* 40(3): 249–265.

Oberlin Solomon, A. (2011). *The role of households in solid waste management in East Africa capital cities.* PhD thesis. Wageningen: Wageningen Academic Publishers.

Office of the Auditor General (2010). *Value for money audit report on solid waste management in Kampala.*

Okot Okumu, J. (2012). Solid waste management in African cities – East Africa. In L.F.M. Rebellon (Ed.) *Waste Management – An Integrated Vision.* INTECH. Retrieved from http://www.intechopen.com/books/waste-management-an-integrated-vision

Okot Okumu, J. & Nyenje, R. (2011). Municipal solid waste management under decentralisation in Uganda. *Habitat International,* 35: 537–543.

Okurut, T. O. (2000). *A pilot study on municipal wastewater treatment using a constructed wetland in Uganda.* PhD Thesis. Rotterdam / Wageningen: International Institute for Infrastructure, Hydraulics and Environmental Engineering / Wageningen University.

Oyake Ombis, L. (2012). *Managing plastic waste in Urban Kenya.* PhD Thesis. Wageningen: Wageningen University.

Polprasert, C. & Rajput, V. S. (1982). Septic tanks and septic systems by ENSIC review committee on septic systems. *Environmental Sanitation Reviews* (7/8). Bangkok, Thailand: Environmental Sanitation Information Center.

Potter, A., Klutse, A. et al. (2011). *Assessing sanitation service levels* (2nd ed.). IRC International Water and Sanitation Centre, The Hague, The Netherlands.

Raman, V. & Chakladar, N. (1972). Upflow filters for septic tank effluents. *Journal Water Pollution Control Federation,* 44 (8): 1552–1560.

Reinhart, D., McCreanor, P.T. et al. (2002). The bioreactor landfill: Its status and future. *Waste Management and Research,* 20 (2): 172–186.

Salukele, F., Mgana, S. et al. (2011). Municipal solid waste management diagnosis of rapidly growing cities: Case of Mwanza City, Tanzania. *26th International Conference on Solid Waste Technology and Management,* Philadelphia, USA, March 28–30.

Sawyer, R., Simpson-Hébert, M. et al. (1998). *PHAST step-by-step guide: A participatory approach for the control of diarrhoeal disease.* Geneva: WHO.

Scheinberg, A., Spies, S. et al. (2011). Assessing urban recycling in low- and middle-income countries: Building on Modernised Mixtures. *Habitat International,* 35 (2): 188–198.

SEI, South African Knowledge Node on Sustainable Sanitation et al. (2011). *What happens when the pit is full? Developments in on-site faecal sludge management; seminar report.* http://www.ecosanres.org/pdf_files/WhatHappensWhenThePitIsFullFSMSeminarReportSouthAfricaNodeMarch2011.pdf

Strauss, M., Larmie, A. et al. (1997).Treatment of sludges from on-site sanitation – low-cost options. *Water Science & Technology,* 35 (6): 129–136.

Szanto, G.L., Letema, S. et al. (2012). Analyzing sanitation characteristics in urban slums of East Africa. *Water Policy,* 14 (4): 613–624.

Tchobanoglous, G., Theisen, H. et al. (1993). *Integrated solid waste management: Engineering principles and management issues* (McGraw Hill International Editions, Civil Engineering Series). Singapore: McGraw Hill.

Tilley, E., Lüthi, C. et al. (2008). *Compendium of sanitation systems and technologies.* EAWAG.

Toubkiss, J. (2010). Meeting the sanitation challenge in sub-Saharan cities: Lessons learnt from a financial perspective. In B. Van Vliet, G. Spaargaren & P. Oosterveer (Eds.), *Social Perspectives on the Sanitation Challenge* (pp. 163–176). Dordrecht: Springer.

UNICEF (2013). *Joint monitoring report 2012.* http://www.unicef.org/media/files/JMPreport2012.pdf

Van Buuren, J. & Potting, J. (2011). ISSOWAMA deliverable 3.1, relevant potential impacts and methodologies for environmental impacts assessment related to solid-waste management in Asian developing countries. *Integrated Sustainable Solid Waste Management in Asia.* Bremerhaven: T. Bremerhaven.

Van Buuren, J.C.L. (2010). *Sanitation choice involving stakeholders Wageningen.* PhD Thesis. Wageningen: Wageningen University.

Van Haandel, A. C. & Lettinga, G. (1994). *Anaerobic sewage treatment, a practical guide for regions with a hot climate.* Chichester: John Wiley & Sons.

Viet, N. A., Morel, A. et al. (2008). *Baffled septic tank system – 9 years' experience of laboratory and field research. sanitation options in the Asia Pacific.* Hanoi, Vietnam, South East Asian Water Utilities Network.

Voegeli, Y., Lohri, C. et al. (2009). Technical and biological performance of the arti compact biogas plant for kitchen waste – case study from Tanzania. *Twelfth International Waste Management and Landfill Symposium Sardinia 2009.* S. Margherita di Pula, Cagliari, Italy, CISA Publisher Italy.

WHO & UNICEF (2008). *Progress on drinking water and sanitation, special focus on sanitation.* New York/Geneva.

Wolmarans, B. & De Villiers, G. H. (2002). Start-up of a UASB effluent treatment plant on distillery wastewater. *Water SA,* 28 (1): 63–68.

Zurbrügg, C. (2013). *Assessment methods for waste management decision-support in developing countries.* PhD thesis. Facoltà di Ingegneria, Dipartimento di Ingegneria Civile, Architettura, Territorio, Ambiente e Matematica, Università degli Studi die Brescia.

Zurbrügg, C. & Tilley, E. (2007). *Evaluation of existing low-cost conventional as well as innovative sanitation systems and technologies* (Workpackage 3 – Assessment of Sanitation Systems and Technologies). NETSSAF, Deliverable 22 & 23. Project No. 037099, EAWAG.

4 Recognising and strengthening the role of households in solid waste management

Asia Oberlin Solomon and Gert Spaargaren

4.1 Introduction

In many developing countries, solid waste has become a top priority (Zhu, Asnani, Zurbrügg, Anapolsky and Mani 2008). The efficient delivery of public services and the provision of viable infrastructures are pressing issues for municipal authorities and other key actors in the waste management chain. Improving solid waste management has been recognised as relevant for achieving the Millennium Development Goals (MGDs) and targets (Coad and Gonzenbach 2007; CWG-WASH 2006). Solid waste management (SWM) is costly and complex for local governments, but these services are so essential to the health, environment, and quality of life of poor people in particular that municipalities cannot afford to get it wrong (Schübeler, Wehrle and Christen 1996). Bad waste collection practices and improper solid waste disposal contribute to local episodes of disease, the pollution of water resources, and the emission of global greenhouse gases (Zhu et al. 2008).

Solid waste management services in low-income areas in capital cities of East Africa are inferior to the systems in more prosperous areas. Sub-Saharan Africa is going through a process of rapid urbanization, and the population is expected to grow from 101 million in 1990 to 313 million in 2015 (Kombe 2005; UNDP 2005). Dar es Salaam City in Tanzania is no exception to the rule of high growth rates of the population going together with a rapid urbanization process. In Dar es Salaam, the large majority of migrants from rural and other urban areas live in unplanned or informal settlements. The city is the largest commercial city in Tanzania, and its extensive informal settlements are facing severe solid waste management challenges. Studies show that in Dar es Salaam, over 60% of the population lives in unplanned and informal settlements (DCC 2004; Kyessi 2002; Kyessi and Mwakalinga 2009; Sawio 2008). Consequently, issues related to SWM have become a severe challenge, from health and environmental perspectives in particular. Illegal dumping results from a shortage of adequate waste collection services and infrastructures in densely populated areas. Problems have become aggravated because of an increased per capita generation of domestic solid waste and the lack of land conveniently situated for waste disposal. What results is a deteriorating living environment in which poor environmental health and hygiene have become chronic features, contributing to high mortality rates.

Various studies (Addo-Yobo and Ali 2003; Solomon 2011; Tadesse, Ruijs and Hagos 2008) have documented the fact that the role of households in solid waste management tends to be overlooked or neglected. In addition, in informal settlements of Dar es Salaam, householders are involved in solid waste management practices that are not known to, nor given full recognition by, the municipal authorities.

In the absence of an authority or its contracted agent to provide services in informal settlements, households and informal service providers have devised their own methods of waste collection and disposal in informal settlements, outside the official arrangement. In looking for innovative and effective solutions to the aggravating problem of inadequate management of domestic solid wastes, one needs to realise that households are not just the prime sources of the generation of domestic wastes, but also crucial actors in the so-called primary phase of solid waste management.[1] Their roles in developing and maintaining effective and legitimate solid waste management arrangement can hardly be underestimated. Since the role of actors in the primary phases have been neglected or overlooked by many official authorities, there is a need for detailed knowledge about actual waste management practices of households, such as waste generation, storage, sorting, and collection/transport, as well as knowledge about the perceptions and evaluations of householders on the present and future performance of different actors in waste chains, including their own. Therefore, this chapter aims to increase our understanding of the role of households in solid waste management by looking at the dynamics of household practices that have to be considered and taken into account when designing new interventions, both socially and technically. After presenting the conceptual framework and the methodology (Section 4.2), what follows depicts the actual legislative and operational situation with respect to domestic solid waste management in Kinondoni, Dar es Salaam (Section 4.3). The core of the chapter consists of an analysis of a number of domestic waste management practices in the research area (Section 4.4) and of the perceptions of householders on the performances of different actors in the waste chains that are serving households in Dar es Salaam (Section 4.5). We conclude with a discussion on how to use knowledge about the role of households and informal waste pickers to improve the waste management situation in the near future.

4.2 Conceptual framework and methodology

The 'Modernised Mixture approach' seeks to combine the best characteristics from two formerly separate schools of thought in sanitation and solid waste management: the centralised, high-tech and large-scale approach on the one hand, and the decentralised, low-tech and small-scale approaches on the other. Both in technical and social respects, the key effort is to find an in-between, locally adapted, but, in principle, up-scalable solution to sanitation and solid waste management problems, as described in Chapter 2. Room is made for local solutions put forward by actors who know the situation from within. Informal collection systems could be developed side by side or even in connection with formal systems, differentiated payment systems, technologies and collection schemes. The claim for all MMa-based solutions in solid waste management is that, in principle, they could be scaled up and developed into an integrated waste management system that covers a wider service area and shows differentiated but shared responsibilities between actors operating in the primary and in the secondary phases of a waste management system. Thus, households and other local actors in the primary phase are recognised and given a role in the waste chain in such a way that their activities are complementary to and supported by the activities of the institutional actors in the secondary phase of the waste chains and networks. In our research on the role of households in solid waste management in Kinondoni, the Modernised Mixture approach was applied to define roles, perceptions, practices and expectations of householders in the perspective of the waste management system as a whole.

Kinondoni municipality was selected to be the research area because it is the largest municipality in Dar es Salaam, and 43.6% of the Dar es Salaam City population lives in Kinondoni Municipality. The whole of Kinondoni municipality encompasses an area of 531 km^2, with a population of 1,083,913, according to national census of 2002; the estimate for 2007 is 1,337,875 (Solomon 2011: 23). The municipality is administratively divided into 27 wards, which in turn are subdivided into villages for rural areas and sub-wards commonly known as Mtaa (singular) or Mitaa (plural) in the urban areas. Furthermore, it is the fastest-growing municipality and it covers a wide range of unplanned settlements, with all categories of income levels being represented. The survey samples were obtained from six sub-wards, purposively sampled to cover the households of low-income socioeconomic status living in informal settlements.[2] These six neighbourhoods were purposively chosen as being together representative for poor neighbourhoods with serious problems of solid waste management in Kinondoni municipality.

The households were selected using a random sampling strategy, following a list of households provided by the sub-ward leaders. If the targeted respondent was not available or not interested in taking part in the research, the next household on the list was chosen, in order to attain the desired sample size. A total sample size of 360 households was drawn, following the above mentioned sampling frame. Next to the household questionnaire, personal observation and secondary information gathering were also used as methods. Ten face-to-face interviews were carried out with key informants, such as the Dar es Salaam City Health Officer, the Kinondoni Municipal Health Officer, and five ward/sub-ward leaders and representatives of Community Based Organizations (CBOs) that were providing waste services in the selected sub-wards. Interviews with CBO representatives[3] aimed to generate information on their roles regarding SWM, the support they get from the municipal authority when providing services to households, and the ways in which they interact with households in service provisioning. In addition, their views on how to improve service provisioning were obtained. The main objectives of the interviews with other key informants were to acquire information on their primary roles regarding household waste management and to explore their views and suggestions about the future of household waste management.

The survey questionnaires used in the study gathered information about households' practices of solid waste management. The pretested questionnaire was divided into five parts, with a total of 27 questions related to actual roles and perceptions of householders in different areas of domestic solid waste management.[4] The household survey was conducted simultaneously with a waste characterization study to determine the net per capita amount of daily wastes and the composition of the wastes in terms of some specified fractions.

The direct sampling method for determining the composition of the solid waste stream involves sampling, sorting and weighing the individual components of the waste stream from 360 randomly selected households.

4.3 Solid waste management in Kinondoni municipality: The existing situation

The existing situation can be described as a transition phase in domestic solid waste management chains in a number of respects. There is the transition from national to decentralised governance of solid waste. There is the transition from public services to partly privatized services, and there is one from a free service to a paid-for service for domestic solid wastes. To start with, the existing situation is depicted by looking into the legislative situation and to the actual service delivery on the ground.

4.3.1 Legislative situation

The Local Government Act of 1982 reveals that, to date, there is no policy for SWM at the national level in Tanzania. There are only some scattered pieces of legislation on SWM contained in different municipal policies for other areas and in a number of by-laws. Owing to the state of affairs, the city and municipal authorities in the country handle solid waste management issues according to by-laws they set for themselves. With regard to institutional arrangements, a major piece of legislation which guided solid waste management in Dar es Salaam is the Dar es Salaam (Collection and Disposal of Refuse) by-laws of 1993 that were made under sections 56 and 13 of The Local Government (Urban Authorities) Act No. 8 of 1982 (Nkya 2004). This by-law was passed to enable the privatization of waste disposal system and to introduce Refuse Collection Charges (RCCs) (Kinondoni Municipal Commission 2000). The obligations of residents (beneficiaries of SWM services) and service providers are prescribed as follows: occupiers of premises should maintain receptacles to keep waste; people are prohibited from causing a nuisance and throwing or depositing waste on streets or in open spaces not designated as collection points; beneficiaries are required to provide and maintain to the satisfaction of the DCC a receptacle for domestic refuse, of a sufficient size and fitted with a good and effective lid. The by-law pronounces penalties (fines and/or imprisonment) for defaulters (Kinondoni Municipal Commission 2000), and defines where and how collection charges should be paid by the residents, recognizing different fees corresponding with different amounts generated.

According to Nkya (2004), these regulations were not, however, fully enforced in a uniform way. Enforcement was difficult because until 1994, solid waste management in Dar es Salaam had been a free public service provided by the Dar es Salaam City Council (DCC). Since 1992, the City's solid waste management system has been reformed and contracted out to private sector operators. After reforms in the city council, the Kinondoni Municipality formed its own departments on waste management, responding to the trend of decentralization of waste management activities, and formulated its own waste management by-laws (Kinondoni Municipal Council Waste management and Refuse Collection fees).

4.3.2 Actual waste service delivery in informal settlements

From the interviews and based on participatory observation, we found both formal and informal systems that are delivering solid waste management services to households in the different sub-wards of Kinondoni. The formal system of service delivery consists of registered solid waste contractors with legal contracts for providing collection and disposal services to households. The informal service delivery is offered by waste pickers. This group includes both unregistered and unregulated waste pickers who are engaged in collection and disposal of solid wastes from households.

The main forms of solid waste collection employed by formal solid waste contractors are *door-to-door systems* and *bring systems. Door-to-door* systems involve the collection of the wastes at the doorstep of the households, using wheelbarrows and push carts. The collected wastes are then delivered to the collection point (or transfer station), which is usually a standby trailer. CBOs employ waste collectors to collect and transfer domestic wastes to the transfer station. The use of a handcart is very suitable for conditions prevailing in the low-income areas, such as narrow streets, low generation rates and low wages. Where *bring systems* are in place, householders are responsible for bringing their waste to areas where waste trucks or standby trailers are located. To ensure that the most suitable locations are chosen for the transfer stations, the siting is decided upon by households, waste contractors and the local leader of the respective sub-wards.

Informal arrangements emerge, especially in the collection and delivery of domestic solid wastes to the transfer stations. Householders and service providers over time have developed both formal and informal arrangements and relationships on SWM issues so as to bring significant improvement to solid waste management services in informal settlements. These relationships are not regulated by the municipality because they result from the negotiations and mutual agreements – both formal and informal – between households and waste providers.

4.3.3 Municipal support for domestic solid waste management

The assistance which the municipality gives to solid waste management practices at household levels includes human, technological, legal and financial resources. In terms of technological support, the Kinondoni municipal council supports waste contractors by providing equipment such as moveable standby trailers.

For instance, KIWODET confirmed to have received two standby trailers from the municipal authority in 2007, and TTM also confirmed to have acquired three standby trailers in the same year. The municipal authority delivered these standby trailers to waste contractors through ward executive officers in their respective wards. In the period 2007–2012, the municipal strategic plan was to supply tricycles known as 'Bajaj' to solid waste service providers. These tricycles could help them to increase the efficiency in waste collection in informal settlements, since a Bajaj can easily penetrate into informal settlements because of its small size.

However, at the time of this study, the level of equipment displayed was not sufficient; the amount of waste being collected surpassed the capacity of the available equipment. For instance, KIWODET reported that they were collecting 30–35 tonnes of waste daily with only one waste tipper truck, which can carry seven tonnes per trip. Its maximum number of trips to the disposal site per day is only three. In a similar vein, TTM reported collecting 20 tonnes of wastes per sub-ward per day, and they were able to transport four trips per week. Consequently, solid waste contractors had to hire trucks from private owners or get helped by municipal waste trucks. They complained that the trucks rented out to them were in bad shape, and they sometimes had to spend money on minor repairs. According to KIWODET and TTM, cost for hiring equipment ranges between TZS 40,000 to 50,000 (30–38 U.S. dollars in 2009) per trip.

In terms of human resources, the municipal waste department staff is employed to support waste management services at the household level. The municipality assigns health officers to work on waste management issues at the ward and sub-ward levels, where the operational tasks are performed. In the course of our discussions, the Kinondoni Health Officer indicated that by 2008, 12 Health Officers had been appointed as waste management officers in Kinondoni municipality. The KIWODET spokesperson also affirmed that the health officer in her area of operation does mobilize households to pay solid waste collection and disposal fees, and also promotes the use of proper solid waste storage containers.

In terms of financial resources, it was learned that the municipal council does pay for its waste management workers with funds generated from its general financial resources, originating directly from central-government grants or subsidies or from its own sources of revenues. Another important support to households and other formal service providers from the side of the municipality is the guiding policy framework to be followed in terms of existing municipal by-laws, which spells out the duties and responsibilities of each stakeholder in waste management chains, including that of households. Since the municipality does not recognise the involvement of these waste pickers in household waste management practices, it also does not give any kind of direct assistance or support to illegal waste pickers.

We can conclude here that the municipality gives assistance to household waste management in order to fulfil its day-to-day roles and responsibilities in solid waste management practices. Nevertheless, the waste contractors use grossly inadequate equipment and have too little financial resources to purchase more or better equipment, despite the support provided by the municipality. As a result, waste contractors are unable to provide sufficient and reliable collection services to large segments of the population in informal settlements.

To improve the present situation, improved regulation and institutional arrangements to enforce it are, of course, necessary. As the recent past has taught us, however, the successful implementation of regulation and arrangements is very much dependent on the local situations and the actors who are at the source of generation, separation, collection and transfer of domestic solid wastes in the primary phase of the waste chains-in-development. That is why subsequent sections emphasise more the actual waste practices as enacted by households (Section 4.4) and discuss in more detail the perceptions and assessments of households in Kinondoni (Section 4.5).

4.4 Households and solid waste management: Enacting waste practices

According to the official regulations, citizens in Kinondoni are expected to have receptacles for their domestic wastes, to operate and maintain the waste facilities, to finance the cost of the waste receptacles, to remove all wastes and maintain cleanliness at the front of their houses and to pay for the collection fees. The reality on the ground shows a different picture: Waste receptacles are hardly used, fees are paid irregularly, illegal waste pickers take their share, and the environment is littered with domestic wastes of all kinds. To understand this discrepancy between regulatory theory and empirical reality, the collected field survey data and the results obtained from analysis of conducted interviews reconstruct the waste practices of households in some realistic detail. To start with, the waste practices of households in the primary phase of the waste chain are considered first. These practices are waste generation, the (non)separation of waste at source, the storage of the wastes and the transport of domestic wastes to the transfer station or skip, where they are handed over to the actors operating in the secondary phase of the waste chain.

The practices of generating, collecting, storing, recycling and, in general, handling domestic wastes in and around the homes are the prime responsibility of women, housemaids and children. They are the key waste handling actors in the primary phase of waste management. With the help of our survey, we were able to bring out this crucial role of women and children as waste handlers. From the survey data, it is concluded that in 74.5% of the households, the housemaids or children are responsible for waste management, in 24% the mothers, and in 1.5% other members of the household. Women's main responsibility for SWM is illustrated by the following quote.

> *It is not usual for a father of the house to deal with waste. This is job for children or myself. Sometimes I ask money from my husband to pay tax for waste (ushuru wa taka). (Hananasifu sub-ward respondent, Mama Jamila, April 2008)*

The fact that waste handling practices are very much a gender issue is a factor that should be kept in mind when discussing the different waste practices of households. These practices are bound up with cultural values and power relations within the household, which to an important extent (co)determine the successful implementation of (new) arrangements for the handling of domestic wastes in Kinondoni.

4.4.1 Waste generation

Our waste characterization study carried out in Kinondoni showed that households in informal settlements produce high levels of food, plastic and paper waste, and lower volumes of glass bottles and metal tins. The study found that, on average, the organic kitchen waste generated constitutes a major part (70%) of the total amount of household waste generated. Recyclables (paper, plastics, glass and metal) accounted for 21% of total waste generated. Table 4.1 shows the average percentages of solid waste constituents as obtained from the waste characterization study after separation at source.

Next to the composition of domestic waste, the social dynamics behind the generation of the wastes deserve analytical attention. The main social factors that were found to contribute to the generation of domestic wastes in Kinondoni include daily cleaning routines, cooking and eating habits, and the daily economic activities of households. The households with home-bound economic activities, in particular, tend to generate more domestic waste. Our survey indicated that out of 360 households studied, 281 (78%) operate informal businesses within their household environment. Among these activities, food-related businesses in the household take the highest dominance (52%).[5] Other economic activities are having small shops, selling charcoal, doing repair work (shoes, clocks, electrical facilities) and tailoring. These other economic activities altogether accounted for 26% of all households. According to the survey, 22% of the respondents reported that they are not engaged in any household economic or business activities.

Based on the high number of households involved in these activities, it is expected that waste from these businesses affects the amount and composition of domestic wastes.

Table 4.1 Physical composition of HSW generated in studied sub-wards

Sub-ward name	*Waste category (%)*							
	Kitchen/ food waste	*Paper*	*Plastic*	*Glass*	*Metal*	*Aluminium*	*Residual waste*	*Total*
Hananasifu	67	10	13	1.2	1.0	2	6	100
Makangira	60	17	9	0	0	3	11	100
Kilimahewa	67	5	7	3	5	2	11	100
Makoka	78	5	5	0	1	8	3	100
Mwongozo	80	5	7	0.5	1	0.5	6	100
Ubungo-Kibangu	69	7	8	1	2	2	11	100
Average	70	8	8	1	1	3	8	100

Source: this study, survey carried out in 2008

4.4.2 Waste separation at source

Many households are involved in the recovery of recyclable materials within the household. These activities are enacted because of the (economic) gains that the recycling of valuable materials can bring. Households sort out the materials that they find they can use for various purposes, such as storing oil or medicines. Our findings indicated that 71% of the respondents kept the recyclables for their own use, 7% indicated that they give it to others, and 22% dispose them together with other wastes in storage containers.

The composition of domestic wastes indicates that there exist some further opportunities for waste recovery and recycling at the household level, particularly with regard to the composting of organic food waste and the recycling of plastics and paper. Organic, compostable waste was found to be the largest fraction (70%) of domestic solid wastes. However, practices of recycling and re-use of organic waste in terms of (local) composting schemes are not reported from the data. For all sub-wards included in the research, low levels of waste separation at source were reported, recycling being restricted to direct (re)usable materials only. When asked why, for example, the composting of organic wastes at household or neighbourhood-level was not seriously considered as an alternative, most households report that the lack of source-separation of organic wastes is due to the inconveniences that these activities may bring along. According to the households, encouraging these waste separation practices would need some incentives and/or indication of the benefits of waste separation at source.

4.4.3 Waste storage

As reported above, official regulations exist at Kinondoni Municipal level for the storage of domestic wastes in particular. By-laws oblige households to have two standard storage containers, (one for organic and the other for nonorganic waste) of not less than 40 l fitted with a lid (Collection and Disposal of Refuse By-law 2001 Sections 4 and 5). These by-laws also require the occupiers of premises to have receptacles to store their waste and prohibit people from causing a nuisance and depositing waste on streets or in open spaces not designated as collection points. Despite this detailed official requirement, all kinds of receptacles or solid waste containers not conforming to the official specifications were reported being used by the householders. Wastes are kept and stored mainly in old plastic buckets (17.5%), plastic bags (73.5%) and boxes (7%). The remaining 2% does not have any waste container at all. This situation on the ground turns out to be far removed from the storage practices prescribed by the regulations. A number of factors contribute to this discrepancy between theory and practice. First of all, households are not well acquainted with the fact that municipal by-law obliges them to have standard containers. Second, they do not get (municipal) support for accessing the storage containers, so they have to find them and pay for them on their own. Third, householders report that theft of containers has been a problem in their settlements, so they were forced to use waste storage devices with no value to thieves.

Fourth, there is hardly any space available in and around the house to place waste bins, so informal pickers retrieving the recyclable portions of the waste tend to leave the remaining wastes scattered all over the street. Inside the house, storage of waste is not acceptable for many householders for cultural reasons. For the reasons mentioned, it is obvious that the prescribed rules concerning the storage of domestic wastes are not applicable to the existing situation.

4.4.4 Delivering domestic wastes to transfer stations

The transport and delivery of domestic wastes to the point where the wastes are handed over to actors in the secondary phase of the waste-chain are practices that deserve a separate discussion. They bring along a complex division of responsibilities among different actors in the primary phase of the waste chain. Next to family members, the informal waste pickers are especially important in this respect. Householders can either transport the waste to the transfer station themselves or decide to make use of the services of either waste pickers employed by the formal waste contractors or illegal, informal pickers. Both groups of actors develop parallel activities and deliver similar services, although based on different kinds of social relationships. The waste pickers who are hired by the official waste contractors have a legal contract from the municipal authorities. They are entitled to use a franchise system to collect fees from the households they serve. The rates of monthly payments are set by the municipal authorities. In reality, however, both informal and formal waste pickers negotiate with householders on the price they have to pay for the services. They develop their own agreements on the modes of operations, which are not stipulated in the municipal SWM by-law nor indicated in their contracts. As they reported during the interviews, the waste contractors recognise that it is difficult for some of the households to pay monthly. As a result, households and waste contractors agree on more convenient ways of handling matters, such as to let households pay by instalments. Finally, householders themselves can act as transporters of the waste. Instead of paying the fees, they take responsibility for manually carrying the wastes generated in their households to the transfer stations. This research revealed that, again, women and children are the main responsible actors for performing these tasks.

4.4.5 Conclusions: The skip as material receptacle and set of social relations

In the primary phase of handling domestic wastes, the households themselves – and, in particular, the female members of the households – are responsible for the wastes generated within the households. When the wastes leave the home, waste collectors appear on the stage, and householders start negotiating with both formal and illegal waste pickers about the terms of handling the wastes. The so-called primary phase of waste handling – where practices are under the control of householders and where they follow the life-world rationalities of households and the local networks they are embedded in – ends when the wastes are handed over to actors in the secondary phase of the waste chains, regulated by system dynamics, in particular. The waste transfer stations or skips, in this context, take on a particular role and meaning. They are technical devices with a certain load capacity and at a location where they are more or less accessible for householders. At the same time, they are social devices as well, since they become a meeting point where different waste chain actors meet or cluster together in a certain time-space order. Households, formal and informal stakeholders can become connected in many different ways in the process of collecting and transporting domestic wastes from the households to the transfer station. The skip, container or transfer station becomes an important facility[6] in the SWM chain because it not only receives wastes from households, but it also functions as the point of connection between the primary and secondary phase of the waste chains and its main actors. In all possible configurations before the skip, however, householders are the central actors. This substantiates our claim that households must be regarded as crucial actors in the primary phase of the SWM chains. Householders are the binding factors that integrate formal and informal waste management systems before and around the transfer station.

4.5 Households and solid waste management: Perceptions and assessments of the waste chain and its main actors

Having described the waste practices as they are enacted by householders, we now turn to an analysis of their perceptions and opinions on the present and future organization of the solid waste management chains that they are connected to. Getting to know the perceptions and evaluations of households is important when thinking about improvements to be realized in the future. What kinds of responsibilities are assigned to whom? And who is to be held responsible for the non-functioning of the waste chain? What should happen to informal and illegal waste pickers when modernizing the waste chain in the future? These are the questions that motivated our survey research with the inhabitants of Kinondoni. Main findings of the survey are reported here, with respect to the opinions of householders on the reliability of the service providers, their views on the (best-possible and future) organization of waste services in informal settlements, and their beliefs on the need to confront the role of informal waste pickers and some of the existing informal arrangements.

4.5.1 Reliability of the waste services being delivered

Since the quality of the waste services delivered in the study areas was known to be poor, some questions on the assessment of the services by the householders were included in the survey. They reported irregular solid waste collection by formal waste collectors. In the survey, 60% of the respondents indicated that waste is collected once per week, 12% indicated twice per week, 3% said waste is collected now and then, while 25% could not give any answer. Solid waste collection services were found to be inadequate in all the studied areas. Households reported that, in several cases, waste contractors fail to collect waste on the scheduled days.

They complained about the fact that the uncollected wastes are vandalized by animals such as dogs, leading to the littering of the surroundings and a bad smell of decomposing waste.

Despite having access to formal waste collection services, households in Hananasifu, Makangira and Kilimahewa sub-wards resorted to the use of alternative methods to get rid of their wastes, such as burning, burying and illegal dumping.

These practices were also regularly-used options for households in Ubungo-Kibangu, Mwongozo and Makoka to dispose of their wastes. Households opt for these alternatives as a result of not having a formal and functioning waste collection system in place. These practices were commonly conducted by household members or informal waste pickers in nearby streets or in the open space.

4.5.2 Opinions of households on the (future) organisation of solid waste management

Most householders (52.8%) hold the municipality responsible for (the lack of) waste service delivery. In other words, householders indicate that SWM services are the sole or at least the prime obligatory responsibility of the municipal authorities. They tend to blame the municipal authorities for improper, unsafe and unsustainable forms of domestic solid waste management and claim that the municipality should provide a waste contractor to serve them. This is illustrated in the following statement by a man who said:

> *We want municipality to assign a waste contractor to our areas and should make sure that waste contractors are paid by the households accordingly. (Male FGD participant, 8/01/2009, Dar es Salaam)*

In line with this view, the householders indicate that major improvements are needed, especially of the performances of formal waste actors in the waste chain. If services would become reliable and efficient, then householders would be willing to pay the fees. One young man from Makangira sub-ward said:

> *We don't have a problem with paying; people resist paying for the collection of waste because municipality does not help them. (Male FGD Makangira sub-ward participant 8/01/2009, Dar es Salaam)*

However, when and as long as formal stakeholders do not deliver proper waste services, householders cannot reasonably be blamed for not paying the fees or for developing illegal and unsustainable alternatives. In sum, households recognise that they have a role to play in waste management, but they indicate that this role is conditional: other actors have to perform as well, and householders have to be taken seriously with respect to their demands and opinions.

Taking households seriously means consulting them on issues that affect their waste practices. An illustrative case of their demands to be consulted refers to the issue of the siting of the skips. From the survey, 45.3% of all the studied households indicated they want transfer stations in their neighbourhood. However, households were against the siting of a transfer station in their neighbourhood under the present waste arrangements for reasons of negative externalities, such as health hazards and the bad odour that the overloaded and irregularly collected skips bring along. Health hazards resulting from the unattended transfer station turned out to be the major concern of the households. As one respondent said:

> *It was difficult to control anyone from throwing the waste in; even dead animals were dumped in, and thieves were hiding inside especially at night. (Male FGD Hananasifu sub-ward participant 8/01/2009, Dar es Salaam)*

From the survey and from our focus group meetings with householders, the following picture on the envisaged waste management system emerges. First, households demand a clean neighbourhood. They expressed the view that their living environment should be as clean as possible and without any waste problems. Second, the way to realize this is to improve the quality of the waste services of formal waste actors. Collection frequency should be increased and reliable. Waste collectors should be provided with better equipment, in particular with more and better moveable transfer stations, which are adapted to the local spatial conditions. Third, householders should have a say in the siting of the skips in their neighbourhood. Increased participation is believed to be the way forward to confront also the sometimes contradictory opinions and behaviours of householders. For example, in spite of the fact that they want the municipality to provide more waste transfer stations, they prefer them to be located somewhere not very close to their own homes. The transfer station serves as an important object in the efforts of householders to claim more (co)decision-making powers and to increase levels of participation. Fourth, householders want formal (waste) authorities to connect to the existing, partly informal and illegal practices in more frequent and flexible ways. This need has to be considered; authorities can build on existing relations and practices by specifying the role of illegal waste pickers, in particular, as discussed in the next sub-section.

4.5.3 The need to recognise and formalise the role of informal waste actors and relationships

From conducted participatory research, and the focus group research, in particular, it became clear that informal and formal waste management co-exist in low-income areas of Dar es Salaam. As one respondent explained:

> *We give waste to informal pickers because waste contractor (Mkandarasi wa taka), come to collect our waste only once per month. (Female FGD participant 8/01/2009, Dar es Salaam)*

While not being officially recognised by the municipality, householders recognise the crucial function of the illegal waste-pickers who tend to provide them with other services, too, in addition to the collection and disposal of solid waste. They support waste pickers by paying fees often on the spot as service is delivered. So while not being recognised and accepted as legitimate actors from the side of the official authorities, waste pickers are being recognised and used by householders on a regular basis.

More in general, informal relations and activities turn out to be an inherent and indispensable element of the waste management systems in informal settlements. This is true for the relationships between householders and illegal pickers, and it is also relevant in the context of newly developed Public Private Partnerships (PPP) between formal waste-pickers, Community Based Organizations (CBOs), householders and municipal authorities. According to a UNDP study (2005), PPPs can do a proper job in providing waste services if they are set up properly. In our research area, we found different forms of PPPs being applied at sub-ward levels. Although the experiences have not been uniformly positive, most householders expect significant improvements resulting from such PPP-arrangements in the longer run. Formal PPPs are governed mainly by a legal contract that defines the partnership and that specifies the roles and responsibilities of the partners (municipality and waste contractors) involved. Informal PPPs emerged from the joint efforts of households, waste contractors and local leaders seeking to improve the management of domestic wastes. Waste contractors (waste collectors) and households develop 'on the ground' mutual agreements on the modes of operation. These modes of operation (collection schedule, payment system, etc.) are not indicated in the contracts given to the solid waste contractors. One could say that these local waste arrangements originate from the local social relations and circumstances. These informal PPPs are especially appreciated by the households for their positive contribution to improving the waste services. For that reason, they argue that these informal arrangements could be the basis for developing a legal framework that better fits the local conditions of informal settlements.

4.6 Conclusion

This study shows that solid waste management services are inadequate in the studied settlements for both social and technical reasons. At the technical side, discussions focused on the lack of proper equipment, lack of human resources, inaccessibility of particular areas for trucks, lack of space for the storage of waste and absence of proper (storage, separation, removal) technologies. The social side documented the ill performance of waste actors, lack of income in poor households, established habits of 'alternative waste handling', cultural norms on cleanliness, divisions of roles within households and the low social valuation of waste handling practices. Both technical and social factors contribute to a situation of structurally underperforming waste management systems in informal settlements.

When formal waste management systems do not deliver services at an adequate level, it has been shown that informal practices, actors and relations tend to come into play. And once they are there at play, they tend to develop into established practices with stakeholders and specific interests attached to them. The practices of waste burning, burying and dumping as developed by households in response to the absence of regular waste collection and disposal services tend to gradually develop into socially accepted routines for handling wastes. The activities of illegal waste pickers solving the immediate waste problem for households on a cash-for-delivery basis tend to develop into normal arrangements appreciated by the parties directly involved. As our study has shown, informal relations and activities are an indispensable element of the waste management systems in informal settlements and need to be recognised and dealt with when trying to improve the functioning of these systems in the short run.

The way to start improving the present system is difficult to indicate. In situations of malfunctioning systems, stakeholders tend to blame the other for not performing well. As long as householders and informal pickers stick to some of their established waste handling routines – inability to pay the fee, illegal practices of burning and littering the wastes – improving the functioning of the performances of waste actors in the secondary phase of the waste chain will not deliver progress. On the other hand, as long as the actors that are primarily responsible do not deliver, one should not blame householders for non-cooperation. The way out of this awkward dilemma is to improve the communication and coordination between actors and stakeholders in the secondary and the primary phases of the waste chain. Stakeholders operating at both sides of the skip should become better connected in many different ways. Transparency and reliability of formal waste actors and municipal authorities and a better recognition of the crucial role of householders in making the waste chain work are among the crucial ingredients.

This study aimed to contribute to improving the communication between actors in waste chains in a particular way. The research investigated in some detail what householders do and what they think concerning domestic wastes. It revealed the nature and dynamics of household activities of generating, storing, sorting, separating, transporting and (illegal) disposing of domestic wastes. In doing so, a disparity was found between the municipal requirements on the one hand and the actual practices of households in the SWM chain on the other. This is a discrepancy everyone knows about, without officially recognizing it. Recognizing the existing situation in the Kinondoni sub-wards and taking local conditions into account is a starting point for improving the formal waste management system. The gap between the (legislative and system) rationality of municipal authorities, on the one hand, and the social and life world rationalities of householders, on the other, should be bridged. Although householders tend to be uninformed and not much interested in taking an active role, it is the only way forward to increase cooperation with local actors operating in the primary phase of the waste chains serving informal settlements. Only when the specific nature and dynamic of household practices and opinions are recognised and taken into account can innovations in waste management services in informal settlements be expected to result in a more healthy and improved living environment.

Notes

1. The primary phase of waste chains or networks are those parts that are under direct control of householders who follow rationalities that fit into their everyday lives. The secondary phase refers to those parts that are under direct control of institutional actors and organizations following system rationalities to organise their activities. See Oosterveer and Spaargaren 2010.
2. The selected wards include: Hananasifu, Makurumla, Makangira, Ubungo-Kibangu, Makoka and Mwongozo.
3. CBOs selected for the study included: Kisutu Women Development Trust (KIWODET), based in Hananasifu; Tua Taka Makurumla (TTM), based in Makurumla; and CLN, based in Makangira.
4. Only the data that are useful for this chapter are reported here (for complete data analysis, see Solomon 2011).
5. These activities include preparation and selling of fish, fruits, vegetables by *mama ntilie. Mama ntile* is a Swahili word for *female food vendor(s).*
6. In the context of this study, standby trailers and waste trucks were considered transfer stations (movable); households were bringing their waste to where transfer stations were located.

References

Addo-Yobo, F. & Ali, M. (2003). Households: Passive users or active managers? The case of solid waste management in Accra, Ghana. *IDPR,* 4 (25): 373–389.

Coad, A. & Gonzenbach, B. (2007). *Solid waste management and the millennium development goals.* A Report of the CWG-WASH Workshop on Solid Waste, Health and the MDG's in Kolkata, India. CWG Publication series No. 3, p 38.

CWG-WASH. (2006). *Solid waste, health and the millennium development goals. A report of the CWG international workshop.* Kolkata, India.

DCC (2004). *Dar es Salaam city profile.* Dar es Salaam: Dar es Salaam City Council.

Kinondoni Municipal Commission (2000). Waste Management and refuse collection fees bylaws 2000. Dar es Salaam, Tanzania.

Kombe, W. J. (2005). Land use dynamics in peri-urban areas and their implications on the urban growth and form: The case of Dar es Salaam. *Habitat International,* 29: 113–135.

Kyessi, A. (2002). *Community participation in urban infrastructure provision. servicing informal settlements in Dar es Salaam.* SPRING Research Series No.33; University of Dortmund, Dortmund, Germany, p 405.

Kyessi, A. & Mwakalinga, V. (2009). *GIS application in coordinating solid waste collection: The case of Sinza neighbourhood in Kinondoni municipality.* Dar es Salaam City, Tanzania. Report of Féderation Internationale des Géometres (FIG) Working week. Surveyors Key Role in Accelerated Development. FIG Publication Eilat, Israel, p 19.

Nkya, E. (2004) Public-private partnership and institutional arrangements: Constrained improvement of solid waste management in Dar Es Salaam. Uongozi Journal of Management Development, 16 (1): 1–21.

Oosterveer, P. & Spaargaren, G. (2010). Meeting social challenges in developing sustainable environmental infrastructures in East African cities. In: B.J.M. van Vliet, G. Spaargaren and P. Oosterveer (Eds.), *Social Perspectives on the Sanitation Challenge.* Dordrecht, The Netherlands, Springer, p 11–30.

Sawio, C. J. (2008). Perception and conceptualisation of urban environmental change: Dar es Salaam City. *Geographical Journal,* 174 (2): 149–175.

Schübeler, P., Wehrle, K. & Christen, J. (1996). *Conceptual framework for municipal solid waste management in low-income countries. Collaborative programme on municipal solid waste management in low-income countries.* SKAT/UNDP/UNCHS (Habitat)/ World Bank/SDC. UMP Working Paper Series 9. UMP Publication. Proceedings of the Ittingen Workshop, St. Gallen, Switzerland, p 59.

Solomon, A.O. (2011). *The role of households in solid waste management in East Africa Capital Cities*. PhD thesis. Wageningen: Wageningen Academic Publishers.

Tadesse, T., Ruijs, A. & Hagos, F. (2008). Household waste disposal in Mekelle City, Northern Ethiopia. *Waste Management,* 28 (10): 2003–2012.

United Nations Development Programme, United Nations Environment Programme, The World Bank, World Resources Institute. (2005). *World resources 2005. The wealth of the poor*: Managing Ecosystems to Fight Poverty. Washington DC, USA.

Zhu, D., Asnani, P. U., Zurbrügg, C., Anapolsky, S. & Mani, K. S. (2008). *Improving municipal solid waste management in India: A sourcebook for policy makers and practitioners.* Washington, DC: World Bank.

5 Informality and public-private partnerships in waste and sanitation management

Kees Burger and Mesharch W. Katusiimeh

5.1 Introduction

In the 2004 World Development Report, 'Making Services Work for the Poor', public services in developing countries are – for the most part – shown to be deficient, as they are inaccessible, dysfunctional, of low technical quality, not responsive to their clients and stagnant in their productivity. The report argued that, while there are good reasons why full privatisation may not work for many types of service, a few types and perhaps parts of *all* types can benefit from more market-based incentives for the supply of these services. The private sector was believed to be more flexible, more attuned to the needs of the clients and more innovative. On the other hand, it responds only to purchasing power and not to needs per se, and it typically neglects externalities. So for services that have large externalities, such as dumpsites of solid waste, and services to which access – for reasons of equity or externalities – should not be dependent on client income, such as health care, schooling and waste collection, the private sector by itself would not provide a good outcome. A mixture of public and private actions is then likely to be optimal, but the weights of either partner in this mixture are not easily determined.

The history of most western countries shows that many of the services now routinely handled by the state, such as schooling, health care, social welfare, and even sanitation and waste collection, were completely in private hands in the 19th century. With the growth of the nation state, these services were taken over by the state and thereby made available to a wider group of citizens. This transition took place only gradually, and could be made dependent on the availability of funding to finance these new governmental tasks. In most developing countries, however, the state has had the responsibility for these services from the start. Over time, the financial and organizational burden of supplying these services increased, and when, in the 1980s, government expenditures far exceeded revenues, it became unbearable. Privatisation of services was considered – in fact, as much in developing countries as in western countries, notably the USA and parts of Europe, where a smaller government became a political objective. However, where richer countries went a few steps back on a road already travelled, developing countries ventured into uncharted territory.

Solid waste collection in Kampala city had many aspects that conform to the picture of deficient public services (Okot-Okumu and Nyenje 2011): many (in fact, most) inhabitants lacked access to the services that the Kampala City Council (KCC) provided, those who were served were not served regularly or well enough, equipment was obsolete and not well maintained, clients' voices were not heard, and there was no improvement in performance for many years.

In the 1990s, the first efforts were made to get the private sector involved in waste collection; in the first ten years of this century, the private sector made large inroads and now accounts for the major share of all waste deposited at the municipal dump site.

Yet, this picture of a transition of public to private service providers is incomplete, as it neglects the role of the informal service providers. Public services may be deficient, but the state is not the only provider, precisely because they are deficient. In informal settings, other providers take on the supply of services when these are not formally provided (Medina 2005). This applies to solid waste collection, but also to other services discussed above. Without proper (formal) health clinics, other people stand up to give advice; where there is no school, other people may teach children to read and write; when no solid waste is collected, households dispose of it themselves through burning, burying or dumping, or employ the services of individuals to help them dispose of it. Though these informal services are often of rather low quality, compared to the formal sector, they fill a gap – namely, the gaps resulting from the deficiencies of the public sector or, in a wider setting, those of the formal (public *and* private) sector.

In this chapter, we describe the role of these informal service providers. Based on surveys among clients and a small survey among informal waste collectors in Kampala, we are able to outline the factors behind the demand and the supply for their services. On the customer side, we are able to look back to the situation before privatisation to see any change in the role of the informal service providers. As the public services were based on communal collection points, skips, they actually may have encouraged the demand for informal providers as these could 'fill the gap' by taking – for a fee – the waste from the doorstep to the skip. In this sense, the two services, public and (informal) private, are complementary. This complementarity cannot be found with formal private services, as these need to actually reach the doorstep, if only to collect the fees. This paper details the appreciation of the customers for the services of the private and the informal sector, as well as those of the public sector. We provide evidence on the nature of the services and show how these differ in what is probably 'responsiveness to clients' needs'. On the supply side, we detail how revenues from informal waste collection are not below those of other workers in similar positions.

In the next section, we elaborate on the situation before privatisation of the waste collection in Kampala and compare it to the more recent situation, with an emphasis on the performance of the informal sector. In Section 5.3, we look at the supply side of informal collection services, and in Section 5.4, we provide some details on the extent to which presently the private sector meets the demand from various groups. We end this section with a look at changing roles of informal collectors in poorer areas and arrive at a view on the possibilities for improving their contribution. In Section 5.5, we conclude with a proposal for a *modernised mixture* of public, private and informal services.

5.2 Demand for waste collection services under public and private supply regimes

Before the year 2000, solid waste collection in Uganda's capital of Kampala was the responsibility of the divisions of the city, while the Kampala City Council (KCC) centrally controlled Kiteezi landfill where all household waste is meant to be brought. In 2000, the Kampala solid waste management ordinance was enacted, which provided a legal framework for the operation of the private service providers. Since then, the road to privatisation was investigated with a few experiments involving franchising, in which a company was licensed to set up a commercial waste collection service in an area, and contracting, in which a company would be contracted to collect waste in an area, typically a poorer part of the city. Contracting and franchising did not work out as envisaged, partly because of the private providers' lack of capacity and KCC's failure to play its role, especially related to honouring contractual obligations (Katusiimeh et al. 2011). This resulted in KCC encouraging open or unregulated competition in which KCC allowed registered firms to make private arrangements with users to deliver a service. Before and after privatisation, however, informal waste collectors offered their services to households. They were never part of great schemes and apparently stayed 'below the radar', yet they served quite a few households.

In this section, we investigate their role under the two regimes, public and (mostly) private waste collection. We document the roles of the various service providers based on a survey among households in two divisions of Kampala.

Data collection was done among urban residents in Kampala, specifically in the Kawempe and the Central divisions. These two divisions were chosen because they have a large concentration of mixed households, with low-income, medium-income and high-income staying largely in the same neighbourhood, save a few areas. In this particular survey, we considered the type of house one lived in as criterion for *high-income* or *low-income*. For example, if a man lived in a permanent house with more than two bedrooms, he was considered rich even though he lived in a poor neighbourhood. The questionnaire as a tool for data collection was administered in 2008 to 387 respondents. We collected data relating to the choice and rating of waste disposal method by income category of the area. Evaluations were given on a Likert scale of 1 to 5, related to the recent past (2008) and the past, divided into a period before privatisation (1996–2001) and in the early years after (2002–2007). The lack of longitudinal data required us to use memory and reflexive comparisons. Such methodologies are possible for issues of garbage management; these are hot issues involving debates that get emotional and that stick in the memory of many urban residents (Katusiimeh 2012). The survey also captured the perceptions of residents of Kampala in relation to the removal of communal containers and the satisfaction with the choice of the disposal method.

Later on, we used data that were derived from a related study. This involved 475 respondents of Nakawa and Kawempe divisions. This captured household characteristics, changes in service provision, fees collected and satisfaction with services rendered by different actors in solid waste collection. Questions related to the appropriateness of the skip were also asked. Nakawa was chosen because it is the biggest division with concentrations of rich neighbourhoods, unlike Kawempe. Given the difficulty of eliciting income and expenditures, low-income households were defined as those that reside in poor unplanned neighbourhoods with high population densities, while high-income households were defined as those households situated in areas with low population densities and in planned neighbourhoods.

In both surveys, we employed random sampling. The process of sampling was such that if the target respondent was not available or not interested to be interviewed, we would move to the neighbouring household. There were also many respondents who were not part of the target group because we were interested in only those who had lived in Kampala consistently for a long time, and in that case, we would move to the next household. The sampling strategy, therefore, may not allow us to claim representativeness.

Figure 5.1 shows the main methods of waste disposal in use by households before the privatisation (roughly 1996–2001) and after privatisation (roughly 2002–2007).

We considered five main ways of disposal:

1. Utilise skip: Households utilise skips or other containers placed by the service provider to deposit their wastes. In the case of Kampala, the skips are provided by KCC. KCC picks up the waste at a fixed frequency for transportation to the disposal facility.
2. Bell ringing: The service provider provides a truck that gets to the community at an agreed-upon time, and a signal (a bell) is used to alert the community to carry the waste to the waiting truck.
3. Bring to skip: These are activities of informal collectors (individuals) who practice door-to-door collection by filling a gap in service delivery left by the formal service providers. They deposit garbage in skips, but also, in many cases, just anywhere that is convenient to them.
4. Door to door: The service provider collects the waste from the individual premises. The storage at source is either in bins or plastic bags, which could be provided by the owners or by the service provider. Waste collected is then moved to a waiting truck that transports it to the disposal facility.
5. Dumping: These are heaps of garbage, especially at the road sides in Kampala, deposited by residents who lack skips for their wastes.

Figure 5.1 (a) shows that before privatisation, KCC's service of providing skips was the main way (49%) that households disposed of their waste. But many (30%) households had their own way (dumping), and many others (18%) made use of informal service providers to take their waste away (bring to skip). If we restrict ourselves to residential households, thus excluding those with a home enterprise, the percentages shift in favour of informal service providers: 36% using skips, 28% dumping, and 36% using informal service providers (not shown in the figure). These informal service providers were almost all used by households in the higher income categories.

In Table 5.1, we restrict ourselves to the three major categories: using a skip, using an informal collector to bring it to a skip, or dumping. This is a mild restriction, as only 3% of the households used other services. Table 5.1 provides a distribution of the choices and the ratings of the overall quality of each, and it does so by income category of the household. Overall ratings for the period before privatisation were low for the simple dumping of waste in the street or roadside piles (1.85), whereas the rating of informal services was close to that for the use of the skips (2.49 and 2.53). Choices differed by income category of the neighbourhood: Households in the richer groups (that are also more residential) divided themselves equally over the three disposal methods, whereas in other areas, informal transport to skips (or piles) was hardly used. Dumping occurred in all areas to an equal degree (30% of households).

The choices were consistent with the ratings: highest ratings were given for what was chosen most.

The introduction of private sector services took two forms. One is a system where a car came into the neighbourhood or street and rang a bell, at which time households

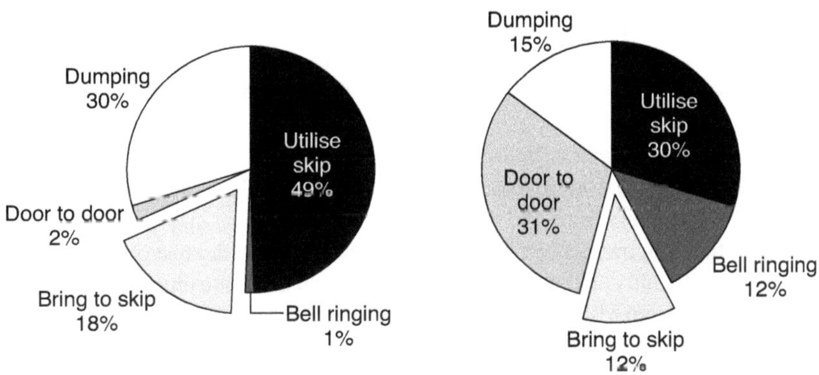

Figure 5.1 Choice of ways of waste disposal: (a) 1996–2001 and (b) 2002–2007

Table 5.1 Choice and rating of disposal method 1996–2001; total and by income category

Choice	*%*	*Overall quality rating*	*% Choice*			*Quality rating*		
			High	*Middle*	*Low*	*High*	*Middle*	*Low*
Utilise skip	51	2.53	33	62	63	2.16	2.44	2.80
Bring to skip (informal collection)	18	2.49	37	8	7	2.60	2.00	2.38
Dumping	31	1.85	30	30	30	1.56	2.07	1.91
	100		100	100	100			

Table 5.2 Choice and rating of disposal method 2002–2007; total and by income category

Choice	*%*	*Overall quality*	*% Choice*			*Quality rating*		
		Quality	*High*	*Middle*	*Low*	*High*	*Middle*	*Low*
Utilise skip	30	3.25	18	31	40	3.05	3.00	3.48
Bell ringing	12	2.65	1	19	20	3.00	2.94	2.41
Bring to skip (informal collection)	12	3.00	10	16	11	3.55	2.64	2.92
Door to door	31	3.10	56	18	16	3.25	2.69	3.00
Dumping	15	2.33	15	16	13	2.41	2.36	2.21

could come and deliver their waste (for a fee); in the other system, waste would be collected from the households directly. In terms of household effort, therefore, the options could be ranked from most to least effort of the client: use skip (most effort), bell-ringing, informal collection, formal door collection (least effort). The pattern that emerged over the period 2002–2007 is given in Figure 5.1 (b) and in Table 5.2, which has the same design as Table 5.1, but now with more rows to reflect the wider range of relevant options. As the ratings and choices refer to a period of 5 years, they should be interpreted as 'impressions'. Those who felt badly served 'some years ago' (roughly coinciding with around 4 years ago) are likely to have given a low rating. Any changes in satisfaction within the period 2002–2007 are not recorded.

The formal private sector (bell-ringing and door-to-door services) gained a market share of 43%, so that more than half of all the households that used some service (85% of total) was served by the formal private sector. In comparison to the period before privatisation, incidence of dumping has halved, and the use of skips has also decreased significantly. This latter change can obviously be attributed to the removal of skips, notably from residential areas. In high-income groups, therefore, their use is reduced to 18%. The more laborious services (skips and bell-ringing) are more popular in lower income groups. Informal service providers are used somewhat less than before, but now also in lower income groups. An analysis of the transition (Katusiimeh 2012: 66) shows that erstwhile users of informal services typically switched to the formal door-to-door system, while erstwhile skip-users now employed informal services to take their garbage (perhaps to a now more distant skip).

In a further analysis, Katusiimeh (2012: 69–70) demonstrates that the choice for an informal service provider is now more related to being a shop-owner than to the income category. The likely reason for this is that high-income households can now use formal private services, but some shopkeepers may prefer individual services, given their specific requirements.

Quality ratings are also shown in Table 5.2. These are generally higher than those for the services in the past, and informal services are rated favourably (3.00). But this rating is not quite translated into a choice in favour of the informal providers.

In low-income groups, the skip retained its popularity expressed by the share of households using it. Its rating also improved and is higher than among richer households. Apparently, the households using skips, which are mostly shopkeepers, appreciate the freedom it offers in terms of weight, size and nature of the waste. Private collectors are more likely to restrict this.

The reasons for the relatively low use of informal collectors could be the nature or the price of their services. When asked to explain low ratings of the quality, households indicated that lack of cleanliness of the informal operators' operations and the distance to the communal container formed problems. Frequent complaints about the formal private sector services were the low frequency and unreliability.

Role of prices

The ratings given to the overall quality of the service may have been influenced by the prices charged for these. Katusiimeh (2012: 81), however, shows that the fee does not significantly influence the quality rating. There is a selection effect that underlies this phenomenon. Normally, high fees should discourage clients. But those that choose to use the expensive service will do so because they rate its quality high. Thus, the ratings are biased, because they were given by the users of the rated services themselves and are not representative for the public at large. Figure 5.2 shows the relationship between the fee per month and the rating of this very fee by the users of the collection modes (informal bring-to-skip providers, formal door-to-door service and formal bell-ringing service). On the horizontal axis is the fee that households paid, and at the vertical axis the score, with 1 being the rating given when the fee was considered very low.

The graph shows three lines that are logarithmic least-squares regression lines through the data points of two private systems (bell-ringing and door-to-door) and

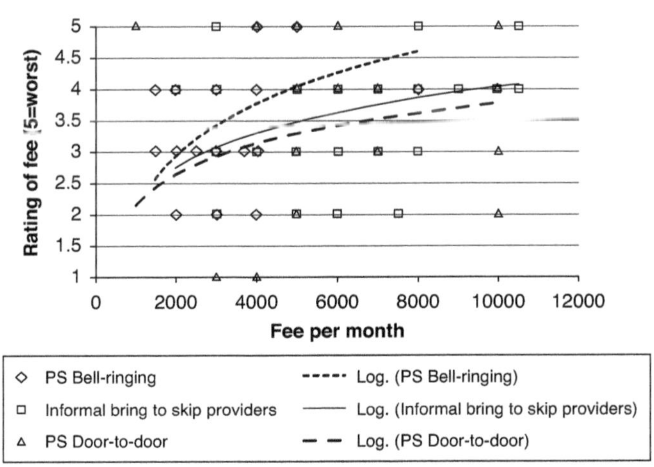

Figure 5.2 Ratings of the monthly fees of three collection systems

the informal bring-to-skip system. It is striking that the 'informal line' lies somewhat to the right of the 'bell-ringing line', implying that customers are prepared to pay a higher fee for informal services: at a level of satisfaction of 3, informal services may command a fee that is higher by 350 Ugandan shillings (UGX) per month. The lower dotted line shows the logarithmic relationship between fees and rating for the door-to-door system, which is the preferred system of the higher-income groups. This curve lies even more to the right, characterised as it is by higher fees and relatively low ratings.

The figure shows that one reason why fewer people employ the informal services, notably in lower-income groups, could be the higher price they charge. The average monthly fees charged for the three systems over the period 2002–2007 are (rounded) 3,500 UGX/m for bell-ringing, 6,400 UGX/m for informal services and 5,100 UGX/m for door-to-door systems (for all systems we dropped the zero and highest fees from the calculation). The estimates for the informal services are more uncertain, however, as fees are not normally collected on a monthly basis.

Summarising this investigation of the demand side of the services by the informal sector, we have seen that 12% of the households make use of their services, which is less than before the privatisation (18%). At that time, residential households in richer areas made most use of them, whereas in recent years it is more the households with trade (such as shopkeepers) that employ their services, and these are located in all income groups. This picture of the use of the informal waste collectors deviates from the stereotype that they serve poor households in low-income groups. It appears that they fill a gap created by the distance between major waste producing households (like shopkeepers) and the waste collection centre. Such centres can be the remaining official skips, but casual observation shows that informal collectors often create equally informal 'waste collection sites' for themselves. The services they render are relatively expensive, but rated quite at par with the services of the private sector.

5.3 Supply of informal services

The data collected from the customers of the service providers show the appreciation for their work from the consumers' point of view. This may bias the outcomes, as consumers cannot be expected to appreciate high prices, and of course would be happy with more frequent services (if at the same price), etc. We therefore also collected information from the informal service providers themselves. To this end, some 30 were selected by going to (informal) waste collection sites and interviewing those who came there 'on business'.

We briefly report here what is published in Katusiimeh et al. (2013).

These informal collectors were rather young men, between the ages of 25 and 45. One in five had no schooling, two out of five completed primary school, and the others had more education. They were in this job for some years and considered it not as casual but structural employment. It was done year-round and seven days a week, although not the full day. In majority, they had other work too, as bicycle taxi driver, guard, hawker for shops or casual work. Some previously worked with Kampala City Council (KCC), now Kampala Capital City Authority (KCCA), but lost the job due to reorganisation.

Almost all did their work in competition with other waste collectors; in half of the cases, they collaborated with the formal sector, such as when hiring a truck from KCC.

On a daily basis, they served some 10 to 20 customers, and, in total, their clientele numbered around 100 per collector. The clients were mostly (60%) residential households; in 30% of the cases, they were shops. The clients were found through personal approaches, and the types of services rendered also varied from one client to the other. Waste collection was supplemented with occasional cleaning work or gardening for clients.

The waste was collected in polythene bags or gunny bags that clients themselves provided. It was brought to (open) collection points some 150 meters away. In some cases (30%), the garbage was sorted to pick plastic, metal or banana peels for separate selling.

Customers were mostly charged per service, typically once a week. The fee ranged from 500–4,000 shillings, and no costs were made to obtain this fee, as bags were not provided by the collector. Collectors used bicycles and wheelbarrows as equipment. A cost of other sorts was that they suffered regular injuries, such as cuts, from handling the waste.

Taking UGX 1,000 as a modal weekly fee, and 10 customers per day, an income can be obtained of 10,000 UGX (some US$ 5) per day, which is substantially above what truck loaders typically get (a daily wage of UGX 3,000–5,000). From this we may derive that these individual waste collectors may obtain reasonable incomes from this activity. It came as no surprise that a majority of them intend to stay in this profession, although some indicated that they would like to be re-employed by KCC. Apparently, there were advantages other than the basic salary that made this attractive: social benefits, such as insurance, certainty and opportunities for moonlighting.

Supply of waste collection services, therefore, appears not to be hindered by income prospects, although the social status it brings may deter people from entering into this business. Yet, those that have the job enjoy the freedom it entails. The interviews confirm that the waste collection service is in most cases partial – that is, the waste is brought to some collection point, but this is not the official eventual dump site. So, additional costs must be incurred by other actors, such as KCC, to really collect the waste, or – in its absence – non-pecuniary costs are incurred in the form of environmental damage. Informal collectors thus partly free-ride on activities of KCC, and partly just shift the environmental burden from client households to other households, namely those that suffer the nuisance from the illegal dump sites.

5.4 A structural role for informal waste collectors?

Solid waste collection was traditionally the responsibility of the municipality, and KCC did have the task of collecting waste in the city. Financial means limited the organisation, and, effectively, collection services were only provided in some parts

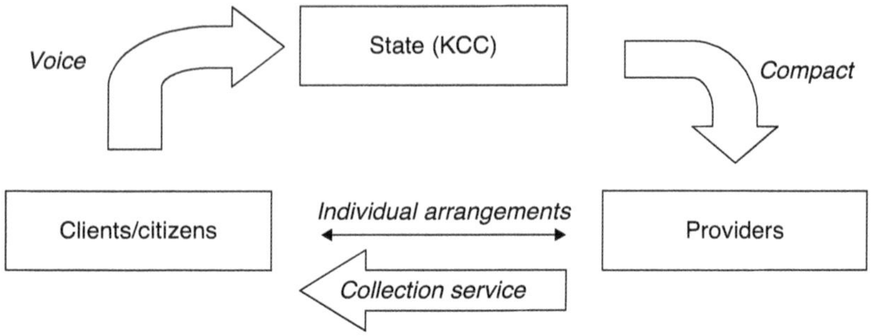

Figure 5.3 The long route of accountability

of the city. The collection method chosen was a relatively cheap one: namely, to put skips in places with high concentrations of people and waste, such as market places and at strategic places in residential areas. In principle, this facilitated waste collection for the households, but only if the skips were within reasonable reach, or if people could be hired to bring the waste there (a role for the informal collectors). The council bore responsibility for the regular replacement of the skips, the transportation to the dump site and the cleaning of the areas around the skips. This was often not done, or not done on time, leading to complaints from the households in the vicinity of the skips. Similar complaints are recorded in other countries (Kawai and Osaka 2013).

The organisation of solid waste collection thus followed what the World Development Report (2004: 49) called the long route of accountability.

Figure 5.3 includes Hirschman's distinction between *voice* and *exit* as ways for clients to express their preferences. The long route is one in which citizens *voice* their concerns and wishes to the state (KCC, in this case) and the state then enters into an arrangement with providers of waste collection services. It may offer these services itself, or make a contract or an (informal) agreement. The complex arrangement between state and provider is indicated by *compact.* The short route of accountability would involve direct contacts between clients and providers. Before privatisation, such a shortcut was not part of the design of the waste collection services. Yet, on the ground, citizens sought ways to circumvent problems, to reduce transaction costs and to find shortcuts where they might be possible. This is where the informal service providers have played a role; they have been technically enabled by the decision to use skips as collecting devices and organisationally useful to limit the dependence of citizens on bureaucracy. Yet, the individual collectors have suffered from the characteristic deficiency of private sector activity: namely, the difficulty of taking the aggregate needs into account. They can do business with individuals, but the common cause is not easily served by private agents. So, while individual problems could be solved by individual arrangements between clients and providers, the major issue of having the filthy skips in the neighbourhood could not be solved in this manner.

The privatisation of waste collection was meant to enable the direct interaction between households and the providers – that is, the short route of accountability.

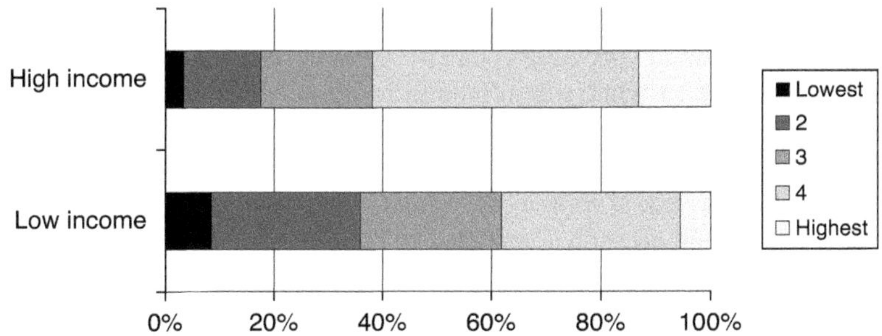

Figure 5.4 Ratings of service 'without skips' for two individual income classes

It was successful in establishing this mechanism. Services to households have changed, as shown by changes and differentiation in frequency of collection, in provision of packaging materials to clients, in differentiated fees and arrangements for their payment. Rather than having to rely on their *voice,* households can now, in many divisions of Kampala, express their preference through *exit,* and switch to other providers in case of dissatisfaction. Households show themselves happy with the present system, and in general prefer this over the old skip-based system. Figure 5.4 shows this for another survey of households in Kampala (Katusiimeh 2012). The graph shows that the rating of the (present) situation without skips is rather high, and even higher for households with higher incomes. An important ingredient in their satisfaction with the change is the removal of the skips and the nuisance they brought.

As the private formal collectors need to have direct contact with their clients to collect the fee for their bell-ringing and door-to-door systems, the private system leaves little room for the individual, informal collectors. For them, opportunities lie either in providing the same services at a cheaper price, or in providing a better, more complex service. The first approach is followed by some, and is made possible by them providing just the basic service of taking the waste away from the household, but not transporting this to the official dump site. The other approach is also feasible because, to achieve some economies of scale, the formal private sector must offer homogeneous services to groups of clients. Individual providers can therefore find a niche in serving clients with needs that are different from the group. With these clients, the informal providers can negotiate prices for a bundle of services of which the price is settled individually, and they weaken, in this way, the market mechanism. Their services become more *discretionary* and more *transaction intensive,* which – as theory has it – limits the operation of the market mechanism (Pritchet and Woolcock 2004).

We now focus on the poorer segments of society, whose needs are not easily met by the private sector, responsive as this is to monetary stimuli. In certain compacts between government and private sector, arrangements are included to stimulate the private sector to serve these areas, while making a profit out of concessions in other, richer parts of the town. Kampala City Council has also experimented with it, but without success. Reasons were twofold. One was the difficulty to actually monitor what the providers were doing in the poorer areas and to arrange payments according to what was (claimed to have been) done. The other was the difficulty of keeping parts of the city reserved for certain licensed providers. Monitoring proved again difficult, and competition between private providers made establishing a spatial monopoly virtually impossible. In a situation where monitoring is difficult, no such compacts can be implemented, with the result that the private sector serves the better-off areas, while the poorer areas of the town may be served less (by informal providers) or not at all, unless the public service provider takes up this role.

In the period 2002–2007, as we have seen in Table 5.2, the lower-income groups were served by KCC for 40%, by the formal private sector for 36% and by individual informal collectors for 11%. The remaining households had their private ways of disposal. The formal private sector has made some inroads, therefore, especially by offering a relatively cheap bell-ringing service. In the high-income groups, its share is 56% (almost all door-to-door), compared with 18% using public sector skips. In both areas, only small shares of 10% are taken by the informal providers.

This is somewhat surprising, as one may expect that with the higher share of households using skips in low-income groups, there would be more scope for individual service providers to handle the waste there. A closer analysis of the data shows the following differences between high-and low-income groups.

Figure 5.5 shows the scores for the various systems in three income groups. The figure shows the fee and the popularity – that is, how many households chose this provider. And it shows how households felt about the fee and quality of the service. This latter 'feeling' was expressed in a rating on a scale of 1 to 5, with 5 being high for the fee, and high for the quality. For this figure, we restricted ourselves to households of which all information (fee, choice and ratings) was available. This led to small changes, compared with Table 5.2.

Important to consider is that most households (56%) in the high-income group are residential households, whereas in other groups, the share of 'commercial' households is large (about 80%). Informal providers have some residential clients in the highest-income group but only shopkeepers in the other groups. This provides an explanation for the rather high fees they charge in these lower income groups. As shown by the competitive fee for high-income groups, the informal providers appear to compete on price in these cases, but in other cases they rely on their capability to supply individualised services, which can command higher fees, but will be suitable for firms rather than (the more homogeneous) residential households. Their rates are considered high and their quality not distinctive.

Where Table 5.2 shows a positive correlation over the high- and middle-income groups between the increased use of skips and increased use of informal providers, this may be related to a common cause (more shops, with likely higher volumes of waste, and more special requirements), rather than to a structural relationship between skips and informal providers (taking waste to the skips).

In this section, we addressed the organization of waste collection. In Kampala, this changed in ten years' time from only public provision to predominantly

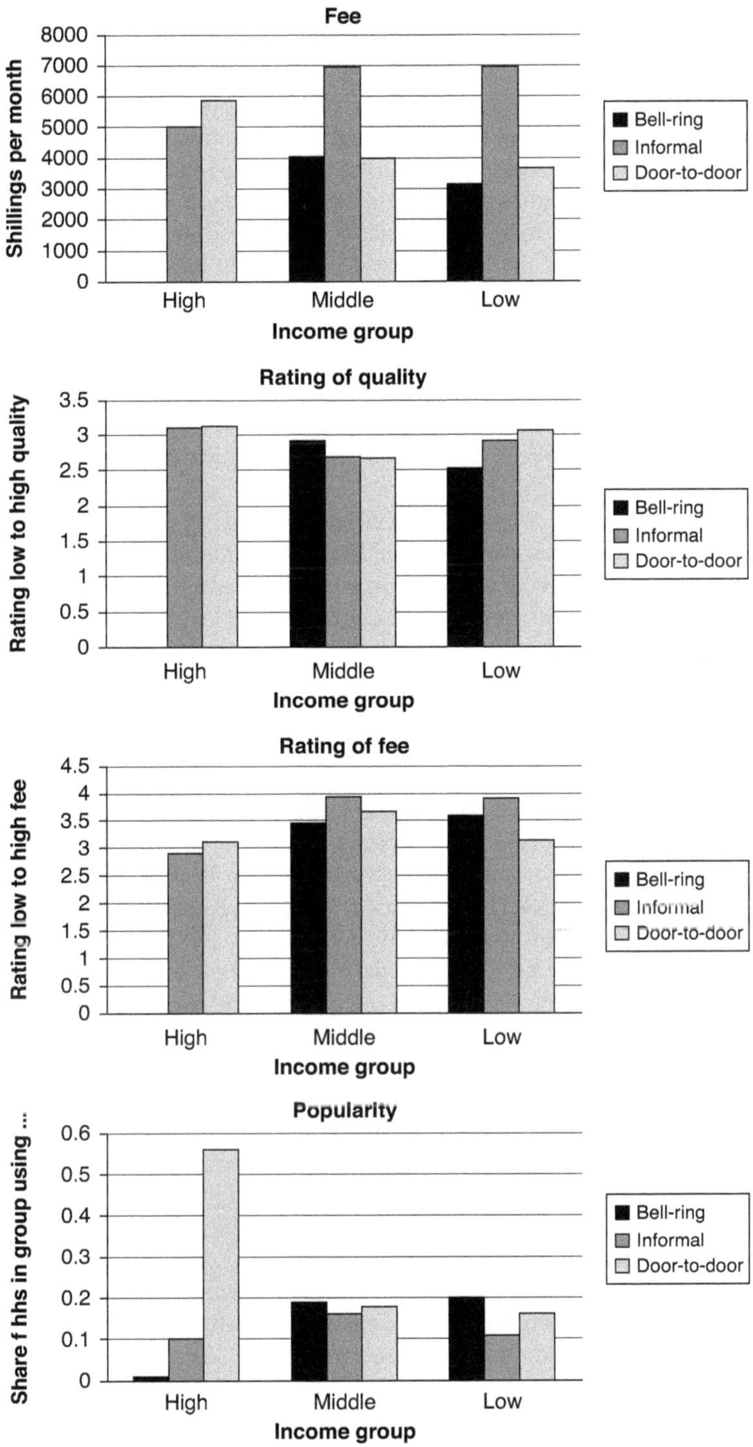

Figure 5.5 Scores of 3 collection systems in 3 income groups

private provision. But at all times, informal providers played a role. In the public system, they offered their services mostly to residential households in the richer income groups. In more recent years, their services are mostly provided to commercial households, and also in poorer income groups. In richer groups, they offer competitive prices, but in other groups their services are more expensive and probably geared toward rendering tailored services. They continue to exist despite the increased market shares of the formal private sector, and appear to have adapted themselves to these new conditions.

An important reason that informal collectors continue to exist can also lie in the mixed nature of households in Kampala and the terrain. While some areas in Kampala city have a big concentration of rich neighbourhoods, generally Kampala is a case of mixed households with both rich and poor staying almost in the same places. Shops are widely spread out, in poor areas also, and these are major waste-producing households. Due to the terrain and poor roads, some of these places are inaccessible to big trucks, offering informal collectors a big role in waste collection to thus fill a gap in service delivery. The combination of impassable roads and scattered households with ability to pay makes it extremely difficult for the formal private sector to operate in many areas of Kampala while maintaining their economies of scale.

In the situation of Kampala and other cities with similar conditions, we can see this co-existence of several providers as a structural feature where private sector, public sector and informal sector are combined in a modernised mixture of services (Oosterveer and Spaargaren 2010; Scheinberg et al. 2011). In this mixture, the market plays either no role (KCC's collection at no fee); or an indirect one (informal providers of tailor-made services); or a direct, price-establishing role (where the formal private sector competes among itself). Informal collectors use simple technologies like wheelbarrows and bicycles that are able to navigate through the terrain of most unplanned and semi-planned settlements, where big trucks of the formal sector cannot easily access; KCC employs the heavy equipment to ship large quantities and the private sector has an amalgam of equipment adapted to their services.

In such a situation, the informal collectors play a useful role, but there is still room for improvement, as they often fail to dispose of their collected waste in an environmentally responsible manner. As indicated above, they either free-ride on KCC or dispose of their collected waste in an illegal way (dumping). More expansion of this free-riding would actually benefit the environment, and it is here that KCCA, i.e., the present public sector, has a task. Providing facilities and incentives to deposit the collected waste in appropriate places are the instruments to enhance the informal providers' roles as environmental agents. This can be realised by acknowledging their contributions, notably in inaccessible areas, and – jointly with them – establish collection centres (transfer points) that are attractive enough. There are several ways to make these attractive: offering infrastructure for waste separation, such as scales and targeted containers for peelings, metals, plastics, hazardous waste, electric equipment, and so on. Informal sector involvement is likely to be greatly enhanced if they co-own such places, or if they are otherwise rewarded for the volume of waste they collect in poor neighbourhoods.

5.5 Conclusions and policy implications

In this chapter, two main observations were made. First, informal collectors fill a gap left by the formal (public or private) providers. The gap is likely due to the distance between major waste-producing households and the waste collection sector, as well as the nature of the waste. These informal collectors operate rather independently. In this sense they form the 'good' informal sector that creates employment for otherwise unemployed (Henry 1982). The second observation is that informal collectors partly free-ride on activities of KCC and partly just shift the environmental burden from client households to other households. Though this sounds as rather unproductive, this free-riding is actually what the public sector should promote and facilitate in areas that cannot be served adequately by the formal private sector.

Provision of communal collection facilities (like skips) has for a long time been associated with the public sector. Its services were hardly appreciated, mostly because timely replacement and cleaning of the surrounding area was not done enough. Yet, this type of service can offer scope for collaboration with informal collectors (and, for that matter, with community-based organisations). It would make their services more environment-friendly. Proper incentives can lie in co-ownership of collective containers, material recovery facilities and direct rewards.

This will reduce illegal dumpsites common in many communities. The typical problem of skips – the nuisance caused by delayed replacement and cleaning of their surroundings – can be reduced by involving private sector in this work. These tasks can be easily described and monitored, making them suitable for contracting.

Thus, we envisage good potential for a modernised mixture of public initiative toward informal collectors, with a view to helping poorer neighbourhoods, and using a technology of collection points, whose negative aspects can be eliminated (or at least reduced) by contracting private agents for replacement and cleaning. This kind of modernised mixture, where large-scale and highly technological solid waste services, typical of public and formal private sectors, mix with small-scale technological solutions of the informal sector, could be a solution to the solid waste problem facing many developing countries. Such systems could improve accessibility and could be ecologically sustainable, improving environmental performance of urban infrastructure in the long run, and thus helping achieve the Millennium Development Goals (MDGs). They are also advocated in the World Development Report (2004), which calls for recognising informal service providers and enabling them to partner with formal public and private operators.

References

Henry, S. (1982). The working unemployed: Perspectives on informal economy and unemployment. *The Sociological Review,* 30 (3): 460–477.

Katusiimeh, M. W. (2012). *Public and private service provision of solid waste management in Kampala, Uganda.* PhD thesis. Wageningen: Wageningen University.

Katusiimeh, M. W., Burger, K. & Mol, A.P.J. (2013). Informal waste collection and its co-existence with the formal waste sector: The case of Kampala, Uganda. *Habitat International,* 38: 1–9.

Katusiimeh, M. W., Mol, A.P.J. & Burger, K. (2011). The operations and effectiveness of public and private provision of solid waste collection services in Kampala. *Habitat International,* 36 (2): 247–252.

Kawai, K. & Osako, M. (2013). Advantages and disadvantages of municipal solid waste collection service for citizens of Hanoi city, Vietnam. *Waste Management & Research,* 31 (3): 327–332.

Medina, M. (2005). Serving the unserved: Informal refuse collection in Mexico. *Waste Management & Research,* 23 (5) :390–397.

Okot-Okumu, J. & Nyenje, R. (2011). Municipal solid waste management under decentralization in Uganda. *Habitat International,* 35: 537–543.

Oosterveer, P. & Spaargaren, G. (2010). Meeting Social Challenges in Developing Sustainable Environmental Infrastructures in East African Cities. In Bas van Vliet, Gert Spaargaren & Peter Oosterveer (Eds.), *Social Perspectives on the Sanitation Challenge* (pp. 11–30). Netherlands: Springer.

Pritchett, L. & Woolcock, M. (2004). Solutions When *the* Solution is the Problem: Arraying the Disarray in Development. *World Development,* 32 (2): 191–212.

Scheinberg, A., Spies, S. et al. (2011). Assessing urban recycling in low- and middle income countries: Building on modernised mixtures. *Habitat International*, 35: 188–198.

World Development Report (2004). *Making services work for poor people.* The World Bank.

6 Local NGOs and CBOs in urban sanitation and solid waste management

Evidence from East African metropolises[1]

Judith T. Tukahirwa, Arthur P. J. Mol and Peter Oosterveer

6.1 Introduction

Both sanitation and solid waste management in developing countries have received noteworthy attention through the Millennium Development Goals (MDGs) and the debate on their follow-up after 2015. Significant improvements in providing these services need to be made if the MDG targets are to be met in African countries. Since the introduction of economic liberalisation policies in the early and late 1990s, sanitation and solid waste management systems have undergone significant reforms in many African countries. Uganda, Kenya and Tanzania have embraced these reforms with a considerable shift from a public sector driven service to diversification of provisioning schemes and involvement of key actors. Hence, from the 1990s onwards, a variety of public schemes, private schemes and public-private mixes can be witnessed in sanitation and solid waste management in East African cities.

This diversification did not only bring private companies to the centre of sanitation and solid waste management services provision, but also enhanced the role of civil society organisations, most notably community-based organisations (CBOs) and non-governmental organisations (NGOs). These organisations have been widely recognised as actors that are philanthropic in nature, often motivated by noble aspirations to improve solid waste management and sanitation conditions of poor communities through direct service provision or through advocating improvements in their situation (Ahmed and Ali 2004; Ahmed and Ali 2006; Beall 1997; Joseph 2006; Klundert and Lardinois 1995; Rathi 2006; Schübeler 1997). Especially, the role of NGOs and CBOs in providing sanitation and solid waste management services to underserved, marginalised, poor or hardly accessible areas and communities is widely celebrated. Fully public and fully private schemes are thought to be less capable and willing to serve these areas and groups effectively.

Some country-level overview studies on NGO and CBO involvement in sanitation and solid waste management in East Africa have been carried out (Schouten and Mathenge 2010; Tukahirwa et al. 2010), but little is known about the actual performance of NGOs and CBOs in service provisioning in East African cities. Still, these country level NGO-CBO studies indicate that the importance, role and performance of these civil society organisations in urban environmental service provisioning differ significantly between Tanzania, Uganda and Kenya. This is surprising, as the three countries have significant similarities – for instance, in their socioeconomic situation. Hence, this chapter explores how and to which extent civil society organisations are involved in urban sanitation and solid waste management services in Kenya, Tanzania and Uganda, and why in some settings NGOs or CBOs are successful in organizing these services (especially for the poor), while under similar socioeconomic conditions elsewhere such models seem to work less successfully.

We provide a comparative analysis of three metropolises in Eastern Africa: Kampala, Nairobi and Dar es Salaam. These three large cities face similar problems with providing sanitation and solid waste management services for significant numbers of poor people. Our comparative research is aimed at understanding and explaining the differences between the role of NGOs and CBOs in these cities, and also provides instrumental suggestions to underpin the improvement of urban sanitation and solid waste management through NGO or CBO involvement. Section 6.2 highlights our perspectives on institutional pluralism, while the applied research methodology is presented in section 6.3. Sections 6.4 and 6.5 cover the historical context of NGOs and CBOs and their current involvement in sanitation and solid waste management, respectively. Subsequently, Section 6.6 compares in more detail the roles of NGOs and CBOs in the urban service provisioning to the poor in the three cities. The final section draws conclusions fundamental to the scale and operations of NGOs and CBOs within, but not limited to, the scope of this research.

6.2 Institutional pluralism in urban service provisioning

One of the main dilemmas of urban sanitation and solid waste management in the large cities of East Africa is the failure and weakness of both large-scale centralised systems that have run relatively successfully in the urban centres of developed countries, and small-scale decentralised systems that are well adapted to the more remote rural areas in developing and transitional countries. Neither of these alternatives has been successfully applied in the East African urban context, leaving a large section of the poor without reliable access to sustainable environmental management services. Recently, scholars have started to work on ideas of what they label *modernised mixtures,* an approach that takes the best features out of both decentralised and centralised systems and (re)combines them into hybrid solutions which better fit specific local (socioeconomic, ecological, technological and political) situations (See Chapter 2 of this volume; Spaargaren et al. 2006; Scheinberg and Mol 2010; Spaargaren and Oosterveer 2010; Scheinberg et al 2011). This Modernised Mixtures approach looks at the degree of consumer involvement, technological advancement and robustness, degree of centralisation, and level of decision-making for implementation, but also at fitting institutional arrangements. With respect to the latter feature, modernised mixture scholars argue for the need to apply less rigid institutional arrangements that govern and run these urban services, and for adapting the institutional structure to the specific conditions prevailing in the area to be served. The concept of institutional pluralism provides us with the tool to analyse varieties in and combinations of institutions involved in these situations.

In its most concise form, *institutional pluralism* refers to situations where individuals or organisations act within multiple institutional spheres. Individuals and organisations are then confronted with two or more sets of 'regime rationalities' at the same time, and hence are subject to and have to cope with multiple regulatory regimes and multiple normative orders. The classical example with respect to developing countries refers to the formal governmental regulatory regime sitting next to a more 'traditional' regulatory regime, both regulating land use or property rights (e.g., Fitzpatrick 2006). Many studies use the notion of institutional pluralism in a slightly different way, especially when studying alternatives for the institutional monopoly of the (central) government or of the market in the provisioning of goods or services (e.g., Blair 2001; Claassen 2009). Institutional pluralism then refers to multiple institutions that provide, through different strategies, services and/or goods at the same time for specific groups of customers in specific areas, often ranging from private firms to community groups, from faith-based organisations to political parties, and from governmental institutions to non-governmental organisations. This comes together with different systems of payment, different systems of accountability, different allocation mechanisms, and different relations between providers and consumers – among other differences.

This latter interpretation, which will also be followed here, brings institutional pluralism close to the literature on how goods and services can be best provided: through the government, through the market, through civil society or through any combination, hybrid or partnership of these sectors (e.g., Glasbergen et al. 2007; Oosterveer 2009). Especially when public goods and services are at stake, debates on institutional preferences are vibrant, such as those on the much-disputed government delegation of public services to private firms and NGOs in Africa (Cohen and Peterson 1999; Katusiimeh et al. 2013). Some scholars argue that institutional pluralism on public good provisioning can enhance effectiveness and legitimacy of the state, as the state can concentrate on other tasks and is no longer solely accountable for providing these services and goods (Esman 1991; Esman and Uphoff 1984). Esman and Uphoff (1984) also found that "multiple tiers of organisations with smaller units at the base yielded greater solidarity, scale and specialised services than the higher levels of organisations acting alone". Others perceive institutional pluralism as an alternative to failed past decentralised efforts and a means to solve the new economic, social and political problems of the twenty-first century by adopting a mix of central, non-central, private sector and NGO initiatives for implementing public sector tasks through market approaches that enhance greater accountability (Cohen and Peterson 1999). Not seldom, analyses and debates are politicised through qualifications of neo-liberalisation, especially when privatisation and markets are involved.

Institutional pluralism studies in the area of public service provisioning have paid relatively little attention to the role of civil society organisations and institutions. In developed countries, the contribution of civil society to sanitation

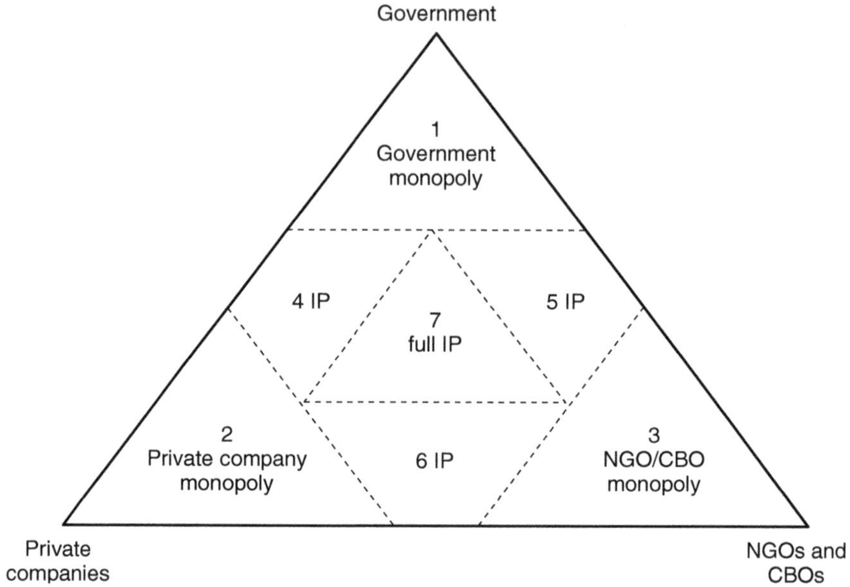

Figure 6.1 Institutional pluralism triangle on urban environmental (IP = Institutional Pluralism)

and solid waste is usually marginal, but in developing countries it often plays a more important role. When we see civil society institutions emphasised in urban sanitation and service provision, it is usually related to peripheral areas and marginal groups: slums and the poor. In studying civil society involvement in urban service provision, we are interested in the degree of involvement and magnitude of service provision by these civil society institutions, the competition and (kind of) collaboration with the institutions of state and market, the question to what extent civil society service provision is limited to the poor, and the differences in all this according to particular time and place.

Figure 6.1 sketches (potential) institutional models based on the arguments above. Subdivisions 1, 2 and 3 portray institutional monopolies where the state, private companies and NGO or CBO institutions operate independently, respectively. Subdivisions 4, 5 and 6 show institutional pluralism involving only two institutions in service delivery. The mixture could be between government and private companies (4) or between NGOs and CBOs and government (5), or between NGOs and CBOs and private companies (6). The most full institutional mixture is between all three institutions (7).

6.3 Methodology

The perspective of institutional pluralism is applied in a study of NGO and CBO involvement in urban service provision in Kampala, Nairobi and Dar es Salaam, the capital cities of Uganda, Kenya and Tanzania, respectively. We analysed NGO and CBO involvement in sanitation and solid waste management in parallel with the other two main service provisioning institutions: governmental schemes and private/market arrangements. Sanitation service refers to safe excreta disposal through both hardware (such as provision of toilets) and software (such as community sensitisation, capacity building, advocacy, and monitoring) activities. Solid waste management services mainly comprise the safe collection, recycling and disposal of waste, as well as carrying out sensitisation activities.

Three inventories were carried out between August 2007 and December 2009 in Kampala, Nairobi and Dar es Salaam. In addition, face-to-face interviews were held in the three cities with key informants from NGOs and CBOs, from relevant Ministries, from local councils or municipalities, from government agencies, and from local and international organisations that linked with NGOs and CBOs. Direct observations were made for identifying some of the major weaknesses and innovative approaches applied by these organisations in sanitation and solid waste management. Annual reports, project and programme progress reports, and evaluation reports – both internal and external – of NGOs and CBOs and of relevant government agencies were collected and reviewed.

During the same period, household surveys were conducted in 12, 6 and 4 (Kampala, Nairobi and Dar es Salaam, respectively) purposively selected informal settlements with the highest number of urban poor and with the most serious sanitation and solid waste problems. Within each neighbourhood of Kampala and Nairobi, 35 households were selected using random sampling following a list of residents provided by local leaders, while 50 households were selected for neigbourhoods in Dar es Salaam because of the large size of the informal settlements. Ultimately, total sample sizes of 337, 206 and 200 households were realised for Kampala, Nairobi and Dar es Salaam, respectively. Data was collected on different aspects, such as respondents' characteristics, their access to NGO and CBO services, as well as their experiences and opinions regarding services of NGOs and CBOs.

6.4 History of NGOs and CBOs in East Africa

NGOs and CBOs as we know them today are a relatively recent phenomenon in East Africa and did not play a significant role in the three countries before the early 1990s. NGOs and CBOs involved in sanitation and solid waste management services are part of wider civil society networks in the three cities/countries. Therefore, to understand and ascertain the similarities and differences among the three cities, the history of these civil society organisations is taken into account.

During the colonial period and until the early 1980s, there was a relatively small NGO sector in Uganda, dominated by charity and religious organisations providing services such as education and medical care (see Makara 2000). During that period, these organisations were not regarded as significant alternative service providers to the (often failing) state. The political and social instability (that led to the death of many people opposing government polices) gave little room for the free organisation of people outside state structures. "Freedom of association was highly circumscribed and associational groups were held suspect by the state"

(Makara 2000). However, the coming into power of the Museveni government in 1986 gave people more freedom to organise themselves and to discuss and form opinions of their own. This led to a significant growth of the NGO sector, which is, however, required to exercise a significant level of self-control to avoid conflict with the government, and the government has often been accused of impeding activities of these organisations (Okuku 2002).

Although there was limited political and social instability in post-colonial Kenya, the (colonial and post-colonial) authoritarian character of the state and the assault to civil society (see Ndegwa 1996; Okuku 2002) hardly allowed for freedom of association in the 1980s. For instance, the head of state president at that time, Moi, set about dismantling civic and political organisations and networks of patronage that had served previous regimes because he felt these had the potential to undermine his power (e.g., Throup 1987 in Ndegwa 1996). The result was a single-party state under which a limited number of civil society organisations operated, mostly adhering to the state rules of that time. Increasing (domestic and international) pressure and suspension of foreign aid later led to opening up of space for NGOs, but these organisations remained targets of direct state control through the 1990 NGO Coordination Act. The introduction of this act further weakened the already sore NGO-state relationship, with NGOs resisting control by the state. The persistent resistance by the NGOs resulted in opening up space for a political multiparty system (Ndegwa 1996) that allowed NGOs to operate freely and independently from the state. This caused an explosion of NGOs, numbers growing from 500 in the 1990s (Ndegwa 1996) to over 3000 by 2004 (Gurgerty 2008).

Tanzania has not witnessed serious political and social instability following independence. Today, Tanzania is still considered a peaceful and stable country which has successfully built a strong national unity (Kayombo 2010: 3). The socialist state sought to bring all non-governmental organisations – both for profit and non-profit ones – under its control (Coulson 1982; Havnevik 1993; Mercer 1999). This successfully crushed many independent organisations, and participation was possible only through the state (Mercer 1999; Tripp 1992). However, the economic and political liberalisation of the mid-1980s led to the adoption of economic adjustment programmes and opened up space for a political multiparty system that encouraged NGO participation in provisioning social services (Mercer 1999). The state still remains suspicious of independent NGO activities and their room for manoeuvre continues to be constrained and manipulated. The government does have an active policy of co-opting the NGO sector in social service provision through establishing collaborations.

Notwithstanding the growth and expansion of the NGO sector in Uganda, Kenya and Tanzania over the last two decades, their governments have been – and often still are – suspicious of NGOs, and consider NGO activities politically sensitive and/or beyond government control. Bratton (1989) and Okuku (2002) indeed see NGOs in Kenya and Uganda as resourceful organisations with a growing autonomy from the state. During economic hardship (e.g., the 1990s) the governments saw donors channelling funds increasingly to NGOs, and the state's diminishing development resources threatened to undermine the state's capacity for political patronage and legitimisation (Clapham 1996; Mol 2001; Ndegwa 1996). The increasing involvement of NGOs in urban service delivery challenges African governments further, as NGO service provision (often funded through donors) competes with and challenges the poorly funded government-run services (Gurgerty 2008). Hence they articulate legitimacy problems for the state institutions, when operating in the same area of service delivery.

In addition, there have been mixed reactions from scholars about the growth and authenticity of these organisations. Fowler (1995), for example, reports that NGOs in East Africa are not so much bottom-up organisations, but structures created by civil servants who lost their jobs. Dicklitch (1998) points to the so-called briefcase NGOs, created by elite with the aim of self-enrichment rather than improving the lives of the poor people. Titeca (2005) reports on frank interviews with directors of Ugandan NGOs who saw NGOs first of all as business opportunities for personal survival. According to Makara, the popular perception of NGOs among the local citizens in these African countries is that of "organizing in order to gain a benefit from donor organisations" (Makara 2000: 178), as well as for personal benefit. This would make the distinction between NGOs and commercial enterprises less sharp and less clear than is often portrayed in the literature.

6.5 Comparing contemporary sanitation and solid waste service institutions

In the three cities, sanitation and solid waste management consist of plural systems with diverse institutions, both formal and informal. The multiplicity of institutions has emerged because of the governments' incapacity to provide adequate services to all citizens and the neo-liberal policies that facilitated privatisation of these public services.

6.5.1 Kampala

Following government failure and the adoption of neo-liberal policies, the government of Uganda started privatisation in urban sanitation and solid waste services and developed regulatory frameworks to guide and enforce the privatisation process. The privatisation processes came with challenges that accelerated the growth of multiple institutions in both systems. The sanitation system in Kampala is heavily dependent on donor funding, and through neoliberal policies and increased donor demands the government increasingly recognised the importance of NGOs and CBOs in the water and sanitation sector. This became evident in the government's recognition and support of the Uganda Water and Sanitation NGO network (UWASNET). UWASNET is an umbrella organisation that coordinates, builds capacity, and ensures collaboration among water and sanitation NGOs and CBOs (and other stakeholders including government). It carries out advocacy and lobbying, research and development, and ensures good governance of its members. The government cooperates closely with UWASNET and engages it in water and sanitation sector planning, monitoring and information sharing, while at the same time allowing it to pursue its activities independently, but within the water and sanitation regulatory framework. UWASNET ensures compliance of its members with governmental water and sanitation policies, guidelines and regulatory framework.

However, the government's interests and priorities are more on rural than on urban water and sanitation service improvement, and this has also directed NGO and CBO activities towards rural service provision. Nonetheless, in some cases NGOs and CBOs, with support from donors, are providing services to the urban poor independently from other institutions, resulting in NGO/CBO institutional monism (subdivision 3, Figure 6.1). In other situations, the government engages NGOs and CBOs in donor-funded projects for sanitation service delivery to the urban poor, leading to cooperation between the two institutions (subdivision 5, Figure 6.1). In addition, governmental agencies also provide services to the urban poor independently (subdivision 1, Figure 6.1). Therefore, in sanitation service delivery there is a typical combination of institutional collaboration and institutional monism, involving government and NGOs or CBOs.

Solid waste management in Kampala is governed through the Kampala City Council *Solid Waste Management Ordinance 2000,* which promotes institutional pluralism in service delivery. It mentions NGOs and CBOs as potential institutions for service delivery, although it does not have a clear strategy or funding for engaging them (e.g., Katusiimeh et al. 2012 and 2013; Tukahirwa et al. 2010). As a result, solid waste service provision is contracted out to only large private companies (subdivision 4, Figure 6.1). However, these companies have hardly been able to provide services in urban poor informal settlements (see Figure 6.2). The inadequacy of services in these locations has prompted a large growth of NGOs and CBOs trying to fill the gap. These organisations work independently in solid waste management, often without formal government recognition, and predominantly service the urban poor (Figure 6.2; Katusiimeh et al. 2013). The contribution of these organisations is hampered by government obstruction. Governmental agencies also try to serve the poor in informal settlements through the provision of trucks, but these can only be accessed by the few households living close or within proximity to the routes taken by the trucks. Hence, solid waste service delivery for the urban poor is fragmented, with institutional arrangements working almost independently next to each other (subdivisions 1 and 3, Figure 6.1) and leaving major parts of the urban poor without access to solid waste services.

6.5.2 Nairobi

Not unlike Kampala, solid waste management in Nairobi is primarily contracted out to large private companies, which have failed to provide services to all neighbourhoods. As a result, the city authority in Nairobi allows and even stimulates open competition where qualified independent small private companies freely compete for solid waste collection services. The increase in the number of private

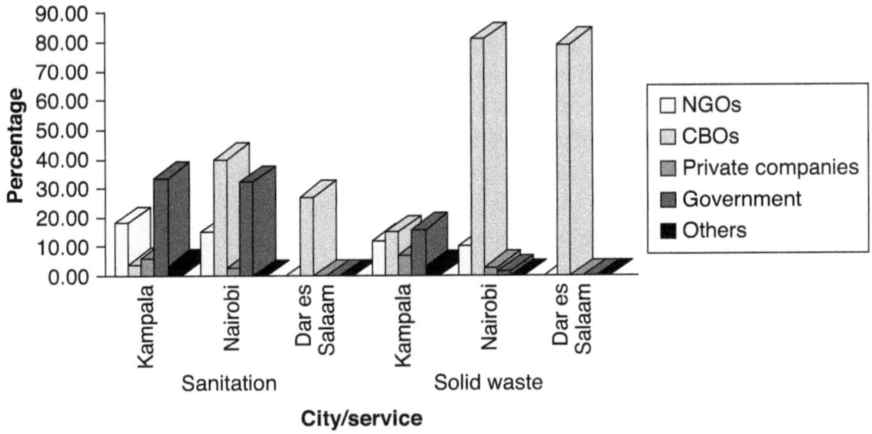

Figure 6.2 Urban poor access to sanitation and solid waste management

companies has not solved the problem of inadequate services provision, especially for the urban poor. The short-falling services of private companies have led to the emergence of other institutional arrangements, including those involving NGOs and CBOs. These organisations work informally, but follow largely similar rules and principles as private companies – and some have evolved into private companies to be able to obtain licenses. NGOs and CBOs also provide services at a lower fee, which has enhanced access of the urban poor to these services (see Figure 6.2). In poor settlements, there is almost a CBO-based institutional monopoly in solid waste service delivery (subdivision 3, Figure 6.1).

Nairobi has a sanitation policy, called *Environmental Sanitation and Hygiene Policy 2007,* which advocates for a people-centred and national participatory approach to sanitation and recognises NGOs and CBOs as important actors. Government and NGOs or CBOs engage in policy dialogues, and the government also recognises the umbrella association Kenya Water and Sanitation Network (KEWASNET). However, the two hardly cooperate in service delivery. In association with KEWASNET, NGOs and CBOs autonomously carry out their activities with support from foreign donors, often to the extent that they are the main sanitation service providers in poor urban settlements. Governmental agencies provide sanitation services independently from civil society organisations. That makes sanitation service delivery for the urban poor a disconnected pluralism between government and NGO or CBO institutions (subdivisions 3 and 1, Figure 6.1).

6.5.3 Dar es Salaam

Dar es Salaam lacks a sanitation policy and instead relies on the National Water Policy 2002. This policy recognises NGOs and CBOs as partners in the sanitation sector. Implementation of sanitation in poor informal settlements is weak, with little cooperation and collaboration between government and NGOs and CBOs. The Tanzania Water and Sanitation Network (TAWASANET) is still in its infancy, and has a preference for and preoccupation with water and sanitation improvement in rural areas. Compared to Kampala and Nairobi, less sanitation service delivery is observed in poor informal urban settlements, all of which is CBO organised (see Figure 6.2). The absence of government (or private company) institutions in sanitation provisioning for the poor is striking and a reflection of the low governmental priority attached to sanitation services.

In contrast, to improve solid waste management Dar es Salaam city has embraced institutional pluralism, formally regulated by the solid waste management by-laws. Solid waste services are franchised to private companies and to CBOs by the local governments and municipalities. The system specifies the roles and responsibilities of each franchisee (similar to institutional pluralism proposed by Cohen and Peterson 1999), ensuring equal service to all clients. Hence, Dar es Salaam has various institutional mixtures involving government, private companies and CBOs. The allocation of specific institutions to specific locations has resulted in high levels of service delivery in the city, including the poor urban settlements. The monopoly of direct service delivery (primary waste collection) in poor, not easily accessible urban settlements is given to CBOs, and this has resulted in large access of the urban poor to waste services (Figure 6.2). However, these organisations cooperate with the government and private companies through the utilisation of their transport means.

6.5.4 Comparison

Different from the formalised institutional pluralism in Dar es Salaam, solid waste service delivery for the urban poor in Kampala and Nairobi is dominated by institutional fragmentation with limited regulation, as well as limited recognition and cooperation with NGOs and CBOs. This is exacerbated by the governments' suspicion in the two cities over the legitimacy, lack of transparency and the informal nature of these organisations. Their authenticity is questioned because many give the impression of being briefcase organisations whose sole aim is to fulfil personal needs (cf. Schaub-Jones et al. 2006; Dicklitch 1998). Hence, these governments mainly contract services out to private companies. Rudimentary institutional pluralism is present in the sanitation service delivery for the urban poor in the three cities. This is propelled by inadequate sanitation policies of the government (Kampala and Dar es Salaam), as well as by poor implementation of the existing policies and legislation (all three cities). Increased NGO or CBO involvement in sanitation service delivery for the urban poor has also been boosted by donor influence.

Overall, the contribution of NGOs and CBOs to sanitation and solid waste service delivery to the urban poor across the three cities is significant. Except for sanitation in Kampala, the contribution of these organisations to serving the poor is higher than that of governmental and private sector institutions. Despite the exclusion of NGOs and CBOs from formal service delivery in Nairobi, their actual contribution to solid waste service delivery is comparable to that of Dar es Salaam.

6.6 Insights in NGO and CBO service delivery

6.6.1 NGO and CBO structures and organisation

The NGO and CBO institutional structures and organisations vary across the three cities, with respect to membership orientation, professionalism, formalisation and funding. There is variation in numbers and types of organisations involved in sanitation and solid waste management. Large numbers of NGOs and CBOs were found in Kampala and Nairobi, but with variations in nature. A total of 44 non-governmental organisations engaged in sanitation and/or solid waste were captured in Nairobi and only 1 of them was a CBO.[2] Likewise, we captured a total number of 44 Kampala NGOs and CBOs involved in sanitation and solid waste management; Kampala also had the largest number (12) of local branches of international organisations among these organisations (Tukahirwa et al. 2010). Dar es Salaam had only 8 NGOs and CBOs in sanitation and solid waste management, most of them providing services to the largest administrative division, Kidondoni. Among these were three local branches of international NGOs, while the rest were CBOs. The large number of NGOs and CBOs in Kampala and Nairobi forms an indication for and a result of the fragmented institutional pluralism, inadequate governmental services as well as the opening up of space for NGO and CBO involvement in urban service delivery. In addition, almost all the NGOs and CBOs captured in our inventory in Kampala and Nairobi are strongly donor-dependent, which may explain the large numbers. The low numbers of NGOs in Dar es Salaam can be explained by the limited space for NGO activities, due to the state's continued suspicion of these organisations (see also Mercer 1999), and by the formalised institutional pluralism that leaves little room for mushrooming organisations aiming to fill the gap in state service delivery.

NGO and CBO evolution shows a clear trend across the years. In Kampala, the local NGOs evolved from CBOs with the aim of serving more communities, as well as a strategy for increasing access to donor funds. However, donor funding has increasingly moved from registered NGOs to unregistered CBOs that manage better to engage the community. Most CBOs are started by community leaders or an elite group within the community, who mobilise the youth to improve the poor sanitation and solid waste management situation. NGOs, especially those that did not start as CBOs, are established by a group of elite men and/or women, such as graduate professionals (e.g., civil engineers) and social workers with trained backgrounds in sanitation and waste management and community development, respectively. The local branches of international NGOs are often made up of professionals, both local and expatriate. Only a few Kampala NGOs and CBOs are membership organisations, composed of both the founding members and ordinary citizens. Membership is then open to the general public, but entails a small fee to help run the organisation. Even so, compliance to payment of membership fee is a challenge, and in most cases, a fee is paid only once, during inception of the organisation.

The majority of CBOs in Nairobi started as groups of informal solid waste pickers that charged a small collection fee for their services. A few were established by an elite group of people. Some of these CBOs have undergone capacity building in sanitation and solid waste management. The NGOs and CBOs involved in sanitation are mostly donor-dependent, and a few are also membership organisations made up of founding members and ordinary members. The founding members are mostly local leaders, executive members of community committees, or professionals, joined by family, colleagues and friends.

The NGOs in Dar es Salaam are mostly local branches of international organisations with both local and expatriate professionals. These NGOs are donor-dependent and mostly implement governmental programs. CBOs in Dar es Salaam started often as (women's) groups that sought to improve the poor solid waste situation. The services of these groups were initially free, which enhanced the trust from local people and the government. Some CBOs registered formally and are now among those being awarded the solid waste franchise by the local government. CBOs in Dar es Salaam normally have undergone capacity building with support from government and international organisations such as ILO. These larger CBOs are membership organisations, but membership is limited to founding members, and they are less open to community membership. They are not donor-dependent, although occasionally they write proposals to fund recycling activities.

6.6.2 NGO and CBO clients, activities and finances

There is variation in the geographical operational scope and target population of NGO and CBO services in the three cities. Some organisations (especially in Nairobi and Dar es Salaam) serve all categories of households (poor/low, middle and high income) located in different neighbourhoods, while those of Kampala provide services mostly to poor and a few middle-income households in informal settlements (Table 6.1). The diversity in NGO or CBO clientele in Dar es Salaam can be explained from the specific form of institutional pluralism, which allows equal participation of institutions in solid waste service delivery. The diversity in Nairobi is a result of the fragmented institutional pluralism that promotes competition among the different service providers.

The most prominent activities of these organisations are garbage collection and community sensitisation. Garbage collection mainly takes place through a door-to-door system using wheelbarrows and push carts, although a drop-off system is also used in some areas, especially in Nairobi and Kampala. Recycling activities are also prominent in the three cities, with activities ranging from composting (mostly in Nairobi) to plastic, paper, glass and scrap recycling (in all three cities). Most of the organisations involved in this have acquired special training for specific recycling activities. For instance, some NGOs in Kampala received training from NGOs and CBOs in Nairobi in briquette making as well as in making construction materials from waste.

Table 6.1 Characteristics of sampled NGOs and CBOs across the three cities

Characteristics	*Kampala*			*Nairobi*		*Dar es Salaam*	
	L/INGOs (12)	*LNGOs (15)*	*CBOs (17)*	*LNGOs (1)*	*CBOs (43)*	*L/INGOs (3)*	*CBOs (5)*
Activities							
Garbage collection	1	6	12	–	34	–	5
Providing communal toilets	8	5	0	–	24	–	1
Recycling	4	9	11	–	25	–	3
Community sensitisation	12	14	13	1	28	–	5
Monitoring	9	4	0		–	–	–
Advocacy	9	2	0		–	–	–
Support to other NGOs and CBOs	9	1	0		–	–	–
Source of finance							
Donors	12	10	13	–	8	3	–
Membership fees	–	7	5	–	6	–	3
Loans	–	–	–	1	4	–	–
Formal solid waste collection	–	–	–	–	–	–	3
Informal solid waste collection	–	6	12	–	34		2
Recycling activities	–	9	11	–	25	–	2
Clients							
Poor/low income	12	15	17	–	33	3	5
Middle income	2	2	6	–	30	0	5
High income	–	–	–	–	6	0	5

Note: L/INGOs refers to local branches of international organisations and LNGOs to local NGOs.

Source: this study

The NGOs and CBOs involved in sanitation carry out similar soft- and hardware services across the three cities. The software services include community sensitisation and capacity building. Advocacy and monitoring activities are most prominent in Kampala and supported by the local branches of international organisations. The hardware services include 'appropriate' pro-poor technologies (both individual and communal toilets). The toilets provided by CBOs in Dar es Salaam are mostly ordinary pit latrines. More advanced and arguably more ecologically sustainable pro-poor technologies are communal biogas generating latrines in Nairobi (cf. Schouten and Mathenge 2010), which combine treatment of human waste with biogas production. NGOs in Kampala provide so-called Ecosan toilets that are also more ecologically sustainable (Hendriksen et al. 2012; Tukahirwa et al. 2010). The difference in the hardware services between the three cities results from donor influences. NGOs and CBOs in Kampala and Nairobi receive considerable donor support for their sanitation activities.

There are similarities and variations among NGO and CBO financing schemes across the three cities (see Table 6.1). Generally all the NGOs and CBOs involved in sanitation services are donor-dependent, and activities commence only when funds are available. Hence, reliance on donor money is a major weakness and danger for sustainable service delivery. NGOs and CBOs in Kampala argue that sustainable sanitation delivery requires government funding, especially in areas in which they have expertise, such as pro-poor technologies and approaches. With respect to solid waste management, NGOs and CBOs depend more on membership fees, recycling activities and collection fees. In Kampala, the finances from solid waste service are inadequate because of lack of payment by (potential) clients (the urban poor). The urban poor argue that NGO services should be free, and therefore they are not keen on paying for services. In Nairobi, the solid waste collection fees vary depending on the areas served, and the fees are determined by NGOs and CBOs based on the quality of service, frequency of waste collection, neighbourhood and local conditions. CBOs in Dar es Salaam have overcome the donor dependency syndrome due to the favourable solid waste service delivery franchise system. The fees for solid waste collection vary according to the area served (low, middle or high income), and the fees are predetermined in by-laws.

6.6.3 NGO and CBO service delivery to poor informal settlements

From our survey in poor informal settlements, no respondent indicated receiving services from NGOs in Dar es Salaam, a reflection of the fact that NGOs' room for manoeuvre in urban services continues to be constrained. For Kampala and Nairobi, the percentages of NGO service recipients are somewhat similar, both for sanitation and solid waste management. In terms of CBO services, Nairobi residents receive the most sanitation services, while Kampala residents received the least. For solid waste services, the majority of the Nairobi and Dar es Salaam respondents receive CBO services (see Table 6.2).

A case study in Kampala on the determinants of poor households' access to NGO or CBO supplied sanitation and solid waste services (Tukahirwa et al. 2011) showed that next to spatial proximity, socioeconomic and perceptional characteristics of households, social proximity also plays an important role. Social proximity refers to the density of social interactions and the 'bonding' of social relations in social networks. The level of social proximity has the potential to strengthen, weaken or even destroy the relationship between the NGOs and CBOs and the user (Bendapudi and Berry 1997). Cooperation between households and NGOs or CBOs is important

Table 6.2 Number of respondents accessing NGOs/CBOs services in percentages

Service	*NGO*			*CBO*		
	Kampala	*Nairobi*	*Dar es Salaam*	*Kampala*	*Nairobi*	*Dar es Salaam*
Sanitation	18% (61)	15% (31)	–	4% (15)	40% (83)	27% (53)
Solid waste	12% (39)	10% (21)	–	16% (53)	81% (166)	79% (158)

Note: N appears between parentheses

Source: this study

in providing solid waste services and securing the trust that is an essential factor explaining access to sanitation. One way to promote access of the urban poor to both sanitation and solid waste services provided by NGO or CBO service providers is to ensure the functioning of social networks and to build trust in those organisations and their services. Spatial proximity is, in some instances, particularly in the case of NGO provided facilities, also a relevant explanatory factor for the level of access of the urban poor. Income differences proved much less important, but this may be due to the relatively marginal differences in income among the poor in these areas.

6.6.4 Comparing recipients of NGO and CBO services

Although our sampled respondents were all selected from poor informal settlements, we expected some differences between the recipients of NGO or CBO services, recipients of governmental services, recipients of private market services and those who never received any institutionalised service. To analyse the differences between households accessing services for sanitation and solid waste in each city, three statistical tests were used (see Tables 6.3, 6.4 and 6.5).[3] To capture the employment status, household heads were asked to mention their type of employment, which was later categorised into formal employment (for instance, working for private companies, public institutions or non-governmental organisations), informal employment (such as home-based workers, street vendors, scavengers) and not-employed. A household head was categorised as employed if (s)he was either formally or informally employed.

In Kampala, households accessing sanitation services from NGOs and CBOs did not significantly differ from those having no access to sanitation services at all (see Table 6.3), indicating homogeneity in household characteristics between the two groups. The situation is only slightly different for access to solid waste services, with differences observed only regarding household size between recipients of NGOs or CBOs services and non-recipients of solid waste services (at 1% significant level). Recipients of NGO or CBO solid waste services had larger household sizes, which are prone to generate more waste and thus may be compelled to seek solid waste services.

Compared with households accessing governmental and private market sanitation services, those accessing NGO or CBO services only differed significantly

Table 6.3 Comparison of households in Kampala receiving sanitation and solid waste services by NGOs or CBOs, by other service providers, and receiving no services

Characteristics	*Access NGO/CBO services and those without access to services*						*Access to NGO/CBO services and access other service providers*					
	Sanitation			*Solid waste*			*Sanitation*			*Solid waste*		
	NGO/CBO (N = 76)	*No access (N = 117)*	*Test*	*NGO/CBO (N = 92)*	*No access (N = 158)*	*Test*	*N1GO/CBO (N = 76)*	*Other providers (N = 144)*	*Test*	*NGO/CB0 (N = 92)*	*Other providers (N = 87)*	*Test*
	Means (standard deviation)						Means (standard deviation)					
Age (years)[a]	35.6 (11.9)	33.4 (9.9)	1.425	36.1 (12.3)	34.0 (10.5)	1.417	35.6 (11.9)	35.3 (11.3)	0.170	36.1 (12.3)	34.5 (10.5)	0.896
Monthly income (US$)[a]	91.0 (114.1)	75.1 (63.3)	1.153	86.3 (94.2)	76.4 (88.1)	0.793	91.0 (114.1)	78.5 (73.5)	0.940	86.3 (94.2)	80.1 (46.6)	0.527
Education (years)[b]	4 (4.6)	3.3 (3.7)	0.763	4.7 (5.0)	3.(4.0)	1.655	4.0 (4.6)	4.6 (5.0)	–0.542	4.7 (5.0)	4.1 (4.7)	0.816
Household size[b]	4.1 (2.4)	4.5 (2.6)	–0.759	5.1 (2.8)	4.(2.5)	2.549***	4.1 (2.4)	4.8 (2.6)	–2.368**	5.1 (2.8)	4.6 (2.3)	1.110
	Percentage						Percentage					
Gender[c]												
male	65.8	59.8	0.696	57.6	63.3	0.791	65.8	64.0	0.078	57.6	67.8	1.989
female	34.2	40.2		42.4	36.7		34.2	36.0		42.4	32.2	
Employed[c]												
yes	88.2	85.5	0.285	91.3	88.6	0.454	88.2	96.5	5.848***	91.3	94.2	0.577
no	11.8	14.5		8.7	11.4		11.8	3.5		8.7	5.8	

Note: [a, b] and [c] denote characteristics analysed by the t-statistics, two-sample Wilcoxon rank-sum (Mann-Whitney) test, and chi square test, respectively. *** and ** represent significant differences at 1% and 5% levels, respectively.

Table 6.4 Comparison of households in Nairobi receiving sanitation and solid waste services by NGOs or CBOs, by other service providers, and receiving no services

Characteristic	*Access NGO/CBO services and those without access to services*						*Access to NGO/CBO services and access other service providers*					
	Sanitation			*Solid waste*			*Sanitation*			*Solid waste*		
	NGO/CBO (N = 114)	*No access (N = 20)*	*Test*	*NGO/CBO (N = 187)*	*No access (N = 10)*	*Test*	*NGO/CBO (N = 114)*	*Other providers (N = 72)*	*Test*	*NGO/CBO (N = 187)*	*Other providers (N = 9)*	*Test*
	Means (standard deviation)						Means (standard deviation)					
Age (years)[a]	40.3 (10.4)	33.1 (6.3)	2.979***	39.9 (9.1)	33.7 (5.8)	2.156	40.3 (10.4)	40.8 (6.5)	–0.3205	39.9 (9.1)	42.7(10.6)	–0.864
Monthly income (US$)[a]	138.1 (55.4)	63 (43.9)	5.720***	161.2 (170.4)	80.8 (46.2)	2.855**	138.1 (55.4)	212.8 (250.5)	–2.970***	161.2 (170.3)	172.8(18.2)	2.093
Education (yr)[b]	9.8 (3.6)	9.6 (3.3)	0.248	10.4 (3.7)	11.2 (4.0)	–0.832	9.8 (3.9)	11.8 (3.2)	–3.937***	10.4 (3.7)	11.1 (2.8)	–0.379
Household size[b]	6.9 (2.3)	6 (1.9)	1.622	6.7 (2.1)	5 3 (1.41)	2.185**	6.9 (2.3)	6.5 (1.8)	0.770	6.7 (2.1)	7.7 (1.9)	–1.472
	Percentage						Percentage					
Gender[c]												
male	69.3	75.0	0.264	70.6	50.0	1.899	69.3	72.2	0.181	70.6	100.0	3.679**
female	30.7	25.0		29.4	50.0		30.7	27.8		29.4	0.0	
Employed[c]												
yes	93.0	100.0	1.492	95.7	100.0	0.446	93.0	100.0	5.279**	95.7	100.0	0.401
no	7.0	0.0		4.3	0.0		7.0	0.0		4.3	0.0	

Note: [a, b] and [c] denote characteristics analysed by the t-statistics, two-sample Wilcoxon rank-sum (Mann-Whitney) test, and chi square test, respectively. *** and ** represent significant differences at 1% and 5% levels, respectively.

Table 6.5 Comparing households in Dar es Salaam receiving sanitation and solid waste services by CBOs with those receiving no services

Household characteristics	*Sanitation*			*Solid waste*		
	CBO access (N = 53)	*No access (N = 147)*	*Test*	*CBO access (N = 158)*	*No access (N = 42)*	*Test*
	Means (standard deviation)			Means (standard deviation)		
Age (years)[a]	42.2 (13.7)	43.3 (14.0)	–0.468	41.5 (13.4)	48.6 (14.2)	–3.051***
Monthly income (US$)[a]	90.0 (116.5)	75.9 (86.2)	0.819	80.1 (99.4)	77.5 (48.2)	0.100
Education (years)[b]	7.8 (3.1)	7.0 (2.8)	2.127**	7.3 (2.7)	6.6 (3.7)	1.317
Household size[b]	4.6 (4.1)	3.9 (2.2)	0.804	4.2 (3.0)	3.7 (1.9)	0.512
	Percentage			Percentage		
Gender[c]						
male	64.2	64.0	0.001	68.35	47.62	6.192***
female	35.8	36.0		31.65	52.38	
Employed[c]						
yes	84.6	74.8	2.102	88.54	35.71	52.829***
no	15.4	25.2		11.46	64.29	

Note: [a,b]and [c]denote characteristics analysed by the t-statistics, two-sample Wilcoxon rank-sum (Mann-Whitney) test, and chi square test, respectively. *** and ** represent significant differences at 1% and 5% levels, respectively.

in having smaller household sizes (at 5% level) and fewer employed household heads (at 1% level). Further investigation is needed to determine the exact cause of this result. The differences in employment levels can be explained from the philanthropic nature of NGOs and CBOs, who target the most vulnerable in the community (Gibbs et al. 1999; Hailey and James 2004), including the less employed. There are no significant differences between recipients of NGO or CBO solid waste services and those accessing government and private sector solid waste services.

In Nairobi, there is a very clear and significant relation between income and access to both sanitation and solid waste services. Households with no access to any service had significantly lower incomes compared to those having access to NGO or CBO provided services, while those accessing governmental and private services had again significantly higher incomes than those accessing NGO or CBO services. This clear relationship in Nairobi is in contrast to the other two cities and relates to the heterogeneity of economic status of inhabitants of poor informal settlements in Nairobi (see Huchzermeyer 2008; K'Akumu and Olima 2007). The lack of affordable housing compels the majority of the middle- and poor-income individuals to occupy the relatively cheap houses in informal settlements, making income levels in Nairobi informal settlements more diverse than those in the other two cities.[4]

Similarly to Kampala, households with larger families accessed significantly more NGO or CBO solid waste services. But numbers are quite small, so we should be cautious with interpretations. The same caution is valid for the gender difference between NGO or CBO services recipients and the recipients of market and governmental services.

Recipients of sanitation services provided by government and private market providers have significantly more years of education and more are employed. Together with their higher incomes (the three factors are highly correlated), it explains that these households both can afford and find it important to have more expensive and reliable private and public sanitation services. Compared to those who access no sanitation services, the household heads with NGO or CBO sanitation services are significantly older, and this is highly correlated with income levels.

In Dar es Salaam, no governmental or private market sanitation and solid waste services were received by our respondents in the poor informal settlements. For solid waste services, the absence of the other two institutions reflects successful institutional pluralism in solid waste services, where specific locations are allocated to each franchisee. For sanitation services, it rather reflects the low priority given by the government and the private market to supplying sanitation in poor settlements. Recipients of CBO sanitation services had significantly more years of education compared to household heads having no access to sanitation services. For solid waste services, statistically significant differences are observed in age, gender and employment status, where household heads with CBO services are younger, mostly male and more often employed.

Overall, these results indicate that within similar settings (poor informal settlements of metropolises in East Africa), there are differences and similarities in socioeconomic characteristics of NGO or CBO service recipients and non-recipients. In settlements with homogenous income levels, as in Kampala and Dar es Salaam, no major income differences were found between recipients and non-recipients of NGO or CBO services. In Nairobi, however, with larger income differences in informal settlements, access to CBO- or NGO-based sanitation and solid waste services varied among income categories. Employment status has two effects: recipients of NGO- or CBO-based sanitation services are less often employed than those receiving government and market services (Kampala and Nairobi), reflecting the philanthropic nature of the former; and those receiving CBO solid waste services are more often employed than those without access to such services (Dar es Salaam). The influence of age, education, gender and household size may vary across the three cities, as well as between accessing sanitation and solid waste services of NGOs and CBOs.

6.6.5 Recipients' opinion on NGO/CBO services

Although NGOs and CBOs are increasingly playing an important role in providing sanitation and solid waste services to the urban poor, the perceptions of the urban poor receiving these services are hardly known. To assess these perceptions

Table 6.6 Percentages of households having positive perceptions of NGO/CBO sanitation services

Factors	*NGO provisioning*		*CBO provisioning*		
	Kampala (N = 61)	*Nairobi (N = 31)*	*Kampala (N = 15)*	*Nairobi (N = 83)*	*Dar es Salaam (N = 53)*
Trust in service	82% (50)	71% (22)	73% (11)	77% (64)	75% (40)
Reliability	72% (44)	61% (19)	73% (11)	72% (60)	83% (44)
Participation	92% (56)	55% (17)	93% (14)	70% (58)	92% (49)
Satisfaction	59% (36)	100% (31)	40% (6)	96% (80)	49% (26)
Anticipated future use	92% (56)	81% (25)	47% (7)	89% (74)	85% (45)

Note: Actual numbers of households appear between parentheses

Source: this study

on NGO or CBO services and intentions to continue using them, respondents were asked to rate different perceptional factors using a 5-point Likert scale, ranging from strongly agree (1) to strongly disagree (5). Tables 6.6 and 6.7 report on the perceptions of current NGO/CBO services and household intentions to continue using these services, based on the summation of 'strongly agree' and 'agree' (1 and 2 levels).

There is generally high trust (>70%) among recipients in sanitation services provided by NGOs and CBOs. Those who lack trust mentioned shortcomings related to gender, religion and distance. Similarly, over 60% of the recipients agree that the services of these organisations are reliable, although a minority alleges failure to maintain sanitary facilities (especially in Kampala and Nairobi). Participation between households and the civil society service providers is lowest among respondents in Nairobi. NGOs and CBOs in Nairobi often provide services without consultation and involvement and only ask citizens to pay for them. Household

Table 6.7 Percentages of households having positive perceptions of NGO/CBO solid waste services

Factor	*NGO provisioning*		*CBO provisioning*		
	Kampala (N = 39)	*Nairobi (N = 21)*	*Kampala (N = 53)*	*Nairobi (N = 166)*	*Dar es Salaam (N = 158)*
Trust in service	59% (23)	48% (10)	38% (20)	72% (119)	84% (132)
Reliability	56% (22)	33% (7)	26% (14)	64% (107)	87% (137)
Participation	69%(27)	33% (7)	49% (26)	64% (106)	100% (158)
Satisfaction	41% (16)	90% (19)	53% (28)	98% (163)	63% (100)
Anticipated future use	62% (24)	62% (13)	81% (43)	93% (155)	100% (158)

Note: Actual numbers of households appear between parentheses

Source: this study

satisfaction levels are low in both Kampala and Dar es Salaam. Across the three cities, except for CBOs in Kampala, there is high anticipation for continuous and future utilisation of NGO- or CBO-based sanitation services.

Perceptions on solid waste services contrasted at various points with those on sanitation. Notable is the overall low appreciation of NGO (in Nairobi) and CBO (in Kampala) solid waste services. The main reasons are the invisibility of these organisations, the infrequent service provision, unreliability and low community involvement. As expected, CBO services in Dar es Salaam are highly valued, although with lower levels of satisfaction as recipients consider services of some CBOs infrequent and expensive. Overall, expectations of continued future use of these services are higher among CBO provisioning than on NGO provisioning in the three cities.

6.7 Conclusion

Sanitation and solid waste service delivery in the three East African capital cities of Kampala, Nairobi and Dar es Salam consists of pluralistic systems, in which NGOs and CBOs have their specific positions, besides other institutional arrangements of state and market. Across the cities and across the two systems (sanitation and solid waste management), there are variations in institutional mixtures that serve urban citizens. However, these plural institutions do not always reach the citizens in poor informal settlements in the three cities.

In Kampala and Nairobi, privatisation increasingly determines how solid waste management services are run across the city. The privatised and rigid institutional arrangements fail to provide adequate services to the poor in informal settlements. This has accelerated the growth of NGO and CBO interventions in solid waste collection and management in these settlements, often working independently from and unregulated by governmental and private solid waste management institutions. In some cases, boundaries between private market and NGO- and CBO-based solid waste management institutions have gotten blurred, with the latter redirecting their orientation and servicing to only those who can afford to pay. In such situations, the plural institutions get disconnected, leaving too many poor inhabitants without services (especially in Kampala). This is reflected in perceptions of the urban poor in the functioning of NGO- or CBO-run solid waste services. In Dar es Salaam, CBO institutions are formally included in solid waste services by the government, resulting in clear allocations of solid waste services for the different institutions. Although the latter model does not necessarily result in higher levels of access (comparing Nairobi with Dar es Salaam), it does seem to result in more positive perceptions of households accessing solid waste services.

Similar trends of institutional pluralism are observed for sanitation service delivery systems in the three cities. This is propelled by inadequate sanitation policies (Kampala and Dar es Salaam), by low governmental priority for sanitation, and by poor implementation of the existing policies and legislation (all three cities). Increased involvement of NGOs and CBOs in sanitation is boosted by donors, which has led to significant NGO or CBO contributions to sanitation service delivery to the urban poor across the three cities. Again, Dar es Salaam provides a formalised and legalised model of institutional pluralism, where CBO institutions have a major role (especially – but not only – serving informal settlements and the poor), but are connected to other institutions through a general framework.

The differences among informal settlement inhabitants, and in connections and coordination among the different sanitation and solid waste institutional arrangements, as well as in historical backgrounds, make it unwise to strive for harmonisation in the involvement of civil society institutions in urban services across the three countries – let alone to formulate one uniform (best practice) model of institutional pluralism that can be universally applied (across, for instance, sub-Saharan Africa) in each of the two sectors of urban service provision. The Modernised Mixture approach has taught us that contextual factors are too important to allow for the design of universal models that can be applied in every context. But that is not to say that the three cities cannot learn from each other in governing urban environmental services. For instance, what can be learned from Dar es Salaam is how CBOs can be fully included into the formal urban service provisioning system by contracting them to provide solid waste and sanitation services. This seems all the more relevant as, compared to developed countries where civil society contributions to sanitation and solid waste are marginal, NGOs and CBOs will remain major and legitimate institutions in adequate urban environmental service provisioning, not in the least regarding the urban poor.

Notes

1. This chapter is based on Tukahirwa, J. (2011).
2. These numbers are based on data collected during our field work in the reported period. It was not easy to capture information on the local branches of international NGOs in Nairobi because of the protocols involved. The actual number of CBOs and NGOs in each of the three cities is higher. There is no complete registry or database in any of the three cities on CBOs and/or NGOs. Hence, it is impossible to estimate what proportion is captured in our inventory (hence the external validity).
3. To assess the influence of household size and education, we used the Wilcoxon Rank sum test (or Mann-Whitney U Test) because it does not assume normality, and data on the two attributes was mostly ordinal. For gender and employment attributes, which are categorical, we used the chi-square test to test for differences. A *t* test was used to analyse differences in age and income characteristics, which are continuous and assumed to be normally distributed.
4. The situation is different for Kampala and Dar es Salaam, where housing facilities within the city periphery are cheaper and affordable to middle-income earners, which explains the absence of middle-income earners in the city poor informal settlements.

References

Ahmed, S. A. & Ali, M. (2004). Partnerships for solid waste management in developing countries: Linking theories to realities. *Habitat International,* 28 (3): 467–479.

Ahmed, S. A. & Ali, M. (2006). People as partners: Facilitating people's participation in public-private partnerships for solid waste management. *Habitat International,* 30 (4): 781–796.

Beall, J. (1997). Policy Arena. Social capital in waste – a solid investment? *Journal of International Development,* 9 (7): 951–961.

Bendapudi, N. & Berry, L. (1997). Customers' motivations for maintaining relationships with service providers. *Journal of Retailing,* 73 (1): 15–37.

Blair, H. (2001). Institutional pluralism in public administration and politics: Applications in Bolivia and beyond. *Public Administration and Development,* 21: 119–129.

Bratton, M. (1989). Beyond the state: Civil society and associational life in Africa. *World Politics,* 41: 404–430.

Claassen, R.J.G. (2009). Institutional pluralism and the limits of the market. *Politics Philosophy Economics,* 8 (4): 420–447.

Clapham, C. (1996). *Africa and the international system. The politics of state survival.* Cambridge: Cambridge University Press.

Cohen, J. M. & Peterson, S. B. (1999). *Administrative Decentralization. Strategies for Developing Countries.* West Hartford, Connecticut: Kumarian.

Coulson, A. (1982). *Tanzania: A political economy.* Clarendon Press: Oxford.

Dicklitch, S. (1998). *The elusive promise of NGOs in Africa: Lessons from Uganda.* Basingstoke: Macmillan Press.

Esman, M. J. (1991). *Management dimensions of development: Perspectives and strategies.* West Hartford, Connecticut: Kumarian.

Esman, M. J. & Uphoff, N. T. (1984). *Local organizations: Intermediaries in rural development.* Ithaca, NY: Cornell University Press.

Fitzpatrick, D. (2006). Evolution and chaos in property rights systems: The third world tragedy of contested access. *The Yale Law Journal,* 115: 996–1048.

Fowler, A. (1995). NGOs and the globalization of welfare: Perspectives from East Africa. In J. Semboja & O. Therkildsen (Eds.), *Service Provision Under Stress in East Africa* (pp. 51–69). London: James Currey.

Gibbs, C., Fumo, C. & Kuby, T. (1999). *Nongovernmental organizations in World Bank – supported projects: A review.* Washington DC: The World Bank.

Glasbergen, P., Biermann, F. & Mol, A.P.J. (Eds.) (2007). *Partnerships, governance and sustainable development. Reflections on theory and practice.* Cheltenham: Edward Elgar.

Gurgerty, M. K. (2008). The effectiveness of NGO self-regulation: Theory and evidence from Africa. *Public Administration and Development,* 28: 105–118.

Hailey J. & James, R. (2004). "Trees die from the top": International perspectives on NGO leadership development. *International Journal of Voluntary and Nonprofit Organizations,* 15 (4): 343–353.

Havnevik, K. J. (1993). *Tanzania. The limits to development from above.* Motala: Motala Grafiska A B.

Hendriksen, A., Tukahirwa, J. T., Oosterveer, P. & Mol, A.P.J. (2012). Participatory decision-making for sanitation improvements in unplanned urban settlements in East Africa. *Journal of Environment and Development,* 21 (1): 98–119.

Huchzermeyer, M. (2008). Slum upgrading in Nairobi within the housing and basic services market: A housing rights concern. *Journal of Asian and African Studies,* 43: 19–39.

Joseph, K. (2006). Stakeholder participation for sustainable waste management. *Habitat International,* 30 (4): 863–871.

K'Akumu, O. A. & Olima, W.H.A. (2007). The dynamics and implications of residential segregation in Nairobi. *Habitat International,* 31: 87–99.

Katusiimeh, M. W., Burger, C.P.J. & Mol, A.P.J. (2013). Informal waste collection and its coexistence with the formal waste sector: the case of Kampala, Uganda. *Habitat International,* 38: 1–9.

Katusiimeh, M. W., Mol, A.P.J. & Burger, C.P.J. (2012). The operations and effectiveness of public and private provision of solid waste collection services in Kampala. *Habitat International,* 36 (2): 247–252.

Kayombo, C. G. (2010). *Formulation of policies, plans and strategies for reform of public administration and state institutions: The case of Tanzania.* 6th Pan-African Forum on the Modernization of Public Services and State Institutions. Assessment and Prospects of Administrative and Institutional Reforms in Africa, Rabat, Morocco (7–8 June 2010).

Klundert van de, A. & Lardinois, I. (1995). Community and private (formal and informal) sector involvement in municipal solid waste management in developing countries; Background paper for the UMP workshop in Ittingen 10–12 April 1995; Waste The Netherlands

Makara, S. (2000). *NGOs in Uganda: Their typologies, roles and functions in governance: The limited expansion of Uganda's third sector.* London: Civil Society and Governance Programme, Institute of Development Studies.

Mercer, C. (1999). Reconceptualizing state-society relations in Tanzania: Are NGOs 'making a difference'? *Area,* 31 (3): 247–258.

Mol, A.P.J. (2001). *Globalization and environmental reform. The ecological modernization of the global economy.* Cambridge, MA/London: MIT Press.

Ndegwa, S. (1996). *Two faces of civil society: NGOs and politics in Africa.* West Hartford: Kurmarian Press.

Okuku, J. A. (2002). Civil society and the democratization processes in Kenya and Uganda: A comparative analysis of the contribution of the church and NGOs. *African Journal Political Science,* 7 (2): 81–97.

Oosterveer, P. (2009). Urban environmental services and the state in East Africa; between neo-developmental and network governance approaches. *Geoforum,* 40 (6): 1061–1068.

Oosterveer, P. & Spaargaren, G. (2010). Meeting social challenges in developing sustainable environmental infrastructure in East African cities. In B. van Vliet, G. Spaargaren & P. Oosterveer Eds., *Social perspectives on sanitation challenge.* Springer: Dordrecht/Heidelberg/London/New York.

Rathi, S. (2006). Alternative approaches for better municipal solid waste management in Mumbai, India. *Waste Management,* 26 (10): 1192–1200.

Schaub-Jones, D., Eales, K. & Tyers, L. (2006). *Sanitation partnerships: Harnessing their potential for urban on-site sanitation.* London: BPDWS.

Scheinberg, A. & Mol, A.P.J. (2010). Multiple modernities; transitional Bulgaria and the ecological modernisation of solid waste management, *Environment and Planning C,* 28 (1): 18–36.

Scheinberg, A., Spies, S., Simpson, M. H. & Mol, A.P.J. (2011). Assessing recycling in Low- and Middle-income Countries: building on modernized mixtures. *Habitat International,* 35 (2): 188–198.

Schouten, M.A.C. & Mathenge, R. W. (2010). Communal sanitation alternatives for slums: A case study of Kibera, Kenya. *Physics and Chemistry of the Earth,* 35 (13,14): 815–822.

Schübeler, P. (1997). Reports and reviews: International report: A conceptual framework for municipal solid waste management in developing countries. *Waste Management & Research,* 15 (4): 437–446.

Spaargaren, G., Oosterveer, P., Van Buuren, J. & Mol, A.P.J. (2006). *Mixed Modernities: towards viable urban environmental infrastructure development in East Africa.* Wageningen University Environmental Policy group discussion paper.

Titeca, K. (2005). *The Political Economy of Civil Society Organizations at a Local Level. Case-Study Kasese District, Uganda.* Paper presented at the Africa-Europe Group for interdisciplinary studies (AEGIS) Conference, London (29 June-2 July).

Throup, D. W. (1987). The construction and destruction of the Kenya state. In Michael Schatzberg (Ed.), *The Political Economy of Kenya* (pp. 57–64). New York: Praeger Publishers.

Tripp, A. M. (1992). Local organizations, participation and the state in urban Tanzania. In: G. Hyden and M. Bratton (Eds.), *Governance and Politics in Africa* (pp. 221–242). Boulder, CO: Lynne Rienner.

Tukahirwa, J. T., Mol, A.P.J. & Oosterveer, P. (2010). Civil society participation in urban sanitation and solid waste management in Uganda. *Local Environment,* 15 (1): 1–14.

Tukahirwa, J. T., Mol, A.P.J. & Oosterveer, P. (2011). Access of urban poor to NGO/CBO-supplied sanitation and solid waste services in Uganda: The role of social and spatial proximity. *Habitat International,* 35 (4): 582–591.

Tukahirwa, J. (2011). *Civil Society in Urban Sanitation and Solid Waste Management: The Role of NGOs and CBOs in Metropolises of East Africa.* PhD thesis. Wageningen: Wageningen University.

7 Local governments and regional alliances in the delivery of municipal environmental services

Lessons learnt from municipalities in the Lake Victoria Basin of East Africa

Christine Majale, Peter Oosterveer and Caleb Mireri

7.1 Introduction

Although governments are generally expected to provide environmental services such as sanitation and solid waste collection for their citizens, in most Sub-Saharan African cities, the (municipal) authorities are not able to provide these services solely by themselves. Without ignoring lack of material resources caused by poverty, there are other structural causes, as well, for this failure, including their particular understanding of the role of the state (Oosterveer 2009). This situation has created considerable room for non-state actors to move into these traditional state tasks (Mol 2001; Tukahirwa et al. 2008). These developments create challenges for establishing an appropriate balance between the role of municipal authorities and non-state actors in municipal environmental service provision in East Africa.

Non-state actors start developing their own sets of rules or standards to fill 'institutional voids' when rules to guide their conduct are needed but not provided by the state. Hence, the types of arrangement for service provision today are highly diverse and range from self-provision through collective action independent of external agencies to indirect state provision through sub-contracting to other agencies, such as NGOs, private for-profit companies, and user groups (Joshi and Moore 2004). For East Africa in particular, the 1990s were marked by governmental reconfigurations, many of which had a powerful 'local' governance orientation, aiming at decentralizing tasks from central to district and municipal levels. Innovative arrangements included resurgent regional organisations and public-private partnerships in infrastructure creation and maintenance and in service delivery (Olukoshi 2005).

Today, however, where real privatisation of municipal services in solid waste management to commercial enterprises has actually taken place in some municipalities, such as Nairobi and Kampala, it has largely been done selectively and piecemeal, serving or operating effectively mainly in the middle- and higher-income residential neighbourhoods that can afford to pay for these services. This process leaves out a large proportion of the poor and low-income neighbourhoods where residents are unable to pay for such privatised services. These neighbourhoods may end up being served by civil society organisations.

Different local authorities that observe that they are confronting similar problems, such as solid waste management, have also pursued the benefits of coordination with other local entities (Kwon 2007), through, for instance, platforms of regional organisations. This chapter seeks to assess these reforms in municipal solid waste management by comparing the involvement of non-state actors in three East African urban centres (Jinja – Uganda; Mwanza – Tanzania and Kisumu – Kenya; see Figure 7.1) and by reviewing the role of regional organisations (Lake Victoria Basin Commission (LVBC) and Lake Victoria Region Local Authorities Cooperation (LVRLAC)) in facilitating the regional alliances in infrastructure provision amongst urban authorities focusing on the Lake Victoria Basin. The overall aim is to draw lessons on environmental service delivery prompted by reforms facilitated by regional organisations aimed at forging regional alliances in infrastructure provision, formulate conclusions on these trends, and identify perspectives for improving the environmental and social performance of these solid waste services.

In the next section, the conceptual tools used to analyse these innovations in municipal solid waste governance are presented and the context of East Africa,

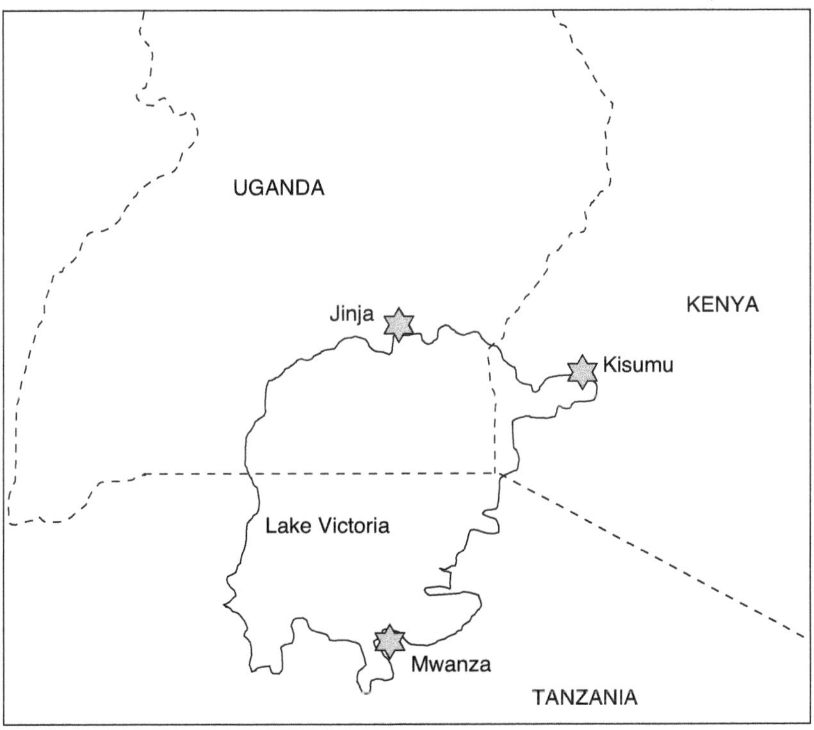

Figure 7.1 Location of the three studied municipalities

where empirical research has been conducted, is sketched as well. Reviewing the role of non-state actors in supplying solid waste services in these three East African cities is the subject of Section 7.3. Before final conclusions are formulated, Section 7.4 presents research findings on the role of regional organisations.

7.2 Study area and methodology

7.2.1 Introduction to the study area

East Africa, encompassing the countries Kenya, Uganda and Tanzania, is going through a phase of change since the 1990s that is characterised by democratisation, decentralisation and privatisation of public services. These developments have not been fully completed in every respect, but they have nevertheless initiated many innovations in recent years. Solid waste, as a domain of municipal governance, has drawn attention as a domain where privatisation seemed to be possible without too many complications. Experiences in three important cities in the three countries may illustrate the dynamics that are ongoing: Mwanza, Kisumu and Jinja.

Mwanza is Tanzania's second largest city, located on the southern border of Lake Victoria. The municipality is divided into two districts, and each has urban and rural wards. Every urban ward receives solid waste services either from a community-based organisation (CBO) or a private company.

Kisumu, located in southwestern Kenya, also borders Lake Victoria and is the third largest city in this country. Officially, all SWM services are provided from the municipality because non-state actors are formally not authorised to operate here, but unofficially they still provide services. Community self-help groups are common in low-income areas; private companies dominate high-and middle-income areas.

Jinja, Uganda, is the country's second largest city and borders Lake Victoria at the north. In Jinja, SWM services have been contracted out per division to two private operators.

These three cities combined will offer a varied impression of the urban SWM services provided in East Africa.

7.2.2 Methodology

Secondary data were collected through a review of literature, as well as from by-laws and other legislative pieces in Kenya, Uganda and Tanzania. Primary data were obtained from interviews with urban authority officials (public health officers and the Director of Environment at Jinja Municipal Council, public health officers and the solid waste manager at Mwanza City Council and environmental officers at Kisumu City Council). Non-state service providers, both formal and informal, in the three urban centres were also interviewed, as well as representatives from LVBC and LVRLAC. In addition, about 600 questionnaires were administered to households, and given the differences inherent in Jinja, Kisumu and Mwanza, different approaches were taken to select samples for the household survey, as described below.

In Mwanza, urban wards (14 in number) were purposively selected because they receive solid waste management (SWM) services. For the survey, stratified sampling was used, and, on average, 13–14 households were interviewed in each ward, irrespective of their population figures. The goal was to have each ward represented by a minimum number of 10 households and arrive at a maximum total sample of 200 households. Using the population census data and with the help of the ward leaders and the public health officers posted to each ward, households were randomly picked from a list.

In Kisumu, a list of low-, middle- and high-income estates was made. In total, there are 41 estates recognised by the council (11 high-income, 17 middle-income and 13 low-income). The council provides waste management services in only 12 of these estates. To administer 200 questionnaires, about half the number of estates in each income category were randomly selected. Hence, 6 high-income, 9 middle-income and 7 low-income estates were included, and about 10 questionnaires were administered in each of them. The number of households per estate varies from about 3,200 to about 12,000. Selecting households within the selected estates depended on the kind of estate arrangement. In planned estates, such as the Railway estates, the houses are numbered and organised in a certain pattern, so every fourth household was systematically selected. In the informal estates, such as Nyalenda, the houses are not numbered or arranged in any particular order, and therefore one household from each village was randomly selected.

The collected data can be considered to reflect the situation of service provision among the different income categories in the town as a whole.

Jinja has three divisions: Central Division, Walukuba Division and Mpumudde Division. One contractor serves both Central and Walukuba divisions, while another contractor serves Mpumudde division. Central and Mpumudde Divisions were picked in order to determine the differences (if any) in service provided by the two contractors. About 180 questionnaires were randomly distributed in Central and 38 in Mpumudde. These frequencies were more or less in line with the distribution of collection points: 119 skips in Central and 20 in Mpumudde. In total, 218 household questionnaires were administered. With a list of street names (also referred to as roads/avenues/zones), households were randomly selected from each street.

7.3 Non-state actors in waste management

In East Africa, the state is never acting in isolation in SWM, nor are there cases where the non-state actors take the full lead. Important questions are, therefore, whether governmental authorities should be encouraged to take their responsibilities more seriously or whether private companies, non-governmental organisations and local communities should be actively involved in implementing and managing urban environmental infrastructures.

Jinja, Mwanza and Kisumu display significant variations in response to these relationships with the non-state actors in the field of SWM and, therefore, illustrate the advantages and disadvantages of different strategies.

7.3.1 Waste management arrangement

In Mwanza, Tanzania, privatisation of solid waste management resulted in the council awarding contracts to non-governmental groups. Local authorities have secured every urban ward to receive services either from a community-based organisation (CBO) or a private company working under a contract, so all urban areas, irrespective of income levels, receive SWM services. In the financial year 2008/2009, contracts were awarded to CBOs and two private companies. Private companies cover the wards in the Central Business Districts (CBDs) as they have the (financial and human) resources to take on the bigger workload. Further, the CBD areas are well structured and can easily be reached. Returns on investment are likely to be higher in the CBD than in the wards further away from the CBD, which makes it easy to contract out the CBD to the companies. The CBOs cover the other wards, supervised and monitored by the municipality under a more flexible arrangement because their capacity, compared to the private companies, is lower. Like in Jinja, the contracts are annual, which have a negative impact because the contractors are not encouraged to improve on their SWM efforts, as they do not know whether or not they will win the tender the following year. Nevertheless, with this arrangement, of the 296 tons of waste generated daily in the municipality of Mwanza, 261 tons are disposed of at the official dumpsite, which is about 88% of waste generated. In comparison, before privatisation, only 28% of wastes generated were disposed of at the dumpsite.

Unlike Mwanza and Jinja, Kisumu, Kenya, has no formal/official arrangement that involves non-state actors in collecting and transporting waste or in sweeping the roads (Majale 2011). The council does the road sweeping itself, as well as the collection, transfer and disposal of waste, but these council services are concentrated in the CBD, and only a few residential areas also benefit from them. Non-state actors provide services to most of the other residential areas in an unofficial manner. These non-state service providers define their clients on the basis of their income. Hence, community self-help groups are more common in low-income areas, while private companies dominate high- and middle-income areas. The consequence of this situation is that, compared to the other municipalities, SWM in Kisumu is patterned much more along income levels.

The survey revealed the categorisation of the non-state actors as presented in Table 7.1. These actors were involved in collecting, transporting, recycling and reusing solid waste in different residential areas. Out of the 68 groups identified in Kisumu, 31 groups were interviewed.

The number of group members in these groups ranged from 2 to 80. Out of the 31 interviewed groups, the majority 22 (71%) have been working on solid waste for more than five years, meaning they were formed in the year 2005 or before.

Table 7.1 SWM groups in Kisumu City Council and those interviewed

SWM handlers	*Existing numbers*	*Numbers interviewed*
Recyclers	23	6
Groups: CBOs and youth groups	27	17
Private companies/individuals	18	8
TOTAL	68	31

Source: Field work in Kisumu, 2008–2009

This duration of their existence speaks for their stability. These organisations take part in different SWM activities, including:

- Collection of scrap metals and plastics
- Reuse of containers
- Composting household waste
- Recycling plastics and metals from household waste
- Collecting household SW/transporting to transfer stations and dumpsites

With this arrangement, 35–45% of waste generated in the town is collected by both municipal and non-municipal actors and disposed of to the dumpsite each day.

In Jinja, Uganda, waste management is privatised and the arrangement is an annual contract between the municipal council and private entrepreneurs. In the financial year (2008/2009) two contractors won the tenders. Jinja has three divisions and within each division there are parishes, but solid waste management services have been contracted out division-wise, with one contractor serving two divisions and the other only one. These contactors are actually private companies with several employees and casuals, responsible for the waste collection and sweeping. Waste is collected from skips (collection points) and not directly from the households. The contract also involves transportation of the collected waste to the disposal site. Payments from the council to the contractors are made on the basis of the number of skips emptied to the disposal grounds. The contractor earns Ugshs28,000 (US$20) per small skip (3 tons) and Ugshs30,000 (US$21.4) for a bigger skip (3.5 tons) emptied. On average, the contractor serving the two divisions empties 18 skips per day, while the one serving one division empties, on average, 7 skips per day. With this arrangement, 40–60% of all waste generated is collected and taken to the dumpsite every day. This figure is recorded to have gone up compared to the time before privatisation. Service is not structured along income levels, as in Kisumu, nor per ward, as is the case in Mwanza.

7.3.2 Legitimacy and influence on decision making

In Jinja, the legitimacy of the contractors is realised in a number of ways. First, the Jinja Solid Waste Management By-Laws, 2005, in their objectives recognise the role of private companies in the collection and disposal of waste, when this

Table 7.2 Perceived service providers by households in Jinja

Service provider	*Frequency*	*Percentage*
CBO	1	0.5
Municipality	84	38.5
Private company	45	20.6
Others	88	40.4
Total	218	100.0

N = 218

Source: Household survey in Jinja, 2009.

is practiced in a sustainable manner and at a fee. The two contractors (private companies) currently providing services in Jinja Municipality are thus officially recognised by the council, creating a formal legitimacy for their involvement in SW services. The general population, however, to some extent, still has the impression that services are provided by the municipality (38.5%) or others (40.4%) and only 20.6% of the clients claim to be served by private companies (See Table 7.2).

Secondly, legitimacy is enhanced through transparency in the bidding procedures. The tenders for contracts in SWM are advertised through the media, there is open bidding, and contracts for companies that were involved previously can only be renewed on the basis of their past performance. Payments to the contractors are made from the property tax accounts, indicating that they are factored into the council budget. This arrangement is, however, not free from complaints from the contractors, about things such as delayed payments, which affect the robust nature of the system. Adei (2009) points out that such delays can only be prevented if the regulatory framework is changed in such a way as to make delays and inefficiency costly to an official (in this case, the council official in charge) in terms of promotion, remuneration and overall performance assessment.

As far as decision making is concerned, the council is still at the helm of SWM, making policies and seeing to their implementation through monitoring and evaluation, but particularly through their decision to offer a continuation of the annual contract or not. The contractors do not attend council meetings, and are therefore unable to make or influence decision making. From an interview with one of the contractors, it became clear that they nevertheless are free to voice their opinions directly to the town clerk, though these may or may not be taken into account when formulating policies.

In Mwanza, legitimacy is strengthened through the official recognition by the council of the CBOs and the two private companies as legitimate organisations. These service providers are awarded formal contracts after having won through a democratic process, although an interview with one of the public health inspectors revealed that the process is faced with interference from politicians who want to influence the awarding of the contracts.

The groups undergo registration as solid waste management service providers and pay a registration fee of Tshs25,000 (US$17.85), while the private companies also pay taxes to the Tanzania Revenue Authority. Secondly, these contractors are well-known to the people they serve because members of these CBOs are local

Table 7.3 Perceived service providers in Mwanza

Service provider	*Frequency*	*Percentage*
CBO	88	44
Municipal	50	25
Private company	27	13.5
Self	35	17.5
Total	200	100.0

N = 200

Source: Household survey in Mwanza, 2009.

residents in the wards they serve. Of the 82% who responded to interviews as having known who their service provider is, about 60% are aware it is either a CBO or a private company (see Table 7.3).

SWM provides a form of employment to these community groups, and, in turn, they are able to keep their surroundings clean. In the event of non-payment by clients, the contractors can seek redress from the council legal office, but such legal action is expensive and politically sensitive. This is especially the case when political elections are about to take place, as no political aspirant would like to go against his/her voters' interests.

Even with such an arrangement of massive community involvement, which, according to Pierre and Peters (2000), should result in minimum local government engagement, making communities responsible to solve their own problems, the Mwanza city council is still at the helm of service provision, awarding contracts and allocating roles and responsibilities to the private companies and CBOs providing services. As much as the community groups are legitimate outfits with formal contracts and recognition by the relevant societal stakeholders, their role in SWM is weakened through their minimal influence in decision making.

In Kisumu, even with the municipality as the central locus of authority, legitimacy remains a key concern because of the problems to accord a legal mandate to the groups that provide SWM in an informal manner. Most of the groups that participate in SWM are registered by the Ministry in charge of Community Development, but they are not formally recognised by law as actors in the domain of solid waste management. The presence and activities of these groups are nevertheless known by the council, and some even asserted during the interviews that they are operating through some form of 'franchise'[1] in areas allocated to them by the council. In their response to a question on their legitimacy, the groups showed a large variety in informal and some formal arrangements, but nearly half of them had no formal understanding at all legitimizing their activities (see Table 7.4).

With no legal papers to show the arrangements they are part of, most, if not all, of these groups are not legitimate in the SWM arena. This impinges on a number of issues; for instance, seeking legal redress in case of payment defaults becomes a problem for them. Getting donor assistance also becomes complicated because questions will arise concerning their ties to the public, transparency and adherence

Table 7.4 Legitimacy of groups

Form of arrangement	*Numbers*
'Franchise'	11
Quasi contract	1
Partnership	1
Unwritten authority to operate	2
Pay rent to council	1
None	15
TOTAL	31

Source: Field work in Kisumu, 2008–2009.

Table 7.5 Service providers to households in Kisumu

Service provider	*Frequency*	*Percentage*
CBO	21	10.5
Municipality	18	9.0
Private company	54	27.0
Others	107	53.5
	200	100.0

N = 200

Source: Household survey in Kisumu.

to the mission of the group, their representative status and the relationship between the group and the community served. On the other hand, in terms of community support, openness of information, and democratic decision making, these groups can be considered more legitimate than some official actors are. These groups engaged in waste services are composed of local members, some serving their own residential areas and others doing it at no cost. The household survey conducted showed that these groups form the largest percentage of SWM service providers (37.5%) when the percentages on CBO (10.5%) and private company (27%) are combined (see Table 7.5). Responses that were categorised as 'others' and that account for 53.5% of all responses included responses like 'dumping in pits', 'burning' or 'the landlord comes to collect the waste'.

As far as decision making is concerned, as in Jinja and Mwanza, in Kisumu the council remains at the helm of SWM activities; the municipal authorities are responsible for all decision making. The community groups mentioned that are responsible for executing SWM activities do not attend council meetings, nor do they influence official decision making in any other manner.

7.3.3 *Service charges and household satisfaction level*

One aspect of the Jinja strategy for SWM, by which it is distinguished from the cases of Mwanza and Kisumu, is that households do not pay for the service. The reticence to pay for SWM among the citizens of Jinja is high because households are convinced

Table 7.6 Household perceptions towards SWM services in Jinja

Service rating	*Frequency*	*Percentage*
Satisfactory	75	57.7
Very satisfactory	6	4.6
Not satisfactory	49	37.7
Total	130	100.0

N = 130

Source: Household survey in Jinja, 2009.

that it is the responsibility of the council to provide these services at no cost. This conviction remains very strong, so that attempts to introduce a fee of Ugshs2000 (US$1.42) per household per month were not successful. Of the 130 households who responded to be receiving service (either perceived as being provided by the municipality, CBO or private sector), about 62.6% (57.7% – satisfactory plus 4.6% – very satisfactory) answered as satisfied with the services provided. (See Table 7.6.) In cases of filled-up and uncollected skips, households have been able to raise complaints through the local media or report directly to the health inspectors.

In Mwanza, the contractors charge different rates for different land uses, as stipulated in the municipal Refuse Disposal By-Laws (Mwanza City Council (2000), but all households pay a standard fee of Tshs400 (US$0.28) per household per month. These figures were agreed upon following consultations with all stakeholders. The payments are made directly to the contractors, and of the 165 households (82.5%) who responded to receive services either from the municipality, a CBO or a private company, only 3.6% did not pay for these services. Among the households interviewed (n = 200), 1% considered the fees too low, 45.5% considered them low, 32.5% moderate and 21% responded that it was not applicable or gave no answer. From the households that responded to the question (n = 165), 51% answered they were satisfied with the service received. This is a low percentage compared with the results from Jinja and Kisumu, and a possible explanation for this is that the residents in Mwanza have higher expectations, as most of them indicated that the CBOs need to improve their skills and equipment used for waste collection.

Kisumu's scenarios differ from the other two councils when it comes to the payment system. The areas that are served by the municipality have their costs taken care of in the water bill and some of the households responded that they pay for waste as part of their house rent. The private companies are operating in open competition and work purely on a willing-buyer-willing-seller basis. From the survey, it becomes clear that their services are mostly offered in high- and middle-income estates. Payments are made at the end of the month, as per a verbal agreement with the households. CBOs operate mostly in middle- and low-income areas, and they also charge fees agreed upon with each household.

The informal operators charge various fees for waste collection, but the average fees for different residential areas resulting from the household survey are presented in Table 7.7. Out of the 93 households that receive service from either

Table 7.7 Payment rates for SWM services in Kisumu

Residential area	*Payment rates (Kshs./Month)*
Low-income areas	40.00 – 100.00
Middle-income areas	150.00 – 250.00
High-income areas	250.00 – 500.00

Source: Household field survey in Kisumu, 2009.

the municipality, a private company or a CBO, 79.6% pay for this, whereby a high percentage of them (69.7%, where n = 74) consider the fees they pay moderate. The survey also revealed that 70.6% (n = 93) of the households are satisfied with the service they received. In trying to understand this finding, a detailed analysis revealed that of those receiving waste collection services, 58% (n = 93) receive these services from the private companies, and that 87% of them responded to be satisfied with the services provided. This high appreciation of the services offered by the private companies largely explains the general satisfaction rate of 70.6%. Given that the private sector is driven by profit and ingenuity, which keeps it innovative and competitive, it comes as no surprise that the high degree of satisfaction of the service provided is particularly due to private sector involvement.

7.3.4 An emerging 'new' local governmental actor

The field studies reveal that in all three municipal councils, the local governments are still at the helm of SWM, so there is no full 'market-based' governance in the case of Jinja (where only private companies have been contracted), nor is there a complete 'community-based' governance arrangement in the case of Mwanza (where CBOs are the majority of service providers). Municipal governments in the three case studies still enjoy an unrivalled position in the local community, and they remain the obvious loci of political power and authority. Although they have been engaged in some form of negotiation with other significant actors in society, their dominance remains unquestioned. These local governments may become increasingly dependent on other societal actors, but they have remained in control of some unique sources of power, such as legislative powers, powers to award contracts and even the authority to determine service charges. Therefore, there is need for (and perhaps a renewed interest in) recognizing the importance of an active and effective local government in managing SWM. However, to engage in partnerships with non-state actors in joint ventures, local governments have to acquire skills that in the past were associated rather with the private sector: strategic planning and management, effective time management, respect of contracts, and timely delivery of licenses and approvals, among others. Local governments must also have the capacity to transform the laws, rules and regulations dating from an era when the state was looked upon as the sole provider of public goods and even in charge of organizing businesses. Therefore, as much as effective market economies and societal institutions are essential for effective SWM, they require a functioning and capable state (local government) in order to operate and grow.

This emerging 'new' local governmental actor is visible in a municipality that embraces the community and the private sector, whether formal or informal, in order to secure for all income groups access to solid waste management services.

7.4 Regional alliances

As municipalities remain key in contemporary and future SWM in East Africa, they could also consider cooperation at a regional level, especially for rural and small councils that find it difficult to fulfil their responsibilities in this. Compared with their larger urban counterparts, rural and smaller urban councils often have a lower tax base, which means that the resources for financing waste management activities are limited. If such councils would combine their financial, administrative, personnel, and equipment resources (EPA 1994), they could spread the costs of pursuing certain projects among several jurisdictions. Such alliances/cooperation can be facilitated through regional governance organisations, such as regional councils of governments or regional partnerships (Kwon 2007). This section presents an assessment of the role of two such regional organisations in enhancing cooperation in infrastructure provision on SWM amongst municipalities in East Africa: the Lake Victoria Basin Commission (LVBC) and the Lake Victoria Region Local Authorities Cooperation (LVRLAC). This assessment focuses on the level of municipal autonomy in decision making within these regional organisations and on the resources available within these regional organisations to facilitate the role of municipalities in SWM.

7.4.1 Lake Victoria Basin Commission (statutory)

The Lake Victoria Basin Commission (LVBC) is a specialised institution of the East African Community (EAC) and responsible for coordinating the sustainable development agenda of the Lake Victoria Basin. The LVBC is categorised as a statutory body because it was established by the Protocol for Sustainable Development of the Lake Victoria Basin under its Article 33 in 2001 as a permanent apex institution of the community responsible for the Lake Basin. This means that it is legally mandated to perform the activities that are accorded to this institution. The commission seeks to promote, coordinate and facilitate development initiatives within the Lake Victoria Basin. The commission envisages a broad partnership of the local communities around the lake, the East African Community and its partner states, as well as their international development partners.

Municipal autonomy in decision making under LVBC

The organisational arrangement of the LVBC consists of a National Focal Point (NFP) in each partner state (Kenya, Uganda, Tanzania, and recently Rwanda and Burundi) which are the main links between the specific LVBC program(s) and the partner states. The NFPs are also responsible for the coordination and harmonisation of the Lake Victoria Basin activities by the various Ministries, NGOs, special interest groups and other development partners in the different countries.

Essentially, NFPs constitute the lowest level of contact within the LVBC organisaton and portray a centralised arrangement with national ministries from the partner states playing the lead role. This indicates a limited flexibility when it comes to the involvement of local urban authorities in decision making within this organisation. Currently, municipal authorities on their own can neither act collectively nor push for an agenda at a regional level under this organisation's framework. Therefore, infrastructure-related interventions by the LVBC are likely to remain restricted to individual municipal councils. Whenever the LVBC had a local-level project like the Lake Victoria Water and Sanitation Program (LVWATSAN), it had project management units at the national level, project implementation units at the town level, as well as Multi-Stakeholder Forums. It should be noted, though, that participation by these units at the local/town level only comes in largely at the implementation stage of a project, and not at its initial planning and design stage. The result of this situation is that interventions undertaken by the LVBC at the local level may not necessarily respond to the immediate needs of the local authorities; nevertheless, local authorities may simply welcome an intervention because it has been made available to them (see Text Box 7.1 for an example of such interventions).

Resource availability and mobilisation within the LVBC

- *Information/knowledge resources*

Within projects undertaken by the LVBC, urban councils have benefited from knowledge transfers, ranging from technical scientific knowledge presented by experts to experiential knowledge from non-experts shared during workshops (Majale 2011). The LVBC has organised the sharing of this knowledge amongst a number of local authorities, particularly under the LVWATSAN program, through workshops and exchange visits because this program also included small urban centres. The towns involved vary significantly in terms of their institutional strengths and weaknesses and the availability of human and financial resources. Under LVWATSAN, a regional approach to training and capacity building has been introduced so that towns can learn from each other, particularly with regard to case studies, best practices and information on what works and what does not, generated from across the region. Therefore, there has been a free flow of information and knowledge amongst the participating municipal councils, and this is essential for collective learning. The LVBC has also organised transfer of technical knowledge.

- *Material resources*

The primary funding mechanisms for the LVBC are contributions from the partner states. Funding also comes from international development partners. Consider, for instance, the budget for financial year 2007–2008, which was US$2,858,519, whereby the partner states contributed US$1,664,019 and the funding from the development partners totalled US$1,194,500. With these funding sources, the LVBC portrays a secure financial standing even with respect to its role in SWM, compared with a voluntary organisation whose funds are dependent on membership subscription.

The functioning of the national focal points (NFPs) in each partner state requires full-time staff. However, under the current situation, the NFP officers also have other national responsibilities besides those of the LVBC, and hence they are seriously overstretched. On the other hand, these staff are paid by partner states relieving LVBC of this burden and allowing the LVBC to use its resources to undertake other activities, such as capital projects under SWM as exemplified in Box 7.1. LVBC as an organisation is thus able to develop a separate budget that is specifically available for SWM.

Therefore, from the perspective of available (material and non-material) resources, the LVBC is well positioned to intervene in SWM as a regional organisation, but its interventions in infrastructure provision so far have remained primarily oriented towards individual councils and not towards cross-border co-operation.

Typical intervention on SWM

Box 7.1 illustrates the interventions bringing out the supporting role of the LVBC. It is actually providing a back-up to the small urban centres in carrying out their traditional SWM tasks of collecting, transporting and disposal of solid waste. The LVBC has provided transportation vehicles and even built transfer points, but the true success of these interventions can only be measured in the long term.

Box 7.1

Kisii municipality:
Kisii is one of the small towns in Kenya that has benefitted from LVWATSAN. Field work in Kisii town revealed that in October 2008 the council was given waste transfer vehicles. A small pickup, manufactured by NDUME Engineering limited of Gilgil, also in Kenya, uses a two-wheeled tractor as a power source and has been modified to suit UN-Habitat's requirements. It has a flat deck body with a very low loading height. The flat body carries eight bins of waste, which can be lifted onto or off the pickup by hand. These little pickups are to be used to collect waste bins from businesses and residential premises and transfer them into large containers or low loading height trailers, which will then be transported to a disposal site. At the time of data collection – Dec 2008–April 2009 – the vehicles were still packed at the council parking area because they had no number plates (official registration) yet and therefore could not be put on the road to use.

Homabay municipality:

Homabay is another of the small towns found in Kenya that has benefitted from LVWATSAN. Apart from two pick-ups and collection bins like those received in Kisii town, Homabay also has been donated four concrete waste transfer stations (bunkers) built in the town. As already mentioned in Chapter 5, they are located as follows:

one in the market/CBD, emptied daily;

one in Sofia market, away from CBD, emptied weekly;

one in a site service scheme (residential) and another in Makongeni (residential), emptied once a fortnight.

A general outlook is that, as a formal institution, the LVBC has a number of strengths, particularly when it comes to accessing resources. Because its resources are assured, the LVBC is able to develop interventions even in large-scale SWM infrastructure in support of the small urban centres. That there is no place for the municipalities in its organisational arrangement, however, points at the limited autonomy of the municipalities within the LVBC when deciding on the interventions developed, which in turn influences the kind of interventions they receive. This organisational arrangement also makes it nearly impossible for local municipalities to act collectively under the LVBC framework. Though the interventions by the LVBC so far have been addressing individual municipalities only, there are clear indications that its formal structure and the supporting role it so far plays will influence the role it could play in the future when enhancing regional alliance in SWM infrastructure provision.

7.4.2 Lake Victoria Region Local Authorities Cooperation (voluntary)

The Lake Victoria Region Local Authorities Cooperation (LVRLAC) was formed in 1997 as a regional cooperation amongst local authorities in the Lake Victoria Region on the initiative of the mayors of Entebbe (Uganda), Mwanza (Tanzania) and Kisumu (Kenya). LVRLAC's main role is to facilitate local authorities' response to environmental sustainability concerns around Lake Victoria, of which solid waste management is one. LVRLAC can be categorised as a voluntary organisation because its membership is open and authorities are free to join as they deem fit. Because of its flexibility in this respect, LVRLAC has developed into a growing network organisation, involving over 81 local authorities from the Lake Victoria Basin of East Africa – Kenya, Tanzania and Uganda. Since the focus is on urban authorities, LVRLAC's members vary considerably in size, from very big authorities with populations of over 500,000 people to small town councils with a population of less than 100,000 people. Towns and division councils are the majority of LVRLAC's members, probably because there are many more townships compared to cities and municipalities in the lake basin. The diversity of its membership is a key strength for LVRLAC, as this can be a rich source for knowledge and information exchange.

Municipal autonomy in decision making under LVRLAC

As constituting members of the General Assembly of LVRLAC, the top organ within the organisation, the municipal authorities are more actively involved in formal decision making as compared with their position in LVBC. The members have statutory/legislative and administrative instruments at their disposal, which provides them with great potential to enlist policy changes at the local level within the Lake Victoria Region whereby LVRLAC is playing an enabling role. Yet, despite their autonomy in decision making and even the presence of a shared policy agenda on promoting sustainable development in the Lake Victoria Basin, political, administrative and fiscal differences between the members is an impediment to them acting collectively. Whereas acting collectively as LVRLAC would mean deciding on environmental issues of regional concern, such as regional waste treatment policy, and implementing decisions, so far the interventions under a common regional framework related to SWM infrastructure have been carried out by individual urban authorities and not collectively.

Resource availability and mobilisation within LVRLAC

Like through the LVBC, members of LVRLAC have benefitted from technical and experiential knowledge through specific projects. For instance, member local councils who were involved as Environmental Pedagogic Centres (EPCs)[2] received training on how to set up and run such pedagogic centres. Nevertheless, although the organisation is committed to improving information and knowledge sharing among its members (as put down in the LVRLAC strategic framework), not all of them have benefitted from this activity. For instance, so far just seven member councils took part in the pedagogic program because selection requirements inhibit prompt membership. Amongst others, selection requirements include resource endowment of a particular council and having an active department that addresses SWM. Also, despite the existence of a monitoring, evaluation and reporting (MER) system, there is limited practical application of the system due to poor data collection, management and sharing between the LVRLAC secretariats and the member local authorities. Lack of working tools, such as access to modern ICT-equipment, makes effective network performance measurements difficult, as it limits the possibilities for feedback from and continuous dialogue between the organisation and its members.

What could be beneficial, however, in the LVRLAC arrangement is the diversity of its membership, shown in the different sizes of the urban centres involved, which at any one seating can become a rich source of information/knowledge.

The local authorities that are members of LVRLAC have to pay a membership fee of US$1,500 (upon subscription) once and an annual subscription fee. The subscription fee amounts for these contributions depend on the size of the respective local communities; currently, district/city councils pay US$500, municipal councils pay US$400 and town councils/divisions have to contribute US$300 annually.

Any authority, organisation or individual that is interested in promoting the use of Lake Victoria resources for public benefit, but does not meet conditions for full membership, can make use of the possibility of associate membership. LVRLAC cannot, however, rely on the member subscriptions for running the organisation because they are not enough. The organisation has an annual average budget for general operation of US$1 million, so LVRLAC has to raise funds from other sources, such as international donors like SIDA.

LVRLAC maintains a small staff structure and has been working under the assumption that paid staff from the member local authorities will backstop the work of the organisation voluntarily without any extra remuneration. In practice, however, this does not work; for instance, even the identity, role and image of sub-secretariats hosted within the different member local authorities are still unclear and poorly understood by these member local authorities. Furthermore, delays have been experienced even in the provision of office space and services by those members hosting parts of LVRLAC administration.

Generally, both material and non-material resources under LVRLAC appear limited. This has had an impact on its role in promoting more sustainable SWM among the individual urban authorities. Such impacts have already been felt on some projects that have commenced but later stalled, as can be learned from one of the cases in Box 7.2.

Typical intervention on SWM

Compared to LVBC, LVRLAC's role is more supplementary to the traditional tasks of SWM performed by the local authorities in the region, rather than a replacement for them. Their interventions are essentially demonstration centres displaying what can be considered best practices on SWM, such as, for instance, waste reuse. The interventions in smaller towns (Masaka, Homabay and Musoma) presented in Box 7.2 show successful connections with the municipal council departments dealing with environmental issues and the integration with on-going plans and projects. Nevertheless, it remains to be seen whether these centres will still be active in the long term or whether they will stall like the one in Kisumu.

Box 7.2

Kisumu city council in Kenya:

Kisumu was the first environmental pedagogic centre (EPC) to be established and became fully operational in 2004. It reached the most advanced stage as an EPC, but momentum of the project slowly dwindled over time and at the time of field work (2007/08), there was nothing much to show for it on the ground. The reasons for this failure varied, but they include inadequate human capacity, budget restraints (because a lot of money went into paying external consulting agencies) and also a political situation that was violent (including destruction of property after elections).

Masaka municipal council in Uganda:

The EPC was initiated in May 2008, and its status is 85% complete. EPC's new construction is adjacent to the Public Health Department building in the town center, hence highly accessible. Hosted by the environment department, the facility is fully integrated into the functioning of the department and will be applied to demonstrate best practices in environmental management. The EPC constitutes demonstration garden plots, a composting unit, a solar-powered main hall, an exhibitions hall, office space, a resource room and roof catchment rain water harvesting.

Homabay municipal council in Kenya:

The EPC was initiated in March 2007, and its status is completed. Homabay's EPC is very suitably located within the town center at a site earmarked for future expansion of the council offices. It has enrolled participation of a youth group that also uses the center as learning ground on various innovations and environmental practices. The tree nursery supplies the council with seedlings for its town greening program, while schools often use the facility as a practical learning center. The center is constituted of demonstration garden plots, a greenhouse, a tree nursery, rain water harvesting facilities, composting, a solar-powered building and a host of information displays, including one on bio-digesters.

Musoma municipal council in Tanzania:

The EPC was initiated in June 2008, and its status is 90% completed. It is a unique EPC in the sense that it uses the concept of a recreational learning center by establishing different components of the EPC within a park environment. It is strategically located within 200 meters of the town hall, and though not fully completed yet, it has fully established a vibrant tree nursery that is supporting the town greening initiative. It has also attracted partnerships with CBOs dealing with environmental management.

Overall, LVRLAC has given municipal authorities a key place in its organisational arrangement and particularly in its decision making process. The rather informal nature of LVRLAC is associated with the massive political will of its member local authorities. Their numerical dominance notwithstanding, these municipal authorities have not been able to act collectively by cooperating in environmental infrastructure provision. Apart from the differences (politically, administrative and fiscal) inherent in the diversity of its members, the weak state of its resources does not sustain the supplementary role of LVRLAC in developing SWM interventions or in steering collective action between its members. Its interventions so far have remained implemented in individual municipalities only.

7.4.3 Emerging as a 'new' local governmental actor

Without necessarily being consolidated under one unit, local authorities can manage some of the SWM problems across jurisdictions through regional organisations. Regional alliances could thus complement the self-organizing mechanisms of individual local authorities and the knowledge and information sharing efforts from regional organisations. Activities like infrastructure provision remain organised within individual municipalities, in particular because the level of decentralisation differs in the three countries under study. This means that municipalities in the respective countries have distinctive levels of administrative, fiscal and political autonomy. So, at the moment, each urban council within the Lake Victoria basin is managing its own waste (within its own jurisdiction) and develops its own by-laws. There are SWM decisions, however, such as putting up a landfill, that go beyond the level of a municipal authority and require involvement and permission of a national environmental authority like National Environment Management Council (NEMC) in Tanzania or the National Environment Management Authority (NEMA) in Kenya and Uganda. Most local councils, especially in Uganda and Tanzania, are also heavily dependent on central government funds, and therefore priorities for the use of these resources are probably more geared towards national programs than towards international collaboration.

Yet municipal authorities can build on enabling factors, like a supportive legislation at the regional level and even at the national level. This way, a 'new' local governmental actor may emerge in the form of a municipality with autonomy in decision making and the necessary resources to take part in regional alliances towards addressing SWM issues (see Figure 7.2).

7.5 Conclusion

While solid waste management remains a problem for most East Africa local governments, there are cases of urban authorities that have embraced the participation of non-state actors in municipal service delivery. These municipalities, like Mwanza, show higher levels of performance measured by the service coverage, amount of waste collected, service satisfaction, and involvement of non-state actors in decision making, among other criteria. Therefore, an emerging 'new' local government actor is a strengthened municipality whose systems embrace both formal and informal non-state actors.

Further, there exist opportunities to improve on the SWM service delivery by forming regional alliances through existing regional organisations. In the Lake Victoria Basin, there are the 'voluntary' and 'statutory' regional organisations, which present different opportunities for the participating urban authorities. Presently, there is only evidence of regional alliances when it comes to information and knowledge sharing, but this could be broadened to include sharing of infrastructure on SWM as well. Therefore, an emerging 'new' local government actor is a municipality with autonomy in decision making and resources to allow it to form regional alliances with other municipalities sharing common SWM problems.

Notes

1. The word *franchise* is in quotation marks because there are no legal papers to show for it; the arrangement is only a franchise by name, but not in actual sense.
2. The EPCs are part of the Swedish support to the Lake Victoria Initiative. Centres are established with the aim of demonstrating to the population how various environmental issues can be dealt with – for example, through general information on environmental conditions and challenges.

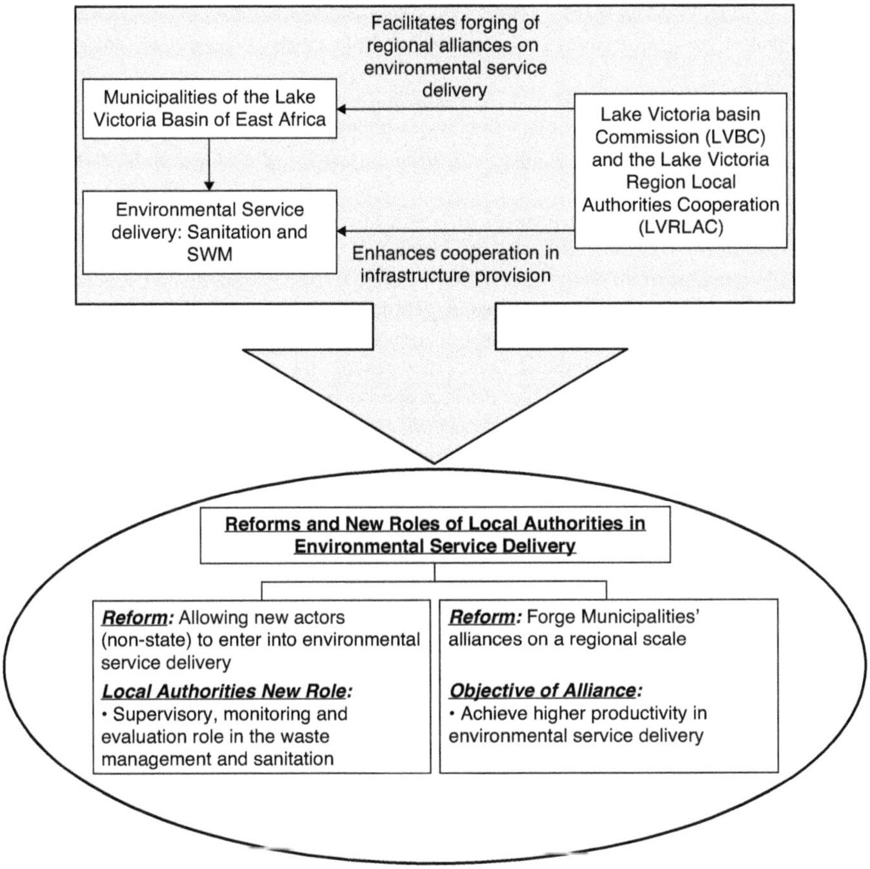

Figure 7.2 Schematic representation of emerging 'new' local government authorities of Lake Victoria Basin in assuming new roles that lead to higher productivity in environmental service delivery

References

Adei, S. (2009). *State and non-state actors' partnership and collaboration: The implications for capacity building in public service.* A paper presented at Africa Public Service Conference of Ministers of Public Service, Dar-es-Salaam, Tanzania, 17–18 June, 2009.

EPA. (1994). *Handbook on joining forces on solid waste management: Regionalization is working in rural and small communities; EPA530-K-93–001.*Washington, DC: US Environmental Protection Agency.

Joshi, A. & Moore, M. (2004). Institutionalised co-production: Unorthodox public service delivery in challenging environments. *The Journal of Development Studies,* 40 (4): 31–49.

Kwon, S.W. (2007). Regional governance institutions and interlocal cooperation for service delivery. *Working Group on Interlocal Services Cooperation.* Paper 28. Wayne State University.

Majale, C. L. (2011). *Modernising solid waste management at municipal level: Institutional arrangements in urban centres of East Africa.* PhD thesis. Wageningen: Wageningen University.

Mol, A.P.J. (2001). *Globalization and environmental reform. The ecological modernization of the global economy.* Cambridge, MA: The MIT Press.

Mwanza City Council. (2000). *Refuse collection and disposal by-laws of 2000.* Mwanza City Council, Tanzania.

Olukoshi, A. (2005). Changing patterns of politics in Africa. In A. A. Borón, G. Lechini (Eds.), *En Libro: Politics and Social Movements in an Hegemonic World: Lessons from Africa, Asia and Latin America.* CLACSO, Consejo Latinoamericano de Ciencias Sociales, Ciudad Autónoma de Buenos Aires, Argentina: Junio (pp. 177–201). Retrieved from http://bibliotecavirtual.clacso.org.ar/ar/libros/sursur/politics/Olukoshi.rtf

Oosterveer, P. (2009). Urban environmental services and the state in East Africa; between neo-developmental and network governance approaches. *Geoforum,* 40 (6):1061–1068.

Pierre, J. & Peters, G. (2000). *Governance, Politics and the State.* London: Macmillan Press Limited.

Tukahirwa, J., Mol, A.P.J. & Oosterveer, P.J.M. (2008). *Participation of NGOs and CBOs in Urban Sanitation and Solid Waste Management in Uganda.* Paper read at Proceedings International IWA Conference. New Sanitation Concepts and Models of Governance, Wageningen.

8 Converging scales of urban sanitation infrastructures and management

Sammy Letema and Bas van Vliet

8.1 Introduction

The previous chapters dealt with the provision of waste and sanitation services by households, informal actors, NGOs and CBOs and local governments. This chapter extends the discussion on scales of management and participation by introducing spatial and technical scales. The Modernised Mixtures approach has been typically developed to include both the technical and managerial dimensions in assessing and evaluating waste and sanitation configurations. This chapter shows what a socio-technical lens may do for the assessment of sanitation infrastructure management in Kisumu (Kenya) and Kampala (Uganda). With the examples of sanitation planning in both cities, it is assessed that diverse scales of sanitation infrastructures, from household on-site, community on-site, to satellite sewers and conventional sewers, require the involvement of different actor configurations for asset ownership, maintenance and management. Data for this research was gathered during field work visits to both cities between 2007 and 2009. Data collection entailed document acquisition, archival retrieval, observations, wastewater sampling, and interviews with sanitation experts, managers, and local authorities in Kampala and Kisumu (Letema 2012).

The study assesses sanitation configurations on four axes: technical scale, management scale, level of flow separation and level of end-user participation. In addition, it presents a judgement of the sustainability of sanitation infrastructures using three criteria: public and environmental health, accessibility and flexibility. These criteria are additional to the set of thresholds which are used in conventional sanitation planning, as they are normally based on per capita water consumption (l/cap*d) or consumption per hectare (m^3/ha*d) to decide on the implementation of certain sanitation infrastructures.

The chapter is built up as follows: the next section distinguishes the kinds and scales of sanitation infrastructures and the different sanitary flows they process. Next, in Section 8.3 the actor configurations around sanitation infrastructures in Kampala and Kisumu are identified. Section 8.4 presents the overall socio-technical assessment – based on the Modernised Mixtures approach – of the typical conventional, traditional and mixed sanitation systems found in both cities. It is followed by an expert judgement of these systems using criteria of public and environmental health, accessibility and flexibility (Section 8.5). Some feasible routes for improved sanitation planning in Kisumu and Kampala are presented in 8.6. Although Kampala and Kisumu cities are unique in many respects, some generalisations in the concluding section (8.7) are made towards East African cities in terms of the feasible variety of sanitary solutions.

8.2 Scales of sanitation infrastructure

Scale of sanitation infrastructure can be defined in many ways. It can relate to the technical size of a sanitation system, to the coverage expressed in population size or to treatment capacity expressed in population equivalents. In spatial terms, scale relates to the area a system can cover or to the size of settlements. In Kampala and Kisumu, sanitation scales are not clearly established, only the size of settlement normally determines the suitable scale of a sanitation system. This is contestable, as also the type of settlement should determine the sanitary option. East African cities are characterised by large segments of informal settlements, comprising 30–70% of the population (Kombe 2005; Nawangwe and Nuwagaba 2002; Olima 1994; UN-Habitat 2008) that are either informal, unplanned or of very low densities. We argue that such diversity of spatial structures calls for provision of different types and scales of sanitary solutions to suit the local conditions.

The study identified six types of sanitation systems of various scales in Kampala and Kisumu (Letema 2012). First, urban sewerage systems are large-scale, as they serve medium urban and large urban settlements. Although in design and practice storm water is separated from sewage flows, because of cross connections via inspection chambers, faulty manholes and infiltration, storm water still ends up mixed with sewage flows in most urban systems. In addition, urban sewage flows are mixed with industrial wastewater and then co-treated with faecal sludge in the central wastewater treatment plant. Second, there are satellite sewerage systems that can be considered of intermediate scale, as they serve communities, neighbourhoods and small urban settlements. They consist of sewer pipes leading waste water to a series of stabilisation ponds. The compositions of sewage flows in satellite systems are specific to the land use, which can be industrial, domestic or institutional. The sewage is collected and treated and discharged close to the point of generation, within the water catchment area.

The third to sixth types are the on-site systems: septic tanks, urine diverting dry toilets (UDDT), bio-latrines and pit latrines. They are small-scale, as they serve households, clusters of households or community settlements (Table 8.1). These on-site sanitation systems differ in the way waste flows are processed in combined or separated modes. In septic tanks, all domestic waste water is processed. Bio-latrines are designed to process only black water. Pit latrines and UDDTs have in common that they deal with human waste without using water. UDDTs, however, divert urine and treat it separately. In pit latrines and UDDTs, excreta are source-separated from the grey water streams.

Table 8.1 shows that scale of settlement is not directly linked to a single sanitary option, except for the largest scale of settlements, where urban sewer systems prevail. The highest diversity of applicable sanitation systems is found in community-size settlements.

Table 8.1 Scales and types of sanitation infrastructure and sanitation flows in Kampala and Kisumu

Scale and type of infrastructure		*Type of sanitation flows processed*				
Settlement scale (population)	*Sanitation type*	*Urine*	*Faeces*	*Grey water*	*Black water*	*Storm water*
Household (5-50)	Pit latrine (TP/VIP)	*	*			
	Septic tank			*	*	
	UDDT	*	*			
Cluster (10-200)	Septic tank			*	*	
	Pit latrine (VIP)	*	*			
Community (50-1500)	Septic tank			*	*	
	UDDT	*	*			
	Bio-latrine			(*)	*	
	Satellite sewer			*	*	
(1500-5000)	Satellite sewer			*	*	
	Urban sewer			*	*	(*)
Small urban (5000-50000)	Satellite sewer			*	*	
	Urban sewer			*	*	(*)
Medium urban (50000-250000)	Satellite sewer			*	*	
	Urban sewer			*	*	(*)
Large urban (>500000)	Urban sewer			*	*	(*)

Note: *indicates scale of sanitation infrastructure applicable and flow processed, (*) indicates the unintended inclusion of flows in these systems.

8.3 Actor arrangements around the diverse sanitation systems

Next to technical or spatial scales, the Modernised Mixtures approach directs us to also assess scales of management and participation. As an input for this assessment, managing actors and their responsibilities for sanitary systems in Kampala and Kisumu were identified. Traditionally, from the 1900s until 1972 in Kampala and from the 1900s until 2003 in Kisumu, local authorities (LAs) provided water supply, sewerage, drainage, solid waste management and faecal sludge management services. Currently, sanitation services provisions are the responsibility of multiple providers (Table 8.2; Figure 8.1). In general, public corporations still provide urban sewerage systems, but asset ownership is separated from operation and maintenance. A public corporation may own the assets, and operation and maintenance could be done by a public service provider or outsourced to a private sector contractor for design, construction, and rehabilitation services. Satellite systems are developed and operated by housing companies, quasi-public institutions (e.g., universities) or the state. These operators are not appointed as sewerage authorities as is required in the regulations, but they nevertheless operate the systems. Only in Ntinda (Kampala) is there a neighbourhood association (CBO) that is responsible for operation and maintenance of the utility (Table 8.2). On-site sanitation systems are developed and operated by a great number of stakeholders: local authorities are involved in group and pilot projects, landlords in the service of rental premises, CBOs and NGOs in group sanitation, and private entrepreneurs take care of single toilets and septic tanks. Besides, countless householders are owner-occupiers of their self-built latrines.

As can be inferred from Table 8.2 and as it is visualised in Figure 8.1, different actor groups are involved in sanitation management in Kampala and Kisumu. First, the roles of the main actor groups are listed.

- Private actors develop, own and operate most of the on-site systems, except for the new sanitation options UDDT and bio-latrines;
- Non-governmental organisations (NGOs) develop and help build septic tanks, UDDT and bio-latrine systems;
- Public authorities are involved in the development, ownership and operation of urban, satellite and septic tank systems;
- Households develop, own and operate septic tanks and pit latrines;
- Quasi-public institutions develop, own and operate satellite, septic tanks and pit latrine systems;
- Marketised CBOs operate and manage septic tanks and UDDT units, whereas welfare CBOs provide and manage bio-latrines, septic tanks and satellite systems.

Table 8.2 shows that sanitation systems are often co-managed by various actor groups: public-public, private-CBO, private-users, NGO/CBO-community, public-CBO, NGO-users.

To illustrate the diverse arrangements of sanitation provision, Figure 8.1 puts the state, private, NGO and household provision at four corners of a square. The second inner square in the figure shows the combined (multi-institutional) configurations that can be observed as well. The figure visualises the assessment (in the sense of characterisation, rather than normative judgement) of the management arrangements for six categories of urban sanitation systems indicated by shadings.

Table 8.2 Actor responsibilities around sanitation services in Kampala and Kisumu

System type	*Management arrangement*				*Nature of end-user participation*
	Developer	*Ownership*	*Operator*	*Management*	
		Urban Sewerage Systems			
Kampala urban	KCCA NWSC	NWSC	KWP	Public-public	Surveys Sensitisation programmes Payment of bills Report issues
Kisumu urban	MCK LVSWSB	MCK LVSWSB	KIWASCO	Public-public	
		Satellite Sewerage Systems			
Bugolobi	NHCC	NHCC	NHCC	Self	Absent
Kyambogo	University	University	University	Self	
Mukono	University	University	University	Self	
Unise	State	Institute	Institute	Self	
Naalya	NHCC	NHCC	NHCC	Self	
Namboole	State	State	SMC	Public-public	
Ntinda	NHCC	NHCC	CBO	Private-CBO	
Molasses	Industry	Industry	Industry	Self	
		On-site Sanitation Systems			
Traditional pit latrine	Household	Household	Household	Self	Development, operation and maintenance of sanitation systems
	Landlord	Landlord	Households	Private-users	
Lined VIP	LAs/SAs	Users	Users	Public-users	
Septic tank	Household	Household	Household	Self	
	Private	Enterprise	Private	Private	
	Landlord	Landlord	Private	Private-users	
	NGOs/ CBOs	Community	CBOs	NGO/CBO-community	
	LAs	Public	Las	Self	
			Private	Public-private	
			CBOs	Public-CBO	
Bio-latrine	NGOs/ CBOs	Community	CBOs	NGO-CBO-community	
UDDT	NGO	Household	Households	NGO-user	
	LAs	Community	CBOs	Public-CBOs	

Abbreviations: KCCA, Kampala Capital City Authority; NWSC, National Water and Sewerage Corporation; MCK, Municipal Council of Kisumu; LVSWSB, Lake Victoria South Water Services Board; NHCC, National Housing and Construction Company; Las, local authorities; NGO, non-governmental organisation; CBO, community-based organisation; KWP, Kampala Water Partnership; KIWASCO, Kisumu Water and Sewerage Company; SMC, Sports Management Council.

8.4 Socio-technical assessment of sanitation configurations

Now that technical scales and actor arrangements of the diverse sanitation systems in Kampala and Kisumu have been addressed, the overall assessment along the dimensions of the Modernised Mixtures approach as presented in Chapter 2 can be made. Again, this is an empirical assessment rather than a judgement. Three typical groups of sanitation configurations for both cities can be identified: *conventional, traditional* and *mixed.*

Urban sewerage systems can be called "conventional" because they are of a large scale, characterised by centralised and combined flows, and under technocratic public management. They can be seen as the materialisation of Western models of infrastructure service provision, commonly applied in the colonial and early post-colonial Africa. The management of urban sewer systems can be characterised as expert-driven and public-utility centred. End-users in most cases only participate in urban system management by paying bills and charges and sometimes by reporting occurring sewage overflows and blockages. In addition, they give their input to occasional surveys and sensitisation programmes held in different parts of both cities.

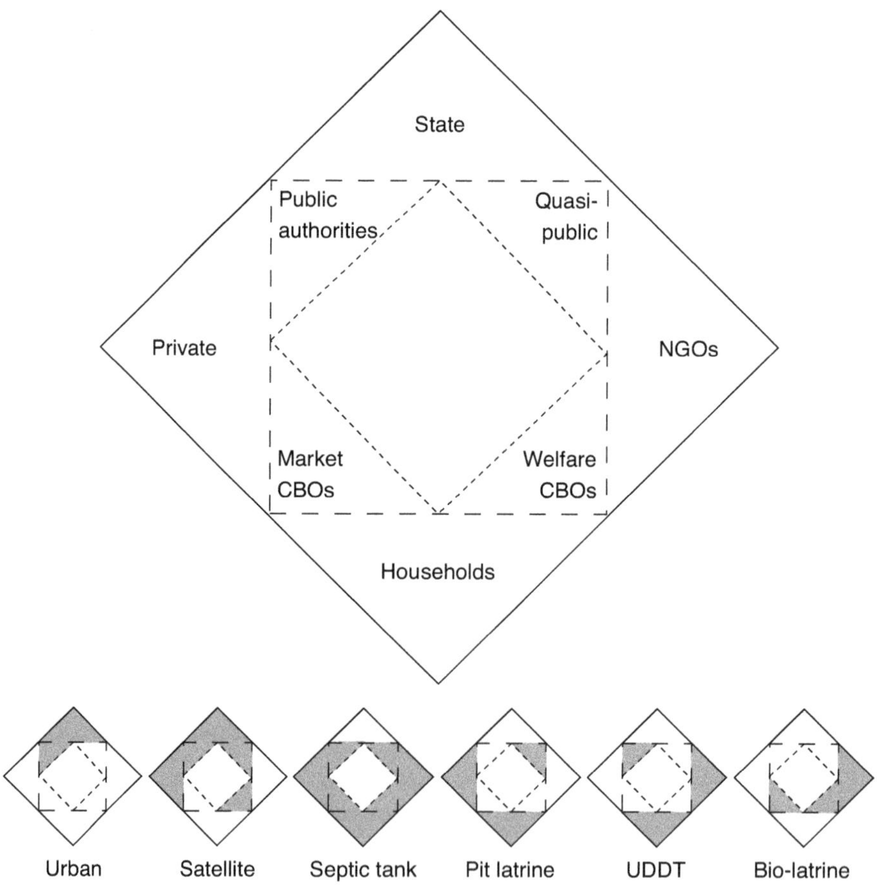

Figure 8.1 Actor arrangements around sanitation in Kampala and Kisumu

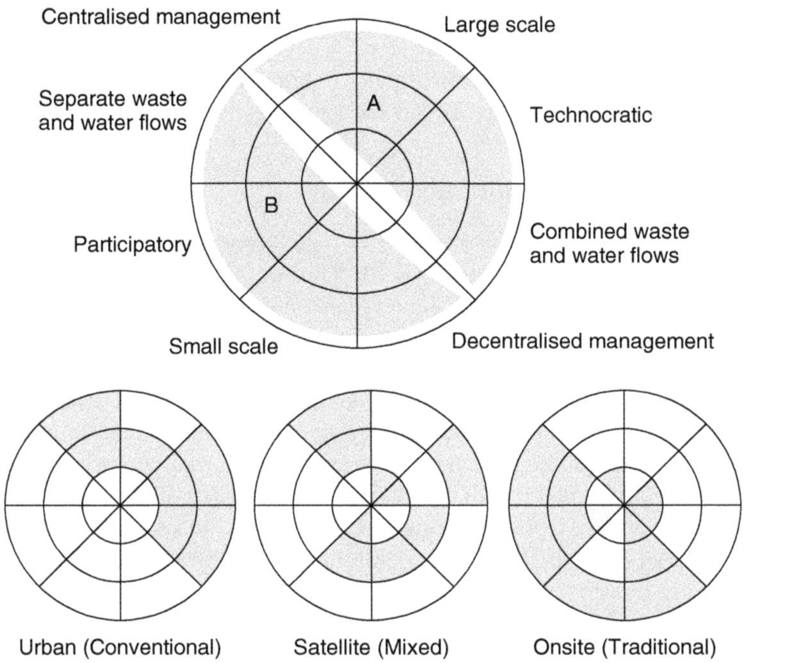

Figure 8.2 Sanitation configurations in Kampala and Kisumu

Most of the on-site systems can be considered 'traditional', as the management of sanitation flows is an individual affair, locally applied by end-users or artisanal local providers. Most of the on-site systems are planned, operated and maintained by end-users, so the systems can be considered participatory. The constructions are made by local artisans, with or without expert design or local authorities' approval. The siting of facilities is mostly done with or by the households or communities using them.

Satellite or community-scale systems can be called mixed (hybrid) systems. Satellite systems are intermediate systems between urban off-site and household on-site scales, applying conventional sewer standards and construction protocols. Satellite systems are developed by various service providers other than sewerage authorities, and end-user involvement is mostly lacking: they do not participate in planning, design and construction. If anything, some users are involved in the (organisation of) operation and maintenance of local treatment ponds. A legal framework for participation of households, communities or NGOs into satellite sanitation systems is, however, absent. Therefore, the management of satellite systems can be characterised as technocratic, too, as end-user participation is on a low level, and the systems apply standards, technologies and construction protocols developed for large-scale sewer systems. Households or communities serviced by sewer systems are not given choices and can therefore be considered captive consumers.

Figure 8.2 shows our assessment on the Modernised Mixtures dimensions of the three typical sanitation configurations. Conventional urban sewer systems resemble the centralised paradigm, (A) in which large technical scale, required expert knowledge and central management are combined. Traditional systems resemble the decentralised paradigm: (B) small, locally made technologies, managed by local (informal) actors and users. The satellite sewer systems combine some of the management and technology characteristics of both paradigms: they are of smaller scale, yet under more centralised, even technocratic, management.

8.5 Sustainability of sanitation systems

Following on the empirical assessments of sanitation configurations along the social and technical dimensions of the Modernised Mixtures approach, six local and international experts[1] from academia and sanitation practice were invited to judge the configurations in Kampala and Kisumu on the criteria of public and environmental health, accessibility and flexibility. The six sanitary systems in Kampala and Kisumu were scored against the three criteria using a regular five-step rating scale of very poor to very good. The judgement showed that the urban sewer and satellite systems scored equal on all three criteria: from poor to very good on public and environmental health, and much lower on accessibility and flexibility. Traditional pit latrines score the opposite: low on public and environmental health, but much higher on accessibility and flexibility. As can be seen in Figure 8.3, septic tanks score average on all criteria.

In terms of public and environmental health, the urban, satellite and bio-latrines systems scored highest. Pit latrines were considered the best accessible systems. Flexibility scores were highest for pit latrines and UDDTs. The poor scores of pit latrines in relation to health can be explained because they are conceived as a rural technology option not suitable for modern cities. They are considered flexible as they don't rely on already established infrastructures, organisational arrangements and planned urban spaces.

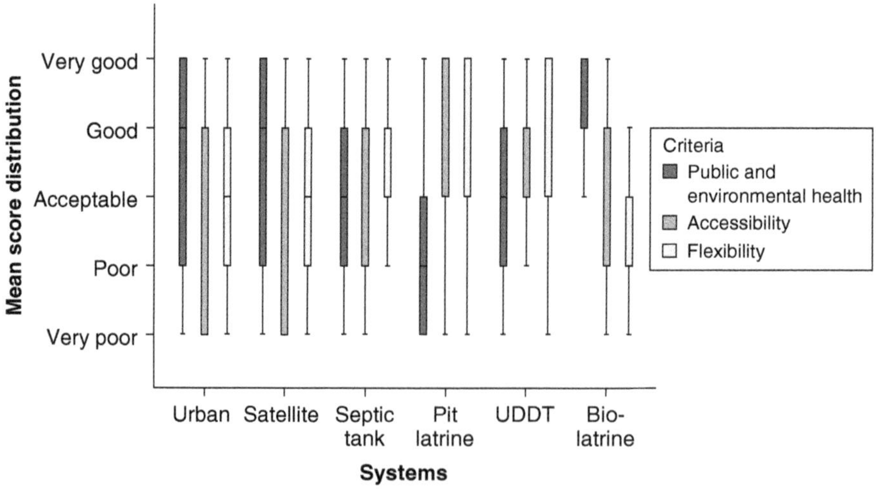

Figure 8.3 Performance rating of sanitation systems per assessment criterion

8.6 Routes for sanitary infrastructure improvement

Based on current insights, the way to enhance the sustainability of existing sanitary mixtures is to shift away from the centralised-decentralised dichotomy to a Modernised Mixtures approach where the strengths of a centralised approach (e.g., economies of scale, efficiency, convenience) are merged with those of a decentralised approach (e.g., accessibility, flexibility and user participation). It opens the way to the development of intermediate systems configurations. Systems on all scales should be gradually 'modernised' in the direction of enhanced accessibility, flexibility and public and environmental health. The latter can, in particular, be achieved by enhancing the recovery of the resources of water, energy, organic matter and nutrients. For Kampala and Kisumu, this would entail:

a) A shift from large-scale sewerage systems to intermediate scales

Shifting from large to intermediate scales in urban sewerage systems reduces the operation and maintenance costs attributed to pumping stations and siphons in large sewer systems. It also eliminates sewage overflows due to mechanical failures and under-capacity of the central treatment plants. Shifting technical scales from large to intermediate level will also affect management configurations: the centralised state-based management is likely to shift to a management configuration including multiple actors – public, private, state and quasi-public actors.

b) Shifting sewerage provision from technocratic to a mix of technocratic and participatory management.

Shifting from technocratic towards participatory management leads to an increased flexibility and accessibility of urban and satellite sewerage systems. Such a shift can be achieved through the combined implementation of technical options depending on local conditions: conventional sewerage, satellite sewerage and traditional on-site sanitation. In residential areas where septic tanks are applied and where the thresholds for on-site sanitation have been exceeded, settled sewers may provide an impetus for septic tank upgrading. It gives households and communities the opportunity to participate in sewerage services provision. The current approach of applying direct connections to sewer lines, wherever these lines are within reach, is typical of a conventional approach without end-user participation. Besides, analysis shows that the discounted cost over ten years resulting from bypassing the septic tank and connecting to a new sewer is much higher than if the property remains connected to a septic tank (NWSC 2004). In areas with shallow rock, shallow sewers are more cost-effective than conventional sewers or on-site sanitation (MWI 2008). In peri-urban slums, household sewer connections are possible through condominial sewers (Mara and Alabaster 2008; UNCHS 1986), including end-user participation in operation and maintenance. In Kisumu, a mix of conventional sewers, condominial sewers and on-site systems are envisaged. Conventional sewers are suitable for planned and high-water consumption zones while condominial and on-site systems suit in the unplanned slum settlements with low water consumption (JICA 1998; LVSWSB 2005, 2008).

c) Servicing households at an intermediate level

Shifting the centralised-decentralised dichotomy to Modernised Mixtures in on-site sanitation systems can be achieved through establishment of intermediate faecal sludge emptying and collection infrastructures at community and small-urban scales. Conventional vacuum tankers can service formal settlements, whereas *Vacutugs* (Parkinson and Quader 2008) and *Gulper* pumps can service informal settlements. Vacutugs and Gulper pumps are being applied in the cities of Nairobi and Dar es Salaam, respectively, and explored as possible solutions in Kampala and Kisumu (LVSWSB 2008; NWSC 2004, 2008). Application of intermediate faecal sludge emptying and collection technologies can transform illegal and insanitary manual emptying to a more hygienic and acceptable service in informal settlements. Local authorities may establish faecal sludge transfer stations where cesspool vacuum tankers, *Vacutug* and *Gulper* operators can empty before haulage to faecal sludge treatment plants at community and small-urban sites. Establishment of faecal sludge treatment plants will enhance resource recovery and reusability of bio-solids. Separate treatment of faecal sludge has some advantages, since it is concentrated and thus suitable for anaerobic digestion, with potentials for energy recovery to be used locally. In addition, recovery of nutrients N and P in concentrated streams is more feasible and can possibly attract commercial consumers for reusing these nutrients. Servicing households at an intermediate level will result in a shift of scales from small to community and small-urban scales. Consequently, management arrangements will shift from household and voluntary sector (NGOs and CBOs) responsibility to public and private entities with bigger capacity, coupled with end-user participation and collaboration between households, private and public agencies.

d) Combining service provision institutions

In sanitation services, there are many different actor arrangements (Table 8.2; Figure 8.2). Urban systems are operated by public authorities; satellite systems by both public and private institutions and private companies; whereas on-site systems are accessible to households, private entrepreneurs, and civil society groups (NGOs or CBOs). Operation by local authorities and sewerage authorities of on-site sanitation systems is limited to a number of pilot projects. Hence, there are no fit-for-all management arrangements that can be adopted in a sanitation mixtures context. A Modernised Mixtures approach deliberately seeks diversified actor arrangements that fit different kinds and scales of sanitation infrastructure. There are three ways to do this. The first is, similar to the plea made in Chapter 4 on waste management, treating households not as serviced consumers alone, but as co-providers of on-site systems such as household- and community toilets. A second way is combining monopolistic and pluralistic institutions to provide or deliver sanitation services in areas and scales that they have comparative advantage in. A third way is combining various provision arrangements in the regulation of on-site and faecal sludge service providers through service contracts in designated service zones. Inclusion of farmers in the sanitation chain, who utilise the sludge-bound nutrients for agricultural production, may stimulate the entire sanitation provision.

The findings in Kampala and Kisumu abound with evidence that urban sewer systems may function well if asset ownership is separated from management, and through flexible public arrangements such as public-public or public-private partnerships. In slum areas, most of the public sanitary pilot projects that survived the project-ending have been implemented by NGOs or CBOs and especially the local companies and small entrepreneurs. These organisations and actors are better integrated in informal slum settlements than most of the public institutions. A technocratic approach – public agencies providing standardised services, with fixed payments and minimal community participation – appears to be hardly tenable in informal slum settlements. NGOs and CBOs have developed capacity and networks for participatory approaches as well as mobilisation, training, and capacity building techniques for such areas. The operation and maintenance of sanitary facilities developed by NGOs and CBOs is done at community level through marketised CBOs and local entrepreneurs, which is a move from a normal welfare to a business approach in sanitary services provision.

One configuration that needs a more flexible management arrangement is the satellite sewer system. Through the introduction of sanitary charges, the appointment of sewerage authorities and opening up the systems for further connections, its contribution to the Millennium Development Goals and "sanitation for all" targets can be enhanced. Private entities, such as companies and local small entrepreneurs, can play a role in the operation and maintenance of decentralised satellite systems. Combining different services in this way will lead to new configurations in sanitation provision.

e) Organising faecal sludge service provision into zones

Zoning can be applied to spatially organise sanitary service providers and infrastructures in the city. Faecal sludge collection service zones can be used in awarding contracts to different service providers depending on their comparative advantages (e.g., related to accessibility, flexibility, personnel capacity and equipment). The more the terms of operation are made flexible, the more service providers will associate in order to win contracts, thus enable a shift from solely decentralised systems to a greater technical and institutional diversity.

Zoning can be used as an instrument for curbing high operation costs inherent in cesspool tankers criss-crossing the city in search for customers through regulation of emptying, collection and disposal. Zoning and service contracts call for city councils to divest themselves from service provision, regulation and enforcement, towards licensing service providers, monitoring and enforcement of contracts and the development of faecal sludge transfer stations and treatment plants. Such organisation will shift faecal sludge handling from household scale to community and small-urban scales, with a concomitant shift in management and actor configurations from household and voluntary sector to a mixture of voluntary sector, private, public and quasi-public actors.

8.7 Conclusion

Sanitation provision in East African cities has moved from a rather strict division between centralised sewerage and rural-style use of pit latrines to more diversified systems, both in technical and institutional respects. Sanitation provision in East African cities is characterised by a mixture of scales of infrastructure and actor configurations. Such mixtures are not sustainable, as such, in the sense that they meet criteria of public and environmental health, accessibility and flexibility. Our findings for Kampala and Kisumu show that intermediate systems and systems where management shifts from single to pluralistic modes of management offer best opportunities to deliver on these criteria. The Modernised Mixtures approach offers an impetus as analytical and prescriptive tool in cities where sanitary mixtures are the norm rather than the exception. It is also very helpful as a conceptual model for organising a research agenda along the four dimensions in the approach (technical scale, scale of management, combining or separating flows and end-user participation) as well as in searching for appropriate intervention pathways along one or more of these dimensions.

Note

1. The experts were a sanitary engineer, a water quality analyst, an environmental engineer practitioner, an environmental engineer/lecturer, and a researcher on sanitation.

References

JICA. (1998). *Kisumu water supply and sewerage system.* Nairobi, Ministry of Local Government and Japan International Cooperation Agency (JICA). Volume 2, Master Plan.

Kombe, W. J. (2005). Land use dynamics in peri-urban areas and their implications on the urban growth and form: The case of Dar es Salaam, Tanzania. *Habitat International,* 29 (1): 113–135.

Letema, S. (2012). *Assessing sanitary mixtures in East African cities.* PhD thesis. Wageningen: Wageningen Academic Publishers.

LVSWSB. (2005). *Kisumu water supply and sanitation feasibility report.* Kisumu: Lake Victoria South Water Service Board.

LVSWSB. (2008). *Long-term action plan: Sewerage design report.* Kisumu: Lake Victoria South Water Services Board.

Mara, D. & Alabaster, G. (2008). A new paradigm for low-cost urban water supplies and sanitation in developing countries. *Water Policy,* 10: 119–129.

MWI. (2008). *Draft practice manual for sewerage and sanitation services in Kenya.* Nairobi: Ministry of Water and Irrigation.

Nawangwe, B. & Nuwagaba, A. (2002). *Land tenure and administrative issues in Kampala City and their effects on urban development.* Kampala: Makerere University.

NWSC. (2004). *Sanitation strategy and master plan for Kampala.* Kampala: National Water and Sewerage Corporation.

NWSC. (2008). *Kampala sanitation program: Feasibility study.* Kampala: National Water and Sewerage Corporation.

Olima, W.H.A. (1994). *The land use planning in provincial towns of Kenya: A case of Kisumu and Eldoret.* PhD thesis. Fachbereich Raumplanung. Dortmund: Dortmund University.

Parkinson, J. & Quader, M. (2008). The challenge of servicing on-site sanitation in dense urban areas: Experiences from a pilot project in Dhaka. *Water Lines,* 27 (2): 149–163.

UNCHS. (1986). *The design of shallow sewer systems.* Nairobi: United Nations Centre for Human Settlements.

UN-Habitat. (2008). *The state of African cities 2008.* Nairobi: UN-Habitat.

9 Conclusions

Bas van Vliet, Joost van Buuren and Shaaban Mgana

9.1 Introduction

Although this volume started with a problem statement on the deplorable state of municipal waste and sanitation services in the fast-growing East African urban centres, it was not the aim of this work to re-emphasise the problems encountered. Rather, the empirical reality of the multifaceted problems in sanitation and solid waste service provision were taken as a starting point to look for reconstruction options for municipal waste and sanitation services through new actor configurations, management practices and technology interfaces. This comprises the empirical heart of this volume.

This concluding chapter reflects on the assumptions put forward in the introduction that both waste and sanitation systems can be more sustainably managed when done by the diversity of players along entire infrastructure chains next to the governmental organisations, private actors or international donors, which are mostly considered the main actors. We also assumed that there is no generic development strategy for infrastructure provision. It means that neither a "small is beautiful" approach nor a simple modernistic roll-out of conventional infrastructures would eventually lead to the achievement of the Millennium Development Goals for sanitation – nor to the (inter-)national standards for safe and environmentally sound waste management. Rather, we studied the potential of network governance of infrastructure development and operation that is adapted to the local circumstances under the complex social, political and economic conditions of Sub-Saharan Africa.

Our assumptions were pillared by the history of infrastructure service provision in Sub-Saharan African states after independence. The urban centres had inherited not only the infrastructures built in colonial times, but also the state institutions and the modes of governance that came along with them. In many cases, this meant that the urban centres were served by sewers and public waste management systems, while the 'African settlements' were left to rely on their own less developed technologies and waste management practices, most of which were considered a continuation of practices commonly known from village life in rural areas. The new independent states tried to overcome this heritage of inequality and exclusion by expanding the infrastructures of the urban centres to the sub-urban areas. This was laid down in the long-term urban planning schemes of the 1960s and 1970s. However, not long after independence, it became apparent that the developmental states did not deliver on their promises of economic growth and nation building and, in similar vein, on the rolling out of modern large-scale urban infrastructures. Although initially backed by international development partner (donor) funding for the (re)construction of infrastructure, the African states lacked the financial resources, technical and managerial capacity to sustain and extend the systems. They also failed to implement proper pay-back tariff systems to cater for the investments made and extend the large infrastructure works to other areas that needed these.

The subsequent Structural Adjustment Programs, instigated by the World Bank and IMF and a wave of privatisation of state-owned companies, including waste management and water and sewer companies, did not substantially change the situation for the growing urban population. Today, urban centres are still served by the sometimes cumbersome and outdated central infrastructures for water, waste and sewerage, while the fast-growing informal settlements are left to provide these services on their own. They are supported by a huge informal sector of waste collectors and pit-emptiers, and a variety of local CBOs, private entrepreneurs and (inter)national NGOs who fill the gaps left by local government.

To achieve the Millennium Development Goals for Water and Sanitation and to safely and sustainably handle domestic waste in urban centres, the role of the state and local government in service provision needs further elaboration. Two directions were discussed in Chapter 2: First, we presented the neo-developmental state, which takes bureaucratic control (again) over the public sector and re-appropriates the infrastructures, the governing institutions and the planning and execution of infrastructure works. Second, we elaborated on the networked state, which sets targets for and facilitates the range of actors that are already (or potentially) involved in waste and sanitation service provision, including the so-far undervalued practices of the informal sector and the households themselves in the private-public partnership mode.

The theoretical perspective of this volume as presented in Chapter 2 was built on this network governance perspective and a number of approaches for technology development in waste and sanitation in developing countries that have been introduced over the last decade. Rather than being an alternative for these approaches, the proposed Modernised Mixture approach (MMa) tries to integrate dimensions of participation of serviced actors, centralised versus decentralised chain management, the separation of flows and technology scales. The MMa is a reflexive modernisation approach to infrastructure provision, beyond the dichotomy of large simple modernistic infrastructure planning versus a small-is-beautiful paradigm that has been dominating the discourse on urban development in Sub-Saharan Africa for a long time. MMa offers a tool for the assessment of contemporary mixtures of technology scales and hybrid governance models in waste and sanitation service provision in an urban context. Apart from being an assessment tool we questioned whether the studied 'modernised mixtures' in waste and sanitation could also be seen as breeding grounds or niches in a long-term transition towards sustainable infrastructure service provision in urban East Africa. Some of our empirical findings contribute to answering this question.

9.2 Empirical findings on waste and sanitation provision in East African urban centres

Chapter 3 analysed the present infrastructure from a technological perspective, with emphasis on access, chain management, environmental performance and the valorisation of recyclable materials. It concludes that in all these respects, current excreta, wastewater and solid waste management practices in East African cities are largely deficient. A striking feature is the strong infrastructure dualism which runs grossly parallel to the off-site versus on-site sanitation approach. A large part of urban population, especially those living in informal settlements, uses sub-standard on-site sanitation facilities and lacks adequate infrastructure for collection, treatment and disposal of wastewater, sludge and solid wastes. In informal settlements, services are currently to a high degree a matter for householders themselves, and to some degree for community organisations. Breaking through the ubiquitous urban dualism would require programs of neighbourhood upgrading focused on housing, roads and the water-related infrastructure. Valorisation of waste streams (e.g., in the form of reuse of biowastes) requires coordinated chain management and the application of technologies like anaerobic digestion and composting, adapted to and selected for local contexts. Rather than enrolling local governments to *provide* the waste and sanitation services (which can be conceived as a developmental state reflex), the envisaged role for local government is clearly to *organise* the closing of material cycles. How to organise this requires insights in the existing and possible future roles of householders, the informal sector, NGOs and CBOs in waste and sanitation services – insights to which the subsequent chapters contribute.

Chapter 4 focused on the crucial roles of householders in informal settlements in the solid waste management chain. The research investigated householders' waste handling practices and what they think concerning domestic wastes. It revealed the nature and dynamics of household activities such as generating, storing, sorting, separating, transporting, and (illegal) disposing of domestic wastes. In doing so, a disparity was found between the municipal requirements, on the one hand, and the actual practices of householders in the solid waste management chain, on the other. The practices of waste burning, burying and dumping, as developed by households in response to the absence of regular waste collection and disposal services, tend to gradually develop into socially accepted routines for handling wastes. The activities of illegal waste pickers solving the immediate waste problem for households on a cash-for-delivery basis tend to develop into normal arrangements appreciated by the parties directly involved. Informal relations and activities have proved to be an indispensable element of managing waste in informal settlements. The huge gap between the (legislative and system) rationality of municipal authorities, on the one hand, and the social and real life-world rationalities of householders, on the other, should be bridged in some realistic way, without imposing the system rationality on householders. Although householders tend to be uninformed and not much interested in taking an active role, enrolling householders and informal waste actors is conceived as the only realistic way forward to increase cooperation with local actors operating in the primary phase of the waste chains that serve informal settlements.

Indeed, the informal collectors fill the gaps left by formal public and private providers as exemplified in Chapter 5. Informal collectors are in many unplanned settlements the only ones collecting, sorting and transporting municipal solid waste. Sometimes they just transfer the environmental burden from their client householders to others, sometimes they free-ride on the activities of local governments – for instance, by utilizing publicly provided skips for trading wastes. The chapter concludes that these kinds of activities should be acknowledged, rather than discouraged, by using public collection points, whose negative aspects can be eliminated (or at least reduced) by contracting private agents for replacement and cleaning. This modernised mixture, where large-scale and highly technological solid waste services, typical for the public and formal private sector, mixes with small-scale technological solutions of the informal sector, is a step towards a solution to the solid waste problem in many developing countries. Such systems improve accessibility and are ecologically sustainable, improving environmental performance of urban infrastructure in the long run.

Apart from householders and private collectors, another important category of actors that is involved in waste and sanitation service provision is that of community-based and non-governmental organisations. Chapter 6 elaborated on the specific positions of NGOs and CBOs in sanitation and solid waste service delivery in the three East African capital cities: Kampala, Nairobi and Dar es Salaam. Increased involvement of NGOs and CBOs in these sectors is boosted by international development partners, which has led to significant NGO or CBO contributions to service delivery to the urban poor across the three cities. The differences in history, organisation and coordination of provision, and in institutional arrangements among the cities under study, make it unwise to strive for harmonisation in the involvement of civil society institutions in urban services across the three countries. The modernised mixture approach has shown that contextual factors are too important to allow for the design of universal models that can be applied in every context. But that is not to say that the three cities cannot learn from each other in how to govern urban environmental services with the involvement of NGOs and CBOs. One important lesson is that they can be fully included into the formal urban service provisioning system by contracting them to provide solid waste and sanitation services.

This is also confirmed in Chapter 7, in a study of the roles of local government in waste and sanitation services in the secondary cities Mwanza (Tanzania), Kisumu (Kenya) and Jinja (Uganda) located on the shores of Lake Victoria. Local governments that embrace both formal and informal non-state actors to service their populations show higher levels of performance in terms of service coverage, amounts of wastes collected and service satisfaction. But the chapter also found there are opportunities for improving service delivery by forming regional alliances and benefiting from the advantages of a larger scale of operation and bigger political clout. Although such regional alliances have not yet taken off, except for initiatives in sharing knowledge and information like the Lake Victoria Basin Initiative, the opportunity is too promising to be missed, most notably in solid waste management. In particular, in the implementation and operation of new landfills such regional alliances could have significant advantages.

Lastly, Chapter 8 assessed that sanitation provision in East African cities is much more complicated than suggested through the dichotomy of large-scale sewer provision for the centre versus locally managed on-site systems in the informal settlements. What is found is a mix of technical scales and actor configurations in sanitation provision. Findings for Kampala (Uganda) and Kisumu (Kenya) show that intermediate systems (such as satellite sewers) and systems where management shifts from single to pluralistic modes of management offer best opportunities to deliver on criteria of accessibility, flexibility and public and environmental health.

9.3 Harnessing social and technical diversity for sustainable development

The findings of this volume show a wide diversity in management scales, technical solutions, governance approaches and actor configurations in practices of waste and sanitation service provision in East African primary and secondary cities. The authors do not dare to claim that this volume captures all the diversity there is. But the variety of studies in terms of disciplinary approach (ranging from engineering to economics, across public administration and science and technology studies) and their social and technical objects (ranging from householders to local governments and from waste skips to sewer systems) does deliver a number of valuable insights concerning pathways for the sustainable development of waste and sanitation systems in East Africa.

Both in sanitation and in waste management chains, we observed emerging cases that may represent a move towards the middle ranges of the dimensions of participation, management, treatment of flows and technical scales. The involvement of the informal sector and of NGOs and CBOs in primary and secondary stages of waste management or in sludge collection from household pit latrines shows that the gaps between centralised and decentralised management have been filled with new services, delivered by a combination of formal, community and informal actors. However, this is done in a highly incoherent and uncoordinated way, based on particular local initiatives. More systematic reflection on these experiences could serve as inspiration for future initiatives.

Diversity was also observed in technological scales in waste and sanitation service provision. Intermediate scales of infrastructure beyond the traditional local and the modern large-scale infrastructures showed some promising solutions for today's problems, such as condominial sewers, waste collection sites in communities, satellite sewers, and mobile vacuum pumps to empty pit latrines and septic tanks in densely populated areas. The insight obtained here is that the intermediate levels of infrastructure are neither the alternative to the small- nor to the large-scale infrastructures. Rather, they represent valuable linkages between the two system rationalities, as they connect – for instance – the numerous individual septic tanks with large scale treatment of sludge in public wastewater treatment plants or – in the case of waste skips – the activities of informal waste collectors with the public waste collection system.

In terms of management scales, between centralised bureaucratic and decentralised local management, some new cases of shared responsibility between central city authorities and local actors were found, such as in the case of satellite sewer systems where management responsibility can officially be transferred to local developers or residential associations. But in most of the other cases, management responsibility is only de facto transferred to local actors, NGOs and CBOs, as legislation is largely lagging behind vested practices of waste and sanitation service provision in urban settlements. In other words, intermediate levels of infrastructure management were found in both waste and sanitation service provision, but only few were supported, let alone legally endorsed, by local or national authorities.

The observed cases of community-based management, NGO activities in sanitation, or informal sector involvement in waste management were geographically spread over the different cities, and there has hardly been any learning from each other's activities, let alone any vision building about a sustainable future. In this respect one cannot yet speak of any strategic niche development towards a regime change in terms of transition theory. There is a huge potential to do things differently, in terms of management scales, actor configurations, involvement of households and the informal sector. But an acceleration towards a sustainability transition in waste and sanitation services provision is not in sight. As it was argued in Chapter 2, such transition depends not only on niches, but on developments at all three levels of niches, landscapes and regimes. Hence not only internal niche processes of learning and actor network building, but also wider trends associated with the landscape play their roles in system innovation. The economic development in East Africa and the rapid growth of urban populations lead to increased socioeconomic differentiation within cities. Over the past decade, international development aid has not only been reduced, but its goals, funding mechanisms and sources haven been changed as well. Especially in the case of development aid for infrastructure development, the emphasis lays on national economic profitability, leading to the expansion of electricity grids, roads and railways, rather than to urban sanitation and waste infrastructures. Growing concerns of sustainability and meeting the Millennium Development Goals may counterbalance such development, but it is clear that current landscape in East Africa at least forms an ambivalent environment for waste and sanitation niches to expand and to lead to long-term regime change.

In any case, such regime change depends for a large part on the position and roles of the state and local government, in particular in providing urban infrastructure services to the urban population at large. The potentially successful initiatives that have been the object of study in this volume do need the support not only from international NGOs and development partners (donors), but especially from local governments. It means that local authorities need to be willing to transfer responsibilities, and endorse and where possible delegate responsibility, to intermediate formal and informal, public and private actors in waste and sanitation service provision. This entails, in other words, a form of network governance. In such a mode of governance, local authorities are crucial for setting the goals for sustainable infrastructure provision, but they need to have the capacity to facilitate and coordinate rather than rule the initiatives taken by actors in society that have for decades taken up responsibilities in waste and sanitation services where local government failed to provide.

9.4 Pathways for East African urban infrastructure policies and research collaboration

The combined analysis by authors in this volume has shown the strengths and opportunities of network governance and chain management in sanitation and solid waste management in East Africa. Future pathways in the domains of governmental policies, international aid and research based on the findings of this volume are the following.

With regard to national and local government, our suggestions concern the fields of legislation, funding mechanisms, strengthening and coordinating the roles of various stakeholders, technology development and capacity building. New legislative and policy efforts should be aimed at taking away the current impediments to cooperation between the stakeholders in the management chains. Instead of harassing informal actors, or denying CBOs access to formal infrastructures of domestic waste and sanitation, urban planning and local by-laws should be adapted to regulate and make efficient use of the existing practices at especially the primary stages of waste and sanitation chains.

As lack of financial resources has shown to be a very persistent bottleneck in development and operation of infrastructure, putting priority to improved and transparent financial mechanisms is strongly advocated. These mechanisms should be geared towards attracting the necessary resources and forwarding these resources to where they are required most productively, likely in expanding the systems. This will enhance access of households to waste and sanitation services and sustain what is already operating. In particular, efforts should be made here to overcome the dire conditions in unplanned settlements and the social and technical dualism in urban infrastructure provision.

Proven feasible and effective forms of collaboration among actors along the waste or sanitation chains should be supported or created, and they should be made responsible for the co-development of technology and infrastructure. First, there is a need to coordinate the efforts of various parties in provision of sanitation and solid waste management, such as state companies, formal private companies, NGOs and CBOs. Government policy should pave the way for private companies and collective sector initiatives to play a stronger role in the recovery and recycling of nutrients and energy from wastewater and wastes.

Alliances of (small) cities within the East African countries and across the national borders could make a difference if they take advantage of a larger scale of operation in waste and sanitation management. Large-scale resource recovery, and the agricultural application of sanitation and waste products on a wider regional scale, requires the cooperation between cities and regions. The existing organisations of regional collaboration, such as the Lake Victoria Basin Commission and the Lake Victoria Local Authorities Cooperation, could be stepping stones in this respect.

With respect to the operation of services, government should stimulate and coordinate monitoring and evaluation of the urban infrastructure residing under its authority. In this way, technical, economic and societal performance can be systematically recorded, resulting in lessons for future infrastructure planning. For operation, monitoring and planning of new infrastructures, further capacity building, especially at the level of local government, will be indispensable, as staff trained for the aforementioned tasks is scarce.

The international donor community could support the East African national and local governments, not by implementing blueprints for sanitation and waste disposal systems, but by supporting the monitoring, research and planning of best practices in waste and sanitation service provision in urban centres, as well as in the unplanned settlements. It would lead to funding what works on the ground, the assessment of which is to be left to local stakeholders, rather than to the international experts alone.

All these suggestions spring from the broader idea as put forward in Chapter 2 and exemplified in the empirical chapters, namely that the pathway towards sustainable waste and sanitation infrastructure in East Africa is that of a *reflexive* modernisation of urban infrastructures. It entails the development of technological options that make a fit with existing and emerging arrangements, and which is done in cooperation with the envisaged users, transporters, traders and managers along the waste and sanitation chains. It requires a network mode of governance that is adaptive to rapidly changing urban settings and networks of actors and which facilitates rather than decides on technology and infrastructure development and operation.

Lastly, this book reviewed much of the current East African literature about sanitation and solid waste management and presented a number of new case studies. Though quite some research has been conducted and is being done in different urban centres in East Africa, it seems that extension of existing and, where necessary, creation of new African research networks would contribute much to African answers to the current challenges. These networks could stimulate the exchange of knowledge within the region, establish a stronger relationship between research and higher education and initiate new African research related to urban environmental management.

Contributor list

Dr Kees Burger is associate professor at the Development Economics Group at Wageningen University, the Netherlands.

Dr ir Joost van Buuren is emeritus academic staff of the Sub-department of Environmental Technology of Wageningen University, the Netherlands.

Dr Mesharch Katusiimeh is a lecturer at the Uganda Christian University, Kampala, Uganda.

Dr Sammy Letema is a lecturer at the Department of Environmental Planning and Management, Kenyatta University, Kenya.

Dr Christine Majale is a lecturer at the Department of Environmental Planning and Management, Kenyatta University, Kenya.

Dr Shaaban Mgana works at Ardhi University (ARU) Department of Environmental Engineering, Dar es Salaam, Tanzania.

Dr Caleb Mireri is a senior lecturer at the Department of Environmental Planning and Management, Kenyatta University, Kenya.

Prof dr ir Arthur P. J. Mol is chair of the Environmental Policy Group at Wageningen University.

Dr Asia Oberlin Solomon is a lecturer at Dar es Salaam Institute of Technology.

Dr James Okot-Okumu is lecturer at Makerere University, Institute of Environment and Natural Resources (MUIENR) in Kampala, Uganda.

Dr ir Peter Oosterveer is associate professor at the Environmental Policy Group of Wageningen University.

Dr Fredrick Salukele Works at Ardhi University (ARU) Department of Environmental Engineering, Dar es Salaam, Tanzania.

Prof dr ir Gert Spaargaren is professor in Environmental Policy for Sustainable Lifestyles and Consumption at the Environmental Policy group of Wageningen University, the Netherlands.

Dr Judith T. Tukahirwa is a deputy executive director of Kampala Capital City Authority, Kampala, Uganda.

Dr ir Bas van Vliet is assistant professor at the Environmental Policy Group of Wageningen University, the Netherlands.

Prof dr ir Grietje Zeeman is professor in New Public Sanitation at the Sub-Department of Environmental Technology of Wageningen University, the Netherlands.

Dr Christian Zurbrügg works at the Swiss Federal Institute of Aquatic Science and Technology, Department of Water and Sanitation in Developing Countries (Sandec), Dübendorf, Switzerland.

Index

Note: Page numbers in *italics* indicate figures and tables.

For Product Safety Concerns and Information please contact our EU representative GPSR@taylorandfrancis.com
Taylor & Francis Verlag GmbH, Kaufingerstraße 24, 80331 München, Germany

www.ingramcontent.com/pod-product-compliance
Ingram Content Group UK Ltd.
Pitfield, Milton Keynes, MK11 3LW, UK
UKHW011017180926
475701UK00004B/793
9781138687172